アメリカ英語ビジネス会話辞典

南雲堂

はしがき

　日本人の英語熱は世界一である。これは1998年の **TOEIC** テストにはっきり反映され，受験者総数約280万人のうち日本人が6割以上の約180万人を占めた。ところが実力は990点満点中，約4割しか取れていない。**TOEFL** の成績になると更に悪く世界でビリに近い163番目である（1997年）。
　TOEIC，TOEFL テストを実施しているアメリカの非営利教育機関が上記の年数以後データを公表していないが，年を追うごとにますます日本人の両テストの成績は非常に悪化していると巷間言われている。

　日本人の英語熱と実力との乖離の原因はいくつかあるが，ここでは特に下記の2点を取り上げたい。

第1　辞典には誤りが多すぎる

　あるべき姿の辞典が市場にないことも非常に大きな原因である。辞典の不備が英語をわざわざ難しくして学習者はその犠牲になっていることを筆者のアメリカ留学時代の苦い経験上断言したい。
　筆者は高校生のとき単語は一語の単語で覚えても意味はなく，辞典の中に出ている例文の中で覚えるべきだと英語の先生に強く勧められた。以来辞典を引くといつも必ず各単語の例文を算数の九九と同様，すらすら口について出てくるまで各文を何度も朗読した。辞書の執筆陣は一流大学の高名な教授たちだったので全幅の信頼を置いていた。誤りがあるとは微塵も考えなかった。ところが，後にアメリカ留学し，レポートを提出したところ全く使われていない **Japanese English** や，ある小説家の独特な表現の例文をたくさん覚え込んでいることを教授たちに指摘された。筆者はこのとき味わった挫折感，失望は長年経った今でも，つい先日のことのようにはっきりと覚えている。まさに地面にたたきつけられた，言葉では言い尽くせない苦い，苦い，苦い経験であった。
　問題なのは筆者が初めて留学してから何十年も経っていながら辞典が旧態依然の状態であることである。この間日本の社会は非常に大きく大きく変わった。特に

1990年代に入ってからは，明治維新，敗戦に次ぐ3番目の大転換期にあると言える。終身雇用をはじめとする多くの社会の制度，また今まで肯定視されてきたありとあらゆる価値観，やり方が大きく見直されている大激動期にある。しかしながら，こと英語の辞典，特に和英辞典は旧態依然である。いや旧態依然どころか更に悪化していると言っても過言ではない。そこに出ている表現は「新和英辞典」「新英和辞典」と「新しい……」というタイトル名で売り出されているにもかかわらず，19世紀，20世紀の初頭までしか使われていない表現を満載しているからである。更に悪いことには英米の区別を明示していないで並記しているのも利用者に不親切である。筆者はこういう辞典を見る度に隔靴搔痒を覚えるどころか，執筆者の学問に対する横柄さに驚きを禁じえない。執筆者はこの不適切な辞典がどれほど利用者を惑わしているかを強く心にとどめるべきである。

　辞典が次々に改訂されたにもかかわらず以前より悪化したと前述したのは執筆陣にネイティブスピーカーの名前を以前と違って大きく出しているからである。これではネイティブがその辞典の中の全文に目を通している印象を読者に与える。しかし筆者はネイティブは参加していないと断言したい。それはネイティブが参加していたらありえない誤りが多すぎるからである。人間のやることには誤りは多少つきまとうであろう。しかし筆者が声を大にして言いたいことは明らかな誤りが多すぎ，利用者を犠牲者にしていることである。執筆者の謙虚さを強く促したい。例を若干紹介しよう。どの辞典（和英のみならず，英和辞典）にも共通する誤りの例をいくつか挙げてみよう。

1「洗濯屋」を和英辞典で調べていると「水洗いの洗濯屋」は laundry，ドライクリーニング店は (dry) cleaner's と区別すると最新の辞典に出ているが利用者を惑わせている。英語では水洗いも，ドライも区別なく There's a cleaners on the corner.（角にクリーニング屋があります）と表現する。以前は cleaner's であったが今は単複関係なく cleaners が使われている。詳細は本辞典の204ページを参照されたい。

2「貿易会社」＝trading company とすべての辞典に書いてあるが，これは「証券会社」の意味。2001年9月11日テロリストに爆破されたニューヨークにあった World Trade Center も「世界貿易センター」と和訳されているが「世界ビジネスセンター」が正しい。日本の辞典は trade＝「貿易」と固く結びつけ利用者を惑わせている。詳細は本辞典の62，70ページを参照されたい。

3 「労働条件」＝working conditions と出ているが誤り。労働条件は job terms を使う。working conditions は「職場環境」という意味。これは英和大辞典の最新版も含めて正しく紹介している辞典がなく利用者を惑わせている。詳細は本辞典の92ページを参照されたい。

4 shipping company＝「船会社」とどの英和にも和英にも書いてあるが，船だけでなく飛行機，トラック，電車による「輸送会社」にも広く使われているので辞典は利用者を惑わせている。詳細は本辞典71ページを参照されたい。

5 辞典では「官僚」＝bureaucrat と出ているが誤り。bureaucrat は「役人」という意味で否定的なニュアンスがある。日本語の「官僚」には否定的ニュアンスはない。詳細は本辞典の29ページを参照されたい。

6 be computer literate＝「コンピューターのエキスパート」という訳語をつけている大英和辞典があるが，これは「コンピューターを使う能力がある」，つまりエキスパートとはほど遠い「かろうじて使える」状態の人を述べるときに使われている。詳細は本辞典の162ページ参照されたい。

7 physician＝「内科医」を出しているが，physician とは doctor の上品な語で「医師」という意味。「内科医」は internist と言う。詳細は本辞典の26ページを参照されたい。

第2　辞典は現代英語を紹介していない

どの辞典を調べても出ていない表現が多数ある。若干具体例を紹介しよう。

1 (彼は私の上司です)
　Ⓐ I work for him.
　Ⓑ He's my boss [supervisor].
　Ⓒ He's my superior.
　Ⓓ He's my higher-up.
　ⒶはⒷと同様非常によく使われているが，どの辞典にも紹介されていない。ⒸⒹ

は使われていないが最新の辞典に出ていて利用者を惑わせている。詳細は本辞典の1ページを参照されたい。higher-up は the higher-ups と複数形で「上層部」＝management の意味で使われている。詳細は本辞典の3ページを参照されたい。

2 (彼は頭の回転がいい)
  Ⓐ He thinks fast.
  Ⓑ He's a fast thinker.
  ⒶⒷ共に非常によく使われているが紹介している辞典はない。詳細は本辞典の13ページを参照されたい。

3 (彼は仕事が速い)
  Ⓐ He's a fast worker.
  Ⓑ He works fast.
  Ⓒ He gets a lot done.
  ⒶⒷⒸいずれも非常によく使われているが紹介している辞典はない。詳細は本辞典の13ページを参照されたい。

4 「会社」＝company はどの辞典にも出ている。しかし firm, business, service, outfit がきちんと紹介されていない。しかし，ほとんど使われていない concern が多くの辞典で紹介されているのは理解に苦しむ。
  (リンダは出版社に勤めています)
  Linda works for a Ⓐ publishing company.
               Ⓑ publishing house ［firm, business, outfit］.
  Ⓐが1番よく使われているがⒷも非常によく使われている。詳細は本辞典の50, 61ページを参照されたい。

5 (ナンシーは大きな車のリース会社に勤めています)
  Nancy works for a big Ⓐ car leasing company.
                    Ⓑ car leasing service.
                    Ⓒ car leasing outfit ［business］.
  Ⓐは1番よく使われている。Ⓑは非常によく使われている。Ⓒはよく使われている。詳細は本辞典の58ページを参照されたい。

6 下記のような「人」で「会社」を表す表現は現代英語でよく使われているが辞典に紹介されていない。

He works for a big stockbroker [travel agent, realtor].
（彼は大きな証券会社〔旅行代理店，不動産会社〕に勤めています）
詳細は本辞典の56，61，74ページを参照されたい。

7 （上司はちょうど出勤してきました）

The boss just Ⓐ walked through [in] the door.
　　　　　　　 Ⓑ came through the door.
　　　　　　　 Ⓒ walked in.

ⒶⒷⒸいずれも非常によく使われている。これは俗語でもなく今後もずっと使われていく表現なのに紹介している辞典はない。これも辞典が現代英語を反映していない一点である。詳細は本辞典の98ページを参照されたい。

　筆者はアメリカに初めて留学して，辞典に夥しい数の誤りがあり，これが英語を必要以上に難しくしていることを知った。以来誤りのない辞典を書き，筆者が味わった挫折感を利用者に味あわせない辞典を書くことが筆者の使命のように思え，長年研鑽してきた。この努力の成果により，あるべき姿の辞典を出版できることになり非常に安堵している。この辞典は利用者に必要以上に英語を難しくしていることから解放し，ひいては日本人の TOEIC，TOEFL の得点力がアップし，日本人全体の英語力向上に大きく貢献するだけでなく，今後出版される英語の辞典にも大きな一石を投ずることになると筆者は強く確信している。

　筆者はすでに第2弾を出す用意もできている。ぜひ読者の皆さんのご感想をお聞かせ下さい。

　この歴史に残る画期的な辞典を出版するに際して南雲堂の南雲一範社長にいろいろご理解を賜り，筆者の執筆意欲を駆り立てて下さったことに対してここで深く感謝申し上げたい。また青木泰祐編集部長には編集面のみならず，その他いろいろとお世話になり心からお礼を申し上げたい。

　最後にボストンアカデミーの福原正子教務部長にも本辞典誕生にいろいろな面で精魂を傾けてくれたことをここで深く感謝申し上げたい。

　　　　　　　　　　　　　　　　　　　　　　　　　　　　市橋敬三

この辞典の特色について

世界標準語に認知されたアメリカ英語

　アメリカ英語とイギリス英語とでは一般に考えられている以上に表現上の差がある。本辞典はアメリカ英語ビジネス会話辞典というタイトル名が示している通りアメリカ英語を紹介している。多くの辞典ではイギリスでしか使われていないのに，その明記なしにアメリカ英語と並記していることは利用者を惑わせている。筆者はイギリス英語は無視せよと言うつもりはないが，日本人にとって外国語である英語を2種類同時に覚えようとすること自体に無理があると断言したい。アメリカ人はイギリス英語を知らない。またイギリス人もアメリカ英語を知らない。英語を必要以上に難しくしている理由のひとつはこれまでの辞典がアメリカ英語とイギリス英語の2種類を説明なしに並記して紹介しているところにもあることを強く指摘したい。従って今後の辞典はアメリカ英語辞典，イギリス英語辞典と別々にすべきである。

　1980年頃から，ビジネスの世界は国境がなくなり始めた。1999年代にインターネットが世界的に普及し始めると共に，ビジネスの世界のボーダレス化は更に加速された。インターネットはアメリカが開発したものなので，世界の諸民族を結ぶ言葉は英語，それもイギリス英語ではなく，アメリカ英語を話せることが過去数年前から全世界的に当然視され始めている。過日の英字紙によると以前イギリス英語を学習してきたヨーロッパの人たちも今はアメリカ英語を学習している。

　インターネットは今後ますます普及するので，アメリカ英語がますます重要視されるであろう。

　以上の理由で日本人はイギリスとビジネスやその他で特別な関係がない限りアメリカ英語に集中して学習することが適切と筆者は考えている。もしイギリス英語も同時に学習すべきと言うのなら，オーストラリア英語，アイルランド英語も同時に学習する必要性が出てくることになる。

インフォーマント

　使用頻度は，別記の米国人インフォーマントから取ったアンケート調査結果に基づいている。見解が割れるときは同一項目について50名以上にアンケートを取り，世代による差もあるのでインフォーマントは30～45歳に限り，全員大卒以上で，南部以外の出身者である。

　従来の辞典では正しい英語か否かを問題にしているが，本辞典では実際にどの位広く使われているかという観点から調査した結果を示した。それは正しくなくとも現在広く使われていることは将来正しい英語として確立していくからである。例を挙げればアメリカ人は slowly, quickly, well（上手にの意味）の代りに slow, quick, good のほうをずっとよく使っているからである。
He speaks English good.（彼は英語を上手に話す）

◎インフォーマント・リスト

Amy Bruni	Andrew Hoge	Ann Hodgkin
Barbara Canover	Barbara Meller	Brian Nelson
Carol Russel	Carolina Harrison	Catherline Edwards
Cathy Adams	Charles Hoffman	Chris Sanders
Christiana Spengler	Cindy O'connor	David Eckholm
Deborah Tyler	Douglas Rhode	Elizabeth Eliot
Frank Harrison	Gerald Gorman	Gregory Kirk
Howard Broad	Jane Dao	Janice Adams
Jean Norris	Jeffrey Russel	Julia Bernstein
Leslie Dale	Lisa Merluzzi	Maria Brooke
Mary Kirkpatrick	Mike Kurz	Nancy Maloy
Nina Bergstein	Norman Alfven	Patricia Milikan
Paul Weber	Richard Fisher	Rose Anderson
Sally Tilton	Sarah Malone	Sarah Wines
Stephen Carter	Susan Cohen	Susan Venable
Thomas Altman	Tom Sanger	Victoria Kinzer
William Fox	William Smith	

以上の他にも多数のインフォーマントの協力を得た。全員アメリカの南部を除く大学卒の米国人。

◎インフォーマントの利用と選択の仕方

インフォーマントの利用に際して次の4点を頭に置く必要がある。

1 アメリカ人の学者は口語英語のインフォーマントとしては不適切

アメリカ人の学者は一般の人よりすぐれた意見を持っていると考えられがちである。しかし日常会話的な表現になると筆者の経験では不適切である。彼らは堅い文章，文学で使う表現やすたれた表現を日常使うからである。これはアメリカ人のみならず日本人にも同じことが言えると思う。

2 日本語が流暢なアメリカ人はインフォーマントとしては不適切

日本語に流暢なアメリカ人は日本人的な英語を話すはっきりした傾向があるからである。このことは日本人で英語が上手な人は英語的な日本語を話すことからもうなずけるであろう。

3 日本在住年数が長いアメリカ人はインフォーマントとしては不適切

日本の在住年数が長いということはアメリカを長く不在していることである。日本語も英語も時代と共に使われる頻度に大きな変化が出てくる単語がある。また全く使われなくなったり，逆に新しく使われ始める語が多数ある。これらは俗語とは限らない。社会状勢の変化によって新しく使われる語がどんどん出てくる。これらの流れは無視できない。

4 若年層（25歳以前）と熟年層（55歳以上）はインフォーマントには不適切

若年層は避けた。筆者の経験上彼らは英語をよく知らないからである。このことは日本人の若年層の日本語を考えれば納得がいくであろう。筆者の経験では「言

質」という表現を知っている日本人の若者（大卒を含めて）は極めて少ない。
　アメリカにおいても熟年層（55歳以上）の人たちは30〜40年前にはよく使われていたが，現在あまり使われていない表現を使う大きな傾向がある。一例を挙げれば現在60歳以上の女性は little woman（妻）と呼ばれると喜ぶが若い女性は怒る。

　日本人はアメリカ人なら誰でも現在使われている英語を話すと思っているようだ。しかしインフォーマントをただ参加させても生きた英語の慣用の事実を引き出せない。彼らの力を十分に引き出すには利用する日本人の側にも文章英語だけでなく，話す英語にも深く精通していることが要求される。従って彼らが分からないときは知ったかぶりをされないで I'm not sure. と言わせるだけの英語力が利用する側にあって，初めて正しい英語の慣用を引き出せることを強く指摘したい。アメリカ人を参加させながら誤りが多い辞典や本が多いのはこの点に原因がある。

構成・使用頻度表示

　本辞典では各見出しの類語を数種類挙げ，それらすべてに使用頻度をつけている。既刊の辞典では皆無である。この点も本辞典の一大特色である。
　各章の中の見出しは状況の流れに応じて構成している。(a)(b)…で語義区分を行ない，必要により下位区分として●，次の区分として1) 2)…を使用。
　（　）印で示した日本語の例文に対する英訳例をⒶⒷⒸ…で掲げ，アメリカ英語における実際の使用頻度を次の記号で表示した。
☆　1番よく使われる
◎　非常によく使われる
○　よく使われる
△　ときどき使われる
▽　まれに使われる
×　使われない
　例文中の [ ] 内は交換可能，( ) 内は省略可能であることを示す。

卑語などについて

　性に関係する語句を用いた表現，呪いの表現，一部の敬虔なクリスチャンが抵抗を示す神を冒瀆する表現なども必要に応じて収録した。これらは従来の辞典では十

分な記述がないことが多かったが，本辞典では使用頻度の高いものはきちんと紹介した。これを知らないとコミュニケーションに支障をきたすからである。多くの場合，注をつけて注意を喚起した。

省略形

　本辞典では，話し言葉で用いられる表現については，be 動詞，have，助動詞などの省略形を用いて表記した。
　　例：This suit's off-the-rack.（is →'s）
　　　　Obesity'll kill you.（will →'ll）
　通常は主語が人称代名詞でないときはこうした省略形では書かないが，本辞典では話し言葉の実際の姿を紹介するために省略形を用いている。

本辞典の内容の一部または全部の無断転載は著作権法違反になります。転載される場合は，南雲堂あて許諾申請をお願いいたします。

目　次

はしがき　iii

この辞典の特色について　viii

第1章　地位に関する表現 …………………………………1
第2章　能力・才能に関する表現 ………………………13
第3章　職業に関する表現 ………………………………24
第4章　会社に関する表現 ………………………………50
第5章　代理店・事務所に関する表現 …………………73
第6章　工場に関する表現 ………………………………77
第7章　…部に関する表現 ………………………………85
第8章　勤務に関する表現 ………………………………91
第9章　職場に関する表現 ………………………………113
第10章　給料に関する表現 ………………………………122
第11章　経営に関する表現 ………………………………127
第12章　コンピューターに関する表現 …………………155
第13章　商品に関する表現 ………………………………165
第14章　広告に関する表現 ………………………………172
第15章　銀行に関する表現 ………………………………176
第16章　電話に関する表現 ………………………………185
第17章　投資に関する表現 ………………………………192
第18章　買物・店に関する表現 …………………………199
第19章　車に関する表現 …………………………………213

INDEX　225

第1章 地位に関する表現

1 「上司」

(a) 一般的に述べる場合
 （ジムは私の上司です）
 ◎ Ⓐ Jim's my boss [supervisor].
 ◎ Ⓑ I work for Jim.
 ○ Ⓒ I report to Jim.
 ◯ Ⓓ I work under Jim.
 × Ⓔ Jim's my (service) superior.
 [注意] Ⓔの superior は軍隊，警察などの組織では非常によく使われている。

(b) くだけた口調で述べる場合
 （上司は外出しているの）
 Is ◎ Ⓐ the head honcho out?
    ○ Ⓑ the top dog out?
    △ Ⓒ the big cheese out?
 [注意] (1) ⒶⒷⒸいずれも会長，社長，専務，部長，課長，支店長，支配人，つまり上司なら誰でも使える。
 (2) He's my head honcho [top dog, big cheese]. のように，ⒶⒷⒸは my のみならず，our, her, his, their, つまり所有格と共に使うことはできない。

(c) 直属の上司
 （ジムは私の直属の上司です）
 ☆ Ⓐ I work directly under [report directly to] Jim.

[1]

◎ Ⓑ Jim's my immediate [direct] supervisor.
○ Ⓒ Jim's my immediate [direct] boss [superior].
○ Ⓓ I work right under Jim.
△ Ⓔ I work immediately under [directly for] Jim.
[注意] Ⓒ superier (上司) は使われていないが immediate [direct] superior はよく使われている。

2 「平社員」
(a) **ホワイトカラー**
  ●客観的に述べるとき
  (ダンは平社員です)
  ◎ Ⓐ Dan's just [only] an (office) employee.
  ◎ Ⓑ Dan just works in the office.
  ◎ Ⓒ Dan isn't in management.
  ○ Ⓓ Dan's just an office worker.
  △ Ⓔ Dan's an ordinary employee.
  △ Ⓕ Dan's just a worker.
  △ Ⓖ Dan's a worker like everybody else.
  ●軽蔑的に述べるとき
  (ダンはただの平社員です)
  ◎ Dan's just a peon.

(b) **ブルーカラー**
  (ダンは平社員です)
  Dan's ◎ Ⓐ just a worker [an employee].
     ◎ Ⓑ a worker like everybody else.
     △ Ⓒ only a worker [an employee].
     △ Ⓓ an ordinary employee.

3 「派遣社員」
  (ボブは派遣社員です)
  Bob's ◎ Ⓐ a temp.
     ◎ Ⓑ (an employee) from a temp agency.
     ○ Ⓒ from a temporary employment agency.
     ○ Ⓓ a member of a temp agency.
     △ Ⓔ on a temp staff.

4 「上層部」
(上層部の許可が必要なんです)
We need the green light from
- ◎ Ⓐ management [upstairs, the higher-ups].
- ○ Ⓑ higher-up.
- △ Ⓒ the administration.

5 「同僚」
(a) **管理職の場合**
(ジムは私の同僚です)
Jim's my ☆ Ⓐ colleague.
　　　　　◎ Ⓑ associate.
　　　　　△ Ⓒ coworker.

[注意] (1) associate は非常にあいまいな語で，出資している場合もある。ⒶⒸには出資しているニュアンスは全くない。
(2) 管理職にも上，中，下がある。Ⓒは下のほうの管理職（課長，係長クラス）ならよく使われている。

(b) **非管理職の場合**
(ジムは私の同僚です)
- ◎ Ⓐ Jim and I work together.
- ◎ Ⓑ I work (together) with Bill.
- ○ Ⓒ Jim's my coworker.
- ○ Ⓓ Jim's my associate.
- △ Ⓔ Jim's my colleague.

[注意] Ⓓの associate は聞こえがいい感じがする。このためホワイトカラーの平社員の間で婉曲的に述べるときによく使われている。

(c) **非管理職で似た仕事に従事しているが依存してはいない場合**
(ジムは私の同僚です)
- ◎ Jim's my fellow worker.

[注意] 互いに依存していないので coworker のように親密感はない。ホワイトカラー，ブルーカラーの両方で使われている。

(d) **同じ会社で働いている場合**
(ジムは私の同僚です)
- ◎ Ⓐ Jim and I work for the same company.

○ Ⓑ Jim's my fellow employee.
［注意］同じ会社で働いてさえいれば地位に関係なく使える。

6 「部下」
(a) 1人の部下に言及する場合
（ボブは私の部下です）
◎ Ⓐ Bob works for me.
◎ Ⓑ Bob's my assistant ［on my staff］.
○ Ⓒ Bob reports to me.
△ Ⓓ Bob works under me.
△ Ⓔ Bob's my subordinate.
［注意］(1) 辞典に inferior, follower が出ているが使われていない。
(2) Ⓐは直属の部下の場合でも直属の部下でない場合でも使われている。ⒸⒹⒺは主として直属の部下に，Ⓑは直属の部下の場合にのみ使われている。

(b) 複数の部下に言及する場合
（部長は部下に人気がないんです）
The General Manager isn't popular with his
  ◎ Ⓐ employees ［staff］.
  ○ Ⓑ people.
  △ Ⓒ subordinates.
［注意］Ⓐの employee は「従業員」「社員」の意味なので，主語が会社の所有者，つまりオーナーのときしか使えないと考えがちである。しかし，現代アメリカ英語では，主語が「社主」の場合だけでなく「上司」の場合でも広く使われている。

7 「下っ端」
(a) 1人しかいない場合
（サリーは職場で1番下っ端なんです）
Sally's ◎ Ⓐ (the) low man on the totem pole at work.
     ◎ Ⓑ just the peon at work.
     △ Ⓒ at the bottom of the food chain at work.
     × Ⓓ low woman on the totem pole at work.
［注意］(1) 女性の場合でも low woman ではなく low man と言う。
(2) ⒶⒷⒸいずれも職種を問わず，ホワイトカラー，ブルーカラーの両方に使われている。

第 I 章　地位に関する表現

(b)　**2人以上いる場合**
　　（サリーは会社で1番下っ端なんです）
　　Sally's ◎ Ⓐ a low man on the totem pole at work.
　　　　　　 ◎ Ⓑ just a peon at work.

8 「会長」
(a)　**男性**
　　（ジムは会長です）
　　Jim's ☆ Ⓐ the Chairman of the board.
　　　　　 ◎ Ⓑ the Chairman (of the board of directors).
　　［注意］アメリカの chairman（会長）は，日本と違って社長（CEO or President）の上司で権限を持っている。

(b)　**女性**
　　（リンダはこの会社の会長です）
　　Linda's ☆ Ⓐ the chairman of this company.
　　　　　　 ○ Ⓑ the chairwoman [chairperson] of this company.

9 「副会長」
　　（ダンは副会長です）
　　Dan's ◎ Ⓐ the Vice-Chairman.
　　　　　 × Ⓑ the Acting-Chairman.
　　［注意］辞典にⒷが出ているが使われていない。「副会長」が病気か，どこかへ出張している間の「臨時副会長」の意味ならよく使われている。

10 「社長」
　　（グレッグは社長です）
　　Greg's ◎ Ⓐ the CEO [the President].
　　　　　　○ Ⓑ the Chief Executive (Officer).
　　［注意］(1) 会社により CEO と President が両方いる場合，または両者が同一職の場合もある。
　　(2) 日本と違うのは会長に選ばれ現場の最高責任者であることである。

11 「取締役」
(a)　**一般的に述べる場合**
　　（ブライアンは取締役です）
　　Brian's ◎ Ⓐ an executive.

[5]

　　　　× Ⓑ a director.
　　[注意] Ⓑは非常にあいまいな語で，部長，課長，支配人なのか不明。従って
　　Ⓑのように述べたとき「取締役」の意味にはならない。

(b) 「会社の取締役」と述べる場合
　　（ブライアンは会社の取締役です）
　　Brian's a ◎ Ⓐ corporate executive.
　　　　　　　 ○ Ⓑ company executive.

(c) 会社名を明示して述べる場合
　　（ブライアンはXYZ会社の取締役です）
　　Brian's ◎ Ⓐ an executive with ［at］XYZ Company.
　　　　　　 ◎ Ⓑ an XYZ Company executive.
　　　　　　 ○ Ⓒ an executive of XYZ Company.
　　　　　　 △ Ⓓ an executive for XYZ Company.

(d) 政策を決定する「取締役理事会の一人」の意味の「取締役」と述べる場合
　　（ブライアンは取締役です）
　　Brian's ☆ Ⓐ on the board of directors.
　　　　　　 ◎ Ⓑ a member of the board of directors.
　　　　　　 ○ Ⓒ a board of directors member.
　　　　　　 × Ⓓ on the board of executives.
　　［注意］(1) executiveは「政策を決定する取締役理事会の一人」の意味には
　　使えない。
　　(2) アメリカの会社は the board of directors（取締役理事会）が会社運営の
　　最高責任者 Chairman（会長）を選び，Chairman が現場の最高責任者で
　　ある the President（社長）を選ぶ。President は会社により CEO
　　（Chief Executive Officer）とも呼ばれる。会社により Chairman が
　　President または CEO を兼任することもある。従って普通日本の会社で
　　名誉職である Chairman はアメリカでは会社の最高責任者である。

12 「銀行の頭取」
(a) 銀行名に言及しない場合
　　（ブライアンは銀行の頭取です）
　　Brian's a ◎ Ⓐ bank president.
　　　　　　　 △ Ⓑ banker.

第1章 地位に関する表現

(b) **銀行名に言及する場合**
(ブライアンはカリフォルニア銀行の頭取です)
Brian's ☆ Ⓐ the president of California Bank.
　　　　 × Ⓑ the president at [for, to] California Bank.
[注意] President of... と大文字で書いても非常によく使われている。

13 「支店長」
(a) **どこの支店ではなく広く一般的に述べる場合**
(グレッグは支店長です)
Greg's a ◎ Ⓐ branch manager.
　　　　　 × Ⓑ branch head.

(b) **支店内，または支店外でも特定の支店を頭に入れて述べる場合**
(グレッグは支店長です)
◎ Greg's the branch manager.

(c) **支店名と共に述べる場合**
(グレッグはシカゴ支店長です)
◎ Ⓐ Greg heads the Chicago branch.
◎ Ⓑ Greg's the manager of [at] the Chicago ...
◎ Ⓒ Greg's in charge of the Chicago ...
◎ Ⓓ Greg's the head of the Chicago ...

14 「副支店長」
(ジムはシカゴ支店の副支店長です)
◎ Ⓐ Jim's the assistant manager of [at] the Chicago branch.
◎ Ⓑ Jim's the second in charge of the Chicago branch.

15 「人事部長」
(ボブは人事部長です)
Bob's ☆ Ⓐ the Personnel Manager.
　　　 ◎ Ⓑ the Personnel Director.
　　　 ◎ Ⓒ in charge of [Bob's head of, Bob heads] Personnel.
　　　 ○ Ⓕ Director of Personnel.
[注意] (1) 人事以外の部長も同じ要領で使える。
(2) 人事以外の部の英語表現は「部」の項を参照されたい。

16 「部長補佐」
(夫は人事部の部長補佐です)
My husband's ☆ Ⓐ the Personnel Assistant Manager.
　　　　　　◎ Ⓑ the Assistant Manager [Director] of Personnel.
　　　　　　○ Ⓒ the second in charge of Personnel.
　　　　　　○ Ⓓ the Deputy Manager of Personnel.
　　　　　　△ Ⓔ the Deputy Director of Personnel.
［注意］人事部以外の「部長補佐」も上の要領で表現できる。「部」の項を参照されたい。

17 「支配人」
(a) **中西部・東部・南部などの大きな地域の支配人**
(彼は中西部の地域支配人です)
　◎ He's the regional manager of the Midwest.
［注意］regional manager は日本の会社にはない地位。このためか英和，和英の辞典には出ていないがアメリカ人の間ではよく使われている。従ってアメリカ人とのコミュニケーションには不可欠。(b)にも同じことが言える。

(b) **中西部・東部・南部などのある州の支配人**
(彼はオハイオの地区支配人です)
　◎ He's the district manager of Ohio.
［注意］district manager は日本の辞典に出ていないがアメリカ英語にはよく出てくる。

(c) **都市・町などの支配人**
(彼はトリド支店の支配人です)
　◎ He's the manager of the Toledo branch store.

18 「工場長」
(a) **自動車・鉄鋼・びん詰・缶詰などの工場**
(彼が工場長です)
　◎ Ⓐ He's the plant [factory] manager.
　◎ Ⓑ He's the manager [head] of the plant [factory].
　◎ Ⓒ He's in charge of the plant [factory].
　○ Ⓓ He heads the plant [factory].
　○ Ⓔ He heads the employees at the plant [factory].

(b) **製紙・繊維・製粉などの工場**
(彼が工場長です)
☆ Ⓐ He's the mill manager.
◎ Ⓑ He's the manager [head] of the mill [factory].
◎ Ⓒ He's the factory manager.
◎ Ⓓ He's in charge of the mill [factory].
○ Ⓔ He heads the mill [factory].
○ Ⓕ He heads the employees at the mill [factory].

19 「副工場長」
(a) **自動車・鉄鋼・びん詰・缶詰などの工場**
(彼が副工場長です)
He's ☆ Ⓐ the assistant plant manager.
◎ Ⓑ the assistant manager of the plant [factory].
◎ Ⓒ the assistant factory manager.
○ Ⓓ the assistant head of the plant.
○ Ⓔ the second in charge of the plant [factory].
[注意] 辞典に acting plant manager が「副工場長」として紹介されているが誤り。副工場長が出張、長期病気の欠勤中の代理的地位で「副工場長代理」が正しい。これはすべての地位に同じことが言える。

(b) **製紙・繊維・製粉などの工場**
(彼が副工場長です)
He's ☆ Ⓐ the assistant mill manager.
◎ Ⓑ the assistant manager of the mill [factory].
◎ Ⓒ the assistant factory manager.
○ Ⓓ the assistant head of the mill.

20 「班長」
(ビルはエンジン組立工程の班長なんです)
☆ Ⓐ Bill's the foreman of the engine assembly line.
◎ Ⓑ Bill heads the engine assembly line.
◎ Ⓒ Bill's in charge of the engine assembly line.

21 「副班長」
(ボブはエンジン組立工程の副班長なんです)
Bob's ☆ Ⓐ the assistant foreman of the engine assembly line.

◎ Ⓑ the deputy foreman ...

22 「病院長」
(a) **経営及び治療の両方に携わっている，またはどちらか不明の場合**
　　（夫は XYZ 病院の院長です）
　　☆ Ⓐ My husband's the head of XYZ Hospital.
　　◎ Ⓑ My husband heads XYZ ...
　　◎ Ⓒ My husband's in charge of XYZ ...
　　○ Ⓓ My husband's the chief of XYZ ...
　　[注意] (1) 辞典に superintendent が出ているが私立病院では全く使われていない。公立病院ではときどき使われている。
　　(2) アメリカでは公立病院は貧しい人が行く。

(b) **経営には関与していない場合**
　　（夫は XYZ 病院の院長です）
　　My husband's ◎ Ⓐ the head doctor of XYZ Hospital.
　　　　　　　　○ Ⓑ the chief doctor ...

23 「外科部長」
　　（夫は外科部長なんです）
　　☆ Ⓐ My husband's the head of Surgery.
　　◎ Ⓑ My husband heads Surgery.
　　◎ Ⓒ My husband's the head surgeon.
　　○ Ⓓ My husband's the chief of Surgery.
　　○ Ⓔ My husband heads the Surgical Department.

24 「最高管理職」
　　（ボブは最高管理職なんです）
　　Bob's ◎ Ⓐ in senior [top] management.
　　　　　× Ⓑ in the highest management.

25 「中間管理職」
　　（ダンは中間管理職なんです）
　　Dan's ◎ Ⓐ in middle management.
　　　　　○ Ⓑ a middle manager.
　　　　　× Ⓒ a middle management member.
　　　　　× Ⓓ a member of middle management.

26 「管理職の下っ端」
（ブライアンは管理職の下っ端なんです）
Brian's ☆ Ⓐ the low man on the totem pole in management.
　　　◎ Ⓑ a low-ranking manager.
　　　○ Ⓒ low man on the totem pole in management.
　　　△ Ⓓ a low man on the totem pole in management.

27 「上の人」
（リンダは上の人から長いお説教をされたんです）
Linda got a long lecture from
　　　☆ Ⓐ management.
　　　◎ Ⓑ the supervisors.
　　　○ Ⓒ upstairs ［the higher-ups, the head honchos, the top-dogs］.

28 「名目上の」
（うちの会長は名目上なんです）
Our Chairman's ◎ Ⓐ in name only ［just a figurehead］.
　　　　　　　△ Ⓑ just in name.
　　　　　　　▽ Ⓒ just a titular head.

29 「前任者」
(a) 支配人
（今度の支配人は前任者よりも物分りがいいね）
The new manager's more understanding than
　　　☆ Ⓐ the old guy.
　　　◎ Ⓑ the guy ［man, person］ before him.
　　　◎ Ⓒ the guy ［man, person］ before.
　　　○ Ⓓ the old one ［the one before him］.
　　　○ Ⓔ the one before.
　　　△ Ⓕ the previous ［the former］ one.

(b) 大統領・首相など地位の高い人
（ブッシュ大統領は前任者より支持率が高い）
President Bush has higher approval ratings than
　　　☆ Ⓐ the previous one.
　　　◎ Ⓑ his predecessor.

◎ Ⓒ the one before him.
○ Ⓓ the one before [the former one].
△ Ⓔ the old one.
▽ Ⓕ the ex-one.

30 「肩書き」
（夫には肩書きがないんです）
My husband ☆ Ⓐ doesn't have a job title.
　　　　　　◎ Ⓑ has no job title.
[注意] 辞典に be titled at work，have a handle to his name が出ているが使われていない。

第2章
能力・才能に関する表現

1 「頭の回転がいい」
（デイヴィッドは頭の回転がいいんです）
- ☆ Ⓐ David thinks fast.
- ◎ Ⓑ David thinks quick [has a quick mind].
- ◎ Ⓒ David's a quick thinker.
- ○ Ⓓ David thinks quickly [has a fast brain].
- ○ Ⓔ David's brain works fast.

2 「頭の回転が遅い」
（デイヴィッドは頭の回転が遅いんです）
- ☆ Ⓐ David thinks slow.
- ◎ Ⓑ David's brain works slow.
- ○ Ⓒ David has a slow mind [brain].
- ○ Ⓓ David's a slow thinker.
- ○ Ⓔ David thinks slowly.
- △ Ⓕ David's brain works slowly.

3 「仕事が速い」
（デイヴィッドは仕事が速い）
- ☆ Ⓐ David gets a lot done.
- ◎ Ⓑ David's productive [a fast worker].
- ◎ Ⓒ David does a lot [works fast].
- ○ Ⓓ David's quick [fast] at work.
- △ Ⓔ David accomplishes [achieves] a lot of work.

4 「計算が速い」
(デイヴィッドは計算が速いんです)
David's ☆ Ⓐ good with numbers.
　　　　◎ Ⓑ quick [fast] with numbers.
　　　　◎ Ⓒ good with math.
　　　　○ Ⓓ quick [fast] at figures [calculations].
　　　　○ Ⓔ good at calculations.
　　　　△ Ⓕ quick at calculating.

5 「統率力がある」
(今度の私たちの上司には統率力があります)
Our new boss
　　　　☆ Ⓐ has [shows] leadership skills.
　　　　◎ Ⓑ shows leadership qualities [abilities, ability].
　　　　◎ Ⓒ has leadership qualities.
　　　　◎ Ⓓ demonstrates leadership skills [qualities, abilities, ability].
　　　　○ Ⓔ has good leadership [has leadership abilities, ability].
　　　　○ Ⓕ shows (good) leadership.
　　　　○ Ⓖ demonstrates leadership.
　　　　△ Ⓗ has leadership.
　　　　× Ⓘ has (the) capacity as a leader.

6 「任せる技術」
(彼は部下に任せる技術を知っています)
He ☆ Ⓐ knows how to delegate.
　　☆ Ⓑ can leave things [stuff] to his staff.
　　☆ Ⓒ lets his staff handle things [stuff].
　　◎ Ⓓ can let his staff handle things [stuff].
　　◎ Ⓔ knows how to use his people [staff].
　　◎ Ⓕ isn't a micro manager.
　　○ Ⓖ knows the art of delegation.
　　○ Ⓗ knows how to leave things [stuff] to his staff.

7 「カリスマ性がある」
(ドゴール大統領はカリスマ性がありました)
President De Gaulle

☆ Ⓐ was charismatic [had charisma].
◎ Ⓑ was charming.
○ Ⓒ had magnetism [was magnetic].
○ Ⓓ had a charismatic [magnetic] personality.

[注意] 強さの点ではⒶのhad charismaが1番，Ⓒが2番，Ⓐのwas charismaticとⒹが3番，Ⓑは1番弱い。

8 「きれる」
(a) 特別高い地位でない人の場合
（私の秘書は非常にきれます）
◎ Ⓐ My secretary's really competent [capable, efficient].
◎ Ⓑ My secretary's really on the ball.
○ Ⓒ My secretary really has it all together.
○ Ⓓ My secretary's really sharp.

[注意] Ⓐのcompetentは「資格がある」という意味が原義なので「きれる」といってもその度合は1番弱い。capableは一般的な意味での「きれる」であるのに対して，efficientは「能率がいい」というニュアンスがある。ⒷⒸⒹは問題の対処の仕方，仕事上のあらゆる面に通じているというニュアンスがある。

(b) 高い地位の人の場合
（彼は非常にきれます）
◎ Ⓐ He really has his act together [has it altogether].
◎ Ⓑ He's really on top of things [on the ball].
○ Ⓒ He's really capable.
△ Ⓓ He's on the top.

[注意] Ⓓは人により使用頻度は大きく変わり，非常によく使う人もいる。

9 「(比喩的な意味で) 財産」
（彼の流暢な英語は将来彼に大きな財産になるでしょう）
His fluent English'll be
　　◎ Ⓐ a great asset to [for] him in the future.
　　◎ Ⓑ a great advantage [benefit] for [to] ...
　　○ Ⓒ a big benefit [asset] for [to] ...
　　○ Ⓓ a big plus for ...
　　○ Ⓔ a great plus to ...
　　△ Ⓕ a big plus to ...

△ Ⓖ a great plus for ...

10 「才能」
(a) 科学上の才能
(彼は科学上の才能があるんです)
☆ Ⓐ He's scientifically gifted.
◎ Ⓑ He's gifted scientifically.
◎ Ⓒ He has a scientific gift [a gift for science].
◎ Ⓓ He's talented scientifically [scientifically talented].
◎ Ⓔ He has a talent for science.
○ Ⓕ He's gifted with scientific talent.
○ Ⓖ He has a scientific flair.
○ Ⓗ He's scientifically inclined.
○ Ⓘ He has an unusual aptitude [flair] for science.
△ Ⓙ He has an unusual ability for science.
[注意] (1) 辞典に He has an unusual endowment [faculty, capability] for science. が出ているが使われていない。
(2) 才能の上ではⒶⒷⒸⒻが1番強い。ⒹⒺが2番, ⒼⒽⒾが3番。

(b) インテリア・デザイン・ファッション・音楽などの才能
(彼はインテリアの才能がすごくあるんです)
He ◎ Ⓐ really has a flair [has a real flair] for decorating.
　　○ Ⓑ really has a gift [talent] ...

(c) 人の上に立つ才能
(彼は人の上に立つ才能がある)
◎ Ⓐ He has a gift for leadership.
○ Ⓑ He has a talent for leadership.
○ Ⓒ He's gifted with leadership.
△ Ⓓ He has a leadership gift.
△ Ⓔ He's gifted leadership-wise.

11 「素質」
(a) 素質を求められる職業に言及する場合
●普通に述べるとき
(バーバラはプロの歌手になる素質があります)
Barbara has

第2章　能力・才能に関する表現

　　☆ Ⓐ what it takes to be a professional singer.
　　◎ Ⓑ the potential [the right stuff] to be a professional singer.
　　◎ Ⓒ the potential [the right stuff] to have a professional singing career.
　　○ Ⓓ what it takes to have a professional singing career.
　　△ Ⓔ the makings to be a professional singer.
　　△ Ⓕ the makings to have a professional singing career.
　　△ Ⓖ the makings of a professional singer in her.
　　△ Ⓗ it in her to be a professional singer.
● 強調して述べるとき
（バーバラはプロの歌手になる素質がすごくあります）
Barbara
　　☆ Ⓐ really has what it takes to be a professional singer.
　　◎ Ⓑ really has the right stuff [the potential] to be a professional singer.
　　○ Ⓒ has a lot of stuff to be a professional singer.
　　○ Ⓓ really has what it takes to have a professional singer.
　　○ Ⓔ really has the right stuff [the potential] to have a professional singing career.
　　○ Ⓕ has a lot of stuff to have a professional singing career.

(b)　**戦力になる期待を見せている場合**
（新入社員は素質がある）
The new employee ◎ Ⓐ shows a lot of promise [potential].
　　　　　　　　　◎ Ⓑ looks promising.
　　　　　　　　　× Ⓒ looks hopeful.
［注意］Ⓒが辞典に出ているが使われていない。

12 「…に向いている」
（ポールはこの種の仕事に向いています）
Paul's ☆ Ⓐ made [cut out] for this kind of work.
　　　　◎ Ⓑ fit [suited] for ...
　　　　○ Ⓒ suitable for ...
［注意］Ⓒは少し改まった響きがある。

13 「セールストーク」
(a)　一般的に述べる場合

(ブライアンはセールストークがものすごく上手なんです)
Brian has really good ☆ Ⓐ sales techniques.
　　　　　　　　　 ◎ Ⓑ sales skills.
　　　　　　　　　 △ Ⓒ sales pitches.

(b) 特定な場面を述べる場合
(あのお客はあなたのセールストークが上手だったからそれを買ったのかもしれない)
That customer might've bought it because your
　　☆ Ⓐ sales pitch was good.
　　○ Ⓑ sales technique was ...
　　△ Ⓒ sales skill was ...
　　△ Ⓓ sales skills were ...
［注意］辞典に sales talk が出ているが使われていない。

14 「上手です」
(a) 語学の場合
● 「ペラペラ」というニュアンスのとき
(娘はオランダ語が上手です)
My daughter speaks ☆ Ⓐ Dutch damn good.
　　　　　　　　　　 ◎ Ⓑ damn good Dutch ［Dutch damn well］.
［注意］(1) Ⓐは正しくないと言われているが，アメリカ人の間で１番よく使われ，「ペラペラ」という日本語の俗語的表現にぴったり。
(2) Ⓑは「ペラペラ」という日本語の俗語的ニュアンスに欠けるが非常によく使われている。
● 「流暢に」というニュアンスのとき
(妻はフランス語が上手です)
☆ Ⓐ My wife speaks fluent ［good］ French ［French fluently］.
◎ Ⓑ My wife's proficient in the French language.
◎ Ⓒ My wife has a good command of the French language.
▽ Ⓓ My wife's a good ［fluent］ speaker of French.
［注意］ⒷⒸの the French language を French としている辞典が多いが，その場合は使用頻度が下がる。

(b) 演説の場合
(リサは演説が上手です)
◎ Ⓐ Lisa's a good speaker.

○ Ⓑ Lisa makes good speeches.
　　△ Ⓒ Lisa's a good orator ［Lisa makes speeches well］.

(c) 楽器の場合
　　（ナンシーはバイオリンが上手です）
　　◎ Nancy's a good violinist ［Nancy plays the violin well］.

(d) スポーツの場合
　　●泳ぐ
　　（妻は泳ぐのが上手です）
　　◎ Ⓐ My wife's a good swimmer.
　　◎ Ⓑ My wife swims good.
　　○ Ⓒ My wife swims well.
　　［注意］厳密にはⒷは正しくないが非常によく使われている。
　　●テニス
　　（1番下の娘はテニスが上手です）
　　◎ Ⓐ My youngest daughter's a good tennis player.
　　◎ Ⓑ My youngest daughter plays tennis good.
　　○ Ⓒ My youngest daughter plays tennis well.
　　●ゴルフ
　　（次女はゴルフが上手です）
　　◎ Ⓐ My second daughter's a good golfer.
　　○ Ⓑ My second daughter plays golf well.
　　△ Ⓒ My second daughter's a good golf player.

(e) 扱い方
　　●部下
　　（ポールは部下の扱い方が上手なんです）
　　Paul ◎ Ⓐ knows how to treat ［take care of, handle］ his staff.
　　　　　○ Ⓑ has a way with his staff.
　　［注意］treat は部下に対する接し方のことを言及している。take care of は treat のニュアンス＋有給休暇のような職場で社員に提供することが求められていることに気を配り，社員があるべき姿で仕事をきちんとしていることをしっかりコントロールしているニュアンスがある。
　　handle は上記の下線部分のニュアンスで使われるのが正しいがしばしば3語は混用されている。
　　have a way with は treat とほぼ同じニュアンスで使われている。

●強調するとき
(私の上司は部下の扱い方が非常に上手なんです)
My boss ◎ Ⓐ really knows how to treat [take care of] his staff.
　　　　 ◎ Ⓑ really has a way with his staff.
　　　　 ◎ Ⓒ knows how to treat [take care of] his staff very well.

15 「さびつく」
(私のオランダ語は最近さびついてきた)
My Dutch ◎ Ⓐ is getting rusty these days.
　　　　　 ◎ Ⓑ isn't what it was [used to be] these days.
　　　　　 ○ Ⓒ is becoming rusty these days.
　　　　　 △ Ⓓ is getting bad these days.

16 「計画性」
(a) 「計画性がある」と述べる場合
　●普通に述べるとき
(ポールは計画性がある)
☆ Ⓐ Paul plans for the future.
◎ Ⓑ Paul's planning for the future.
○ Ⓒ Paul has a good plan for the future.
○ Ⓓ Paul looks towards the future.
△ Ⓔ Paul's future-oriented [future-minded].
[注意] ⒹⒺは「未来志向である」が本来の意味。しかしアメリカ人はⒶⒷⒸの意味でもよく使う。
　●強調して述べるとき
(ポールは非常に計画性がある)
☆ Ⓐ Paul really plans for the future.
◎ Ⓑ Paul's really planning for the future.
○ Ⓒ Paul has a really good plan for the future.
○ Ⓓ Paul really looks towards the future.
△ Ⓔ Paul's really future-oriented [future-minded].

(b) 「計画性がない」と述べる場合
　●普通に述べるとき
(ブライアンは計画性がないんです)
Brian
　　◎ Ⓐ has no plan [doesn't have any plan, doesn't plan] for the

future.
- ◯ Ⓑ isn't planning for the future.
- △ Ⓒ isn't future-oriented [future-minded].
● 強調して述べるとき
(ブライアンには全然計画性がないんです)
Brian
- ☆ Ⓐ has no plan for the future at all.
- ◎ Ⓑ doesn't plan for the future at all.
- ◎ Ⓒ doesn't have any plan [plans] for the future at all.
- ◯ Ⓓ isn't planning for [doesn't look towards] the future at all.
- △ Ⓔ has no plan [isn't planning] for the future whatsoever.
- △ Ⓕ doesn't plan for [look towards] the future whatsoever.

17 「詳しい」
(a) 専門的知識を持っているという意味での「詳しい」
● 普通に述べるとき
(私の上司は金融市場に詳しいんです)
- ◎ Ⓐ My boss's knowledgeable about the financial [money] markets.
- ◎ Ⓑ My boss's well-informed about [of] ...
- ◎ Ⓒ My boss's familiar with ...
- ◯ Ⓓ My boss's well-versed [quite at home] in ...
- △ Ⓔ My boss's well-acquainted [thoroughly acquainted] with ...
- △ Ⓕ My boss has a thorough knowledge of ...
- × Ⓖ My boss's well-posted in ...
- × Ⓗ My boss's conversant with ...
- × Ⓘ My boss has the financial markets at his fingers' ends.
- × Ⓙ My boss has the financial markets at his fingertips.

[注意] (1) 辞典にⒼ〜Ⓙが出ているが使われていない。
(2) Ⓙは辞典に「精通している」で紹介されているが，この意味では使われていない。しかし「情報を容易に得られる」という意味ではよく使われている。

● 非常に詳しいと述べるとき
(私の上司は金融市場に非常に詳しいんです)
- ◎ Ⓐ My boss knows the financial [money] markets really well.
- ◎ Ⓑ My boss's really [very] familiar with the financial [money] markets.
- ◎ Ⓒ My boss (really) knows everything with ...

◎ Ⓓ My boss (really) knows a lot about ...
◎ Ⓔ My boss really knows about ...
◎ Ⓕ My boss (really) knows all there's to know about ...
○ Ⓖ My boss (really) knows a lot of stuff [things] about ...
○ Ⓗ My boss's really knowledgeable about [on] ...
△ Ⓘ My boss's really well-informed about ...
△ Ⓙ My boss's really well-versed in ...
△ Ⓚ My boss's knowledgeable of ...
△ Ⓛ My boss knows the financial markets like the back of his hand.
[注意] ⒸⒹⒻⒼの really は意味上は重複になるが非常によく使われている。

(b) 名詞の前で使う「詳しい」
(私たちはもっと詳しい情報が必要なんです)
We need more ☆ Ⓐ in-depth [detailed] information.
　　　　　　　◎ Ⓑ precise [specific] ...
　　　　　　　○ Ⓒ explicit [exact] ...

18 「大物」

(a) 実業界・政界の場合
●現在の状態
(あの人は政界で大物です)
That's ◎ Ⓐ a big shot in the political world.
　　　　○ Ⓑ a bigwig ...
　　　　○ Ⓒ a big gun ...
　　　　○ Ⓓ an important figure ...
　　　　× Ⓔ a big pot [swell, bug, wheel, noise] ...
[注意] (1) 辞典にⒺが出ているが使われていない。
(2) Ⓓは堅い響きがある。
●未来の予想
(あの人は将来政界の大物になるでしょう)
That'll be ◎ Ⓐ a big shot [an important person] in the
　　　　　　◎ Ⓑ somebody [something] in the
　　　　　　○ Ⓒ a big gun [a bigwig, an important figure] in the
　　　　　　△ Ⓓ a somebody in the
political world in the future.

(b) **スポーツ界の場合**
(彼はフットボール界の大物の1人です)
He's one of ◎ Ⓐ the football superstars [star players].
　　　　　　◎ Ⓑ the star football players.

19 「小物」
(a) **主語が単数の場合**
(あの人は大物ではありません。小物です)
That isn't a big shot. He's ◎ Ⓐ a nobody.
　　　　　　　　　　　　　　◎ Ⓑ a small fry.
　　　　　　　　　　　　　　△ Ⓒ small potatoes.
　　　　　　　　　　　　　　△ Ⓓ nobody [nothing].

(b) **主語が複数の場合**
(あの人たちは大物ではありません。小物です)
Those aren't big shots. Those're ☆ Ⓐ nobody.
　　　　　　　　　　　　　　　　◎ Ⓑ nobodies.
　　　　　　　　　　　　　　　　○ Ⓒ small fries.

第3章

職業に関する表現

1 「アパートの管理人」
(ブライアンはアパートの管理人です)
Brian's a ◎ Ⓐ super.
　　　　 ○ Ⓑ superintendent.
　　　　 × Ⓒ caretaker.
[注意]Ⓒが辞典に出ているがこの意味では使われていない。

2 「医師」
(a) 眼科医
(私の父は眼科医です)
My father's ☆ Ⓐ an eye doctor.
　　　　　　 ◎ Ⓑ an eye specialist.
　　　　　　 △ Ⓒ an ophthalmologist.
[注意]Ⓒは医学界では非常によく使われている。

(b) 肛門医
(私の父は肛門医です)
My father's ◎ Ⓐ a proctologist.
　　　　　　 △ Ⓑ a butt doctor.
　　　　　　 △ Ⓒ an end specialist.

(c) 産婦人科医
(私の父は産婦人科医です)
◎ My father's an obstetrician.

[24]

(d) 耳鼻咽喉科
(私の父は耳鼻咽喉科医です)
My father's ◎ Ⓐ an ear, nose and throat specialist.
　　　　　　○ Ⓑ an ear, nose and throat doctor [man].
　　　　　　△ Ⓒ an ENT doctor.

(e) 小児科医
(私の父は小児科医です)
My father's ◎ Ⓐ a pediatrician [a children's doctor].
　　　　　　○ Ⓑ a doctor for children [kids].
　　　　　　△ Ⓒ a kids' doctor.

(f) 心臓専門医
(私の父は心臓専門医です)
My father's ☆ Ⓐ a heart specialist.
　　　　　　◎ Ⓑ a heart surgeon [doctor].
　　　　　　○ Ⓒ a cardiologist.

(g) 整形外科医
(私の父は整形外科医です)
My father's ☆ Ⓐ a bone doctor.
　　　　　　◎ Ⓑ an orthopedic surgeon [an orthopedist].

(h) 精神科医
●客観的に述べるとき
(私の父は精神科医です)
◎ My father's a psychiatrist.
●否定的に述べるとき
(彼は精神科医です)
He's ◎ Ⓐ shrink.
　　 ○ Ⓑ a headshrinker [a head doctor].
[注意] Ⓑの headshrinker が1番否定的な響きがあり，head doctor が2番目，Ⓐが3番目。

(i) 内科医
(私の父は内科医です)

My father's ◎ Ⓐ an internist.
　　　　　× Ⓑ a physician.

[注意] (1) Ⓑは英和・和英辞典で「内科医」として紹介されているがこの意味では全く使われていない。

(2) Ⓐの internist（内科医）はアメリカの医者，または医療関係者の間では非常によく使われている。しかし一般の人々の間では使われていない。なぜなら一般の人々は日常，内臓のどこかが悪いと感じたときは general practitioner [G.P.]（一般総合医）の所へ行く。general practitioner は family practice（全科医療：約55％），Internal Medicine（内科医学：約35％），Osteopathy（整骨療法：約10％）で構成されている。internal medicine は general practitioner の中に組み込まれているために，一般の人々は internist という言葉を使う機会がないので知らないのである。

(3) general practitioner は文字が示す通り，軽い治療なら内科・外科・耳鼻科などを診る。重い症状のときは各専門医を紹介する。

(4) アメリカ人には internist とは intern（医学研修生）と同意語であると思っている人が多い。前記した理由で internist の存在を知らないからである。

(5) physician を英和辞典で引くと，どれも「内科医」という訳語がつけられ誤訳されている。これは英米の辞典，つまり英英辞典に出てくる physician の定義を明治時代に誤訳したのが，いまだに誤解されたまま，踏襲されているためであることをここで強く指摘したい。参考までにここに定義を紹介しておく。one engaged in general medical practice, as distinguished from one specializing in <u>surgery</u>. 下線部分の surgery（外科）にひっかかって外科の反対の内科，つまり内科医と誤訳したのであろう。

(6) physician には「内科医」の意味がないことを筆者は日米口語表現辞典（研究社，1986年出版）で発表した。このため1987年以降に出版，または改訂された辞典では，筆者が唱えている「医師」の訳語を出している辞典が数冊出始めたが，それでもそれらの辞典で「内科医」という訳語も並記して読者を惑わせているので，ここで physician は「内科医」ではなく「医師」と訳すべきであることを強く，強く指摘したい

(7) physician はアメリカ人の小学生の間では使われていない。つまり doctor（医者）の品位のある語，従って「医師」という日本語に相当する。

(8) surgeon, dentist は普通 physician, doctor の中には入らない。

(j) 脳外科医
（私の父は脳外科医です）
My father's ☆ Ⓐ a brain surgeon.
　　　　　◎ Ⓑ a brain specialist.

　　　　　　　　○ ⓒ a neurologist.
　　　　　　　　△ ⓓ a brain doctor.

(k) 皮膚科医
　　(私の父は皮膚科医です)
　　My father's ☆ ⓐ a skin doctor.
　　　　　　　　◎ ⓑ a dermatologist.
　　　　　　　　○ ⓒ a skin specialist.

(l) 美容外科医
　　●一般の人対象
　　(私の父は美容外科医です)
　　◎ My father's a plastic surgeon.
　　●金持ちの人対象
　　(私の父は美容外科医です)
　　◎ My father's a cosmetic surgeon.

(m) 婦人科医
　　(私の父は婦人科医です)
　　My father's ◎ ⓐ a gynecologist.
　　　　　　　　△ ⓑ a women's doctor.

(n) 麻酔専門医
　　(私の父は麻酔専門医です)
　　◎ My father's an anesthesiologist.
　　[注意] anesthetist が辞典に出ているが使われていない。

(o) やぶ医者
　　(彼はやぶ医者です)
　　He's ◎ ⓐ a quack ［a bad doctor］.
　　　　△ ⓑ an incompetent doctor.
　　[注意] (1) 辞典に quack ［horse］ doctor が出ているが使われていない。
　　(2) quack は bad doctor よりずっと否定的ニュアンスが強い。

3 「犬のブリーダー」
　　(ナンシーは犬のブリーダーなんです)
　　Nancy's a ◎ ⓐ dog breeder.

○ Ⓑ breed of dogs.

4 「営業マン」
(a) **一般的に述べる場合**
(ボブは繊維会社に営業マンとして勤めています)
◎ Bob works for a textile company as a salesman [salesperson].

(b) **相手に聞こえよく言おうとする場合**
(ボブは繊維会社に営業マンとして勤めています)
Bob works for a textile company as a ◎ Ⓐ sales rep.
○ Ⓑ sales representative.

5 「栄養士」
(サリーは栄養士です)
Sally's ☆ Ⓐ a nutritionist.
◎ Ⓑ a nutrition specialist.
○ Ⓒ an expert on nutrition.
△ Ⓓ a specialist on nutrition.

6 「カメラマン」
(a) **新聞・雑誌**
(キャシィーは新聞のカメラマンです)
Cathy's a ☆ Ⓐ newspaper photographer.
◎ Ⓑ press photographer.
○ Ⓒ photographer for a newspaper [for the press].
× Ⓓ newspaper cameraman.

(b) **ビデオ**
(キャシィーはビデオのカメラマンです)
Cathy's a ◎ Ⓐ cameraman.
○ Ⓑ video cameraman.
× Ⓒ camerawoman.

(c) **映画**
(キャシィーは映画のカメラマンです)
Cathy's a ☆ Ⓐ movie cameraman.
◎ Ⓑ cinematographer.

第3章 職業に関する表現

　　　　　○ Ⓒ film cameraman.

7 「観光ガイド」
（メアリーは観光ガイドです）
Mary's a ◎ Ⓐ tour guide.
　　　　△ Ⓑ tour conductor.

8 「監督」
(a) スポーツ
（グレッグはジャイアンツの監督です）
◎ Ⓐ Greg's manager [head coach] of [for] the Giants.
◎ Ⓑ Greg manages the ...
○ Ⓒ Greg heads the ...
○ Ⓓ Greg's skipper of [for] the ....
[注意] 日本と違って head coach が「監督」の意味で使われている。

(b) 映画
（ボブは映画監督です）
Bob's a ◎ Ⓐ movie director.
　　　　○ Ⓑ film director.

9 「官僚」
(a) 単に官僚と述べるとき
●所属官庁名に言及しないとき
（父は官僚です）
My father's a ☆ Ⓐ government official.
　　　　　　◎ Ⓑ public official.
[注意] ⒶⒷ共中央，地方政府に使われている。
●所属官庁名を明示するとき
（ジムは財務省の官僚です）
◎ Ⓐ Jim's a Treasury Department official.
◎ Ⓑ Jim's an official at the Treasury Department.
◎ Ⓒ Jim has a position at the Treasury Department.
◎ Ⓓ Jim has a Treasury Department position.
[注意] ⒶⒷのほうがⒸⒹより地位が高いという響きがある。

(b) 高級官僚と述べる場合

● 所属官庁名に言及しないとき
(ジムは高級官僚です)
- ◎ Ⓐ Jim's a top-ranking [high-ranking, senior] government official.
- ◎ Ⓑ Jim has a top-ranking [high-ranking] government position [job].
- △ Ⓒ Jim has a senior government position [job].
- × Ⓓ Jim's a high-ranking bureaucrat.

[注意] (1) 日本語の「高級官僚」に相当する英語はⒶ～Ⓓである。

(2) どの辞典にもⒹの bureaucrat に「官僚」の訳語が出ている。しかし日本語の「官僚」には否定的なニュアンスはあまりないのに対し、英語の bureaucrat には以下の例のようにいつも否定的な響きがあり、政治家・ロビィストにも広く使われている。

That senator's a typical Washington bureaucrat.
（あの上院議員は典型的なワシントンの官僚政治家なんです）

I lost my passport in France, so I went to the American Consulate. But a guy I talked to first didn't help me. He was such a bureaucrat. I got so angry. I was really sick and tired of him. I finally spoke with the top guy in the section. He was able to help me.
（私はフランスでパスポートをなくしたんです。それでアメリカ領事館へ行きました。でも私が最初に相談した男の人は助けてくれなかったんです。彼はすごく官僚的でした。私は腹が立ち、彼に本当にうんざりしました。ついに私はその課の1番上の人と相談したんです。彼は力になってくれました）。

(3) ⒶⒷⒸいずれも中央政府、地方政府の両方に広く使われている。

● 所属官庁名を明示するとき
(ジムは財務省の高級官僚です)
- ◎ Ⓐ Jim's a top-ranking [high-ranking, senior] official at [in, with] the Treasury Department.
- ◎ Ⓑ Jim has a top-ranking [high-ranking] position at [in, with] the Treasury Department.
- ○ Ⓒ Jim has a senior position at [in, with] the Treasury Department.
- △ Ⓓ Jim has a senior job at [in, with] the Treasury Department.

(c) **下級官僚と述べる場合**
(ジムは下級官僚です)
Jim's a ☆ Ⓐ low-ranking [minor] government official.

◎ Ⓑ low-level government official.
○ Ⓒ low-ranking official.
△ Ⓓ minor-level official.

［注意］Ⓐ～Ⓓいずれも中央政府の意味でも地方政府の意味でも使われている。はっきりさせたいときは Jim's a Treasury Department official. と明示する必要がある。

10 「企業再建屋」
（彼は XYZ 会社の企業再建屋です）
He's
　☆ Ⓐ the guy brought in ［the guy hired］ to turnaround XYZ Company.
　◎ Ⓑ the turnaround specialist working for ...
　△ Ⓒ the turnaround manager ［artist］ working for ...

11 「銀行員」
（キャスィーは銀行員です）
◎ Ⓐ Cathy's a bank employee.
◎ Ⓑ Cathy works for a bank.
◎ Ⓒ Cathy works at a bank.

［注意］(1) 多くの辞典に bank clerk が出ているが今は使われていない。
(2) Ⓑは管理職または管理職の秘書であるというニュアンスがある。この違いは他の職業にも当てはまる。

12 「銀行家」
（ブライアンは銀行家なんです）
◎ Brian's a banker ［a bank executive］.

［注意］banker は以前は Brian owns a bank. の意味でも使われていた。

13 「(銀行の) 貸付係」
（ボブは貸付係です）
◎ Ⓐ Bob's a loan officer.
◎ Ⓑ Bob works in loans.
○ Ⓒ Bob works in the Loan Department.

14 「車の修理工」
（ジムは車の修理工です）

He's ☆ Ⓐ a car mechanic.
　　　◎ Ⓑ an auto mechanic.
　　　○ Ⓒ a car [an auto] repairman.

15 「経営者」
(a) **オーナーを指す場合**
(あの男性がこのホテルの経営者なんです)
◎ Ⓐ That guy owns this hotel.
◎ Ⓑ That guy's the owner of this hotel.
○ Ⓒ This hotel belongs to that guy.

(b) **経営だけに言及する場合**
(あの男性がこのホテルの経営者なんです)
◎ That guy's managing [running] this hotel.
[注意] (1) ホテルを所有しているオーナーなのか，雇われて経営をしているのかには言及していない。経営していることのみに言及している。
(2) be running は小さいビジネスに用いる傾向がある。従ってオーナーであるときは「経営している」という事実だけに言及する場合でも That guy's running this hotel. を使うことが多い。

16 「経済記者」
(ビルは経済記者です)
☆ Ⓐ Bill covers the economy.
◎ Ⓑ Bill covers finance.
◎ Ⓒ Bill's a reporter who covers the economy.
◎ Ⓓ Bill's a reporter who covers finance.
◎ Ⓔ Bill's a reporter for the economics desk.
◎ Ⓕ Bill's a reporter for the financial desk.
◎ Ⓖ Bill's a reporter on the economy.
[注意] ⒷⒹⒻは正しくは金融界を意味する。しかしアメリカ人は混用している人が多い。

17 「刑事」
(ボブは刑事です)
Bob's a ☆ Ⓐ police detective.
　　　　　◎ Ⓑ police investigator.
　　　　　△ Ⓒ G-man.

第3章 職業に関する表現

18 「警備員」
(a) **警備員だと述べる場合**
（ブライアンは警備員です）
Brian's a ◎ Ⓐ security guard.
　　　　　○ Ⓑ watchman.

(b) **警備を担当していると述べる場合**
（LMN がうちの警備をやっています）
　☆ Ⓐ LMN handles [takes care of] our security.
　◎ Ⓑ Our security's (being) handled [run, taken care of] by LMN.
　◎ Ⓒ We contract our security to LMN.
　○ Ⓓ Our security's (being) provided by LMN.
　○ Ⓔ We contract out our security to [with] LMN.
　○ Ⓕ We contract our security with LMN.
　○ Ⓖ We have a contract with LMN.

19 「経理」
（ジムは経理をしています）
Jim's ◎ Ⓐ a bookkeeper.
　　　× Ⓑ an accountant.
[注意] 辞典はⒶを「簿記係」として紹介しているが、日本語では普通「経理」と言う。Ⓑは「経理士」の意味でなら非常によく使われている。

20 「（得意先を訪ねる）広告取り」
（彼はニューヨークポストの広告取りです）
　◎ Ⓐ He's an ad salesman for the *New York Post*.
　◎ Ⓑ He goes out and sells ads for ...
　○ Ⓒ He's an advertising man for ...
　△ Ⓓ He's an adman for ...
[注意] (1) She でも salesman, advertising man, adman を使う。これもアメリカが男性社会であることを裏書きしている一例。
(2) 辞典には an ad solicitor [canvasser] が出ているが使われてもまれ。

21 「公認会計士」
（ボブは公認会計士です）
Bob's ◎ Ⓐ a CPA.

◎ Ⓑ an accountant.
[注意] ⒶⒷは厳密には同じではないが一般には混用されている。

22 「公務員」
(a) **国家公務員**
　●日本の場合
（私は公務員です）
　◎ Ⓐ I work for [I have a job in] the Japanese Government.
　◎ Ⓑ I'm a Japanese Government employee [worker].
　○ Ⓒ I have a position in the Japanese Government.
　○ Ⓓ I'm an employee for [of, in] the Japanese Government.
　○ Ⓔ I work for the government.
　○ Ⓕ I'm employed by the Japanese Government.
　○ Ⓖ I'm a civil servant.
　× Ⓗ I'm a public servant [a government official, government officer].

[注意] (1) Ⓗが多くの辞典に「国家公務員」として紹介されているが，この意味では使われていない。しかし public servant は選挙で選ばれた国会議員，知事，市長，町長などに普通に使われている。従って public servant に相当する日本語はない。government official は政府の「官僚」，state government, county government の「幹部」の意味でなら非常によく使われている。government officer も，government official の意味では使われているが，official のほうが officer よりもよく使われている。
(2) Ⓖの civil servant は多くの辞典に「国家公務員」と紹介されているが，国家だけでなく県庁，市役所，町役場の「公務員」の意味でよく使われている。
(3) Ⓑは高い地位にいる「公務員」として数冊の辞典に紹介されているが，英語のニュアンスを歪曲している。government employee は地位の高低に関係なく使われている。government worker は地位が非常に低い場合にのみよく使われている。
(4) 辞典にⒶは出ていないが，地位に関係なく非常によく使われている。
(5) Ⓒは地位が高いという響きがある。
(6) ⒻはⒷの government worker ほどではないが地位が低いときに使われている。
(7) Ⓔは政府，県庁，市役所，町・村役場，区役所の「公務員」の意味でよく使われている。
(8) アメリカ政府以外の国はすべて Japanese を変えて同じ表現を使う。

第3章　職業に関する表現

●アメリカの場合
1) アメリカ人がアメリカ人に話すとき
(私は公務員です)
◎ Ⓐ I work for the Federal Government.
◎ Ⓑ I'm a Federal Government employee.
◎ Ⓒ I have a job in the (Federal) Government.
◎ Ⓓ I'm employed by [I'm an employee of] the Federal Government.
○ Ⓔ I'm an employee for [I work at] the Federal Government.
○ Ⓕ I'm on the Federal Government payroll.
2) アメリカ人が外国で話すとき
(私は国家公務員です)
◎ Ⓐ I work for the (American) Government.
○ Ⓑ I work for Uncle Sam.
○ Ⓒ I have a job in the Government.
○ Ⓓ I'm employed by the American Government.
○ Ⓔ I'm an American Government employee.
△ Ⓕ I'm an employee of [for] the American Government.
× Ⓖ I work for the Federal Government.
× Ⓗ I'm a Federal Government employee.

(b)　**県庁**
(私は公務員です)
☆ Ⓐ I work for the County (Hall).
◎ Ⓑ I work for the County Government.
◎ Ⓒ I work at [in] County Hall.
◎ Ⓓ I'm an employee at [of] County Hall.
◎ Ⓔ I'm an employee of the County Government.
◎ Ⓕ I'm a County (Government) employee.
× Ⓖ I work for the Prefecture.

[注意] (1) 日本の辞典では「県」=prefectureと出ている。しかしアメリカでは全く使われていない。従って奇妙に聞こえる。countyが日本の県に相当する。
(2) 話し手が働いているcounty (県) 以外で話すときは，I work for a county. のtheではなくaを使う。
(3) countyは小文字も等しくよく使われている。

(c) 市役所
   （私は公務員です）
   ☆ Ⓐ I work for (the) city [town] hall.
   ◎ Ⓑ I work at (the) city [town] hall.
   ◎ Ⓒ I work for the City [the city government].
   ◎ Ⓓ I'm an employee at (the) city hall.
   ◎ Ⓔ I work in (the) city hall.
   ◎ Ⓕ I'm a city hall [a city (government)] employee.
   ◎ Ⓖ I'm employee by city hall.
   △ Ⓗ I work for the municipal government.
   ▽ Ⓘ I'm a city office employee.
   ［注意］(1) city　hall は大文字，小文字共によく使われている。但し town hall は小文字でしか使われていない。
   (2) city hall は全体でいくつかの city office から成り立っている。しかし，一般の会話では city office は city hall の意味でよく使われている。
   (3) Ⓗの municipal government は「町役場」の意味でもよく使われている。

23 「裁判官」
(a) 最高［控訴］裁判所
   （ブライアンは裁判官です）
   Brian's a ◎ Ⓐ justice.
   　　　　　× Ⓑ judge.
   ［注意］最高裁判所はアメリカの各州にひとつあり，連邦最高裁判所がひとつ，合計51ある。

(b) 最高［控訴］裁判以外の裁判所
   （ブライアンは裁判官です）
   Brian's a ◎ Ⓐ judge.
   　　　　　× Ⓑ justice.

24 「作曲家」
(a) クラシック音楽
   （ボブは作曲家です）
   ☆ Ⓐ Bob's a composer.
   ◎ Ⓑ Bob writes music.
   ○ Ⓒ Bob writes classical music.

(b) **ジャズ音楽**
（ボブは作曲家です）
◎ Ⓐ Bob writes (Jazz) music.
○ Ⓑ Bob's a jazz music composer.
○ Ⓒ Bob composes jazz music.
△ Ⓓ Bob's a composer.

(c) **ロック音楽**
（ボブは作曲家です）
☆ Ⓐ Bob writes rock music.
◎ Ⓑ Bob's a rock music composer.
○ Ⓒ Bob writes music.
△ Ⓓ Bob composes rock music.
× Ⓔ Bob's a composer.

25 「実業家」
(a) **一般的**
（グレッグは実業家です）
Greg's a ◎ Ⓐ businessman.
▽ Ⓑ businessperson.
[注意] 一般の「サラリーマン」の意味にも使われている。

(b) **製造業**
（グレッグは実業家です）
◎ Greg's an industrialist.

26 「写真師」
（ジムは写真師です）
Jim's a ☆ Ⓐ photographer.
○ Ⓑ studio photographer.
△ Ⓒ photographer at a studio.

27 「消防士」
（リンダは消防士です）
Linda's a ◎ Ⓐ fireman [fire fighter].
▽ Ⓑ firewoman.
[注意] (1) 女性でもⒶの fireman が非常によく使われている。

(2) 男性のときは④のみが使われている。

28 「照明係」
(ビルは照明係です)
Bill's a ◎ Ⓐ guy who controls [handles, operates, takes care of, works, runs, manages] the spotlight.
　　　○ Ⓑ lightening man.
　　　△ Ⓒ spotlight man.

29 「私立探偵」
(ブライアンは私立探偵です)
Brian's a ☆ Ⓐ private investigator.
　　　◎ Ⓑ private detective [PI].
　　　○ Ⓒ private eye.

30 「政治記者」
(彼は政治記者です)
He's a ☆ Ⓐ political reporter.
　　　◎ Ⓑ reporter who covers politics [the political desk].
　　　◎ Ⓒ reporter for the political desk.
　　　○ Ⓓ reporter on politics [the political desk].
　　　△ Ⓔ newsman who reports on politics.
[注意] 多くの辞典で newsman を最初に出しているが，堅い言葉なので会話ではあまり使われていない。

31 「税務官吏」
(彼は税務官吏です)
He's a ◎ Ⓐ tax official.
　　　○ Ⓑ revenue official.
　　　△ Ⓒ tax officer.
[注意] 辞典に revenue officer が出ているが使われていない。

32 「税務署員」
(ボブは税務署員なんです)
☆ Ⓐ Bob works for a tax office.
◎ Ⓑ Bob's a tax office employee.
◎ Ⓒ Bob's a clerk at the tax office.

○ Ⓓ Bob's a tax office clerk.
△ Ⓔ Bob's on the staff of a tax office.
[**注意**] ⒶⒷⒺは地位に関係なく使えるのに対してⒸⒹは地位が低い人にしか使えない。

33 「税務署長」
(夫は税務署長なんです)
☆ Ⓐ My husband's in charge of [the head of] the tax office.
◎ Ⓑ My husband heads the tax office.
◎ Ⓒ My husband's the supervisor of the tax office.

34 「税務調査官」
(彼は税務調査官です)
He's a ◎ Ⓐ tax auditor.
○ Ⓑ tax specialist.
△ Ⓒ tax inspector.

35 「造園技師」
(ブライアンは造園技師です)
Brian's a ☆ Ⓐ landscape architect.
◎ Ⓑ landscape designer [landscaper].
△ Ⓒ landscape engineer.

36 「測量士」
(彼は測量士です)
He's a ☆ Ⓐ surveyor.
◎ Ⓑ land surveyor.
○ Ⓒ surveying engineer.

37 「大使」
(あの方は駐日オランダ大使です)
◎ That's the Dutch Ambassador to Japan [Tokyo].

38 「タクシーの運転手」
(ボブはタクシーの運転手です)
Bob's a ☆ Ⓐ taxi driver.
◎ Ⓑ cab driver.

△ ⓒ cabbie.

39 「駐車場の係員」
(a) 駐車ビル
　　（ジムは駐車場の係員なんです）
　　◎ Jim's a parking attendant.

(b) 地上の駐車場
　　（ジムは駐車場の係員なんです）
　　◎ Jim's a parking (lot) attendant.

40 「駐車場の係の責任者」
　　（デイヴィッドは駐車場の係の責任者なんです）
　　☆ Ⓐ David's in charge of valet parking.
　　◎ Ⓑ David's the head of valet parking.
　　○ ⓒ David heads valet parking.

41 「（高級ホテル・レストランなどの）駐車場の車の出し入れ係」
(a) 一般的に述べる場合
　　（スティーヴは駐車場の車の出し入れ係なんです）
　　☆ Ⓐ Steve's a valet parking attendant.
　　◎ Ⓑ Steve works at valet parking.
　　○ ⓒ Steve's an attendant at valet parking.
　　○ Ⓓ Steve works for valet parking.

(b) ホテル名・レストラン名を明示する場合
　　（スティーヴはヒルトンの駐車場の車の出し入れ係なんです）
　　☆ Ⓐ Steve's a valet parking attendant at the Hilton.
　　◎ Ⓑ Steve works for valet parking at the Hilton.

42 「調停人」
　　（彼は労使の調停人なんです）
　　He's ☆ Ⓐ the go-between between management and labor.
　　　　　◎ Ⓑ the mediator between ...
　　　　　○ ⓒ the arbitrator between ...
　　［注意］正しくは madiator は自発的に調停役を買ってする人。arbitrator は任命されて調停をする人であるがアメリカ人は混用している。

43 「通訳」

(a) **ただ通訳であることを述べる場合**
   (ナンシーは通訳です)
   Nancy's ◎ Ⓐ an interpreter.
   　　　　 ○ Ⓑ a translator.
   [注意] translator を「翻訳者」としてのみ紹介している辞典がほとんどだが，「通訳」の意味でもよく使われている。

(b) **何語の通訳であるかを述べる場合**
   (ナンシーはフランス語から英語への通訳です)
   Nancy's ◎ Ⓐ a French-English interpreter.
   　　　　 ○ Ⓑ a French-English translator.
   　　　　 ○ Ⓒ an interpreter from French to English.
   　　　　 △ Ⓓ a translator from French to English.

(c) **同時通訳**
   (ナンシーは同時通訳です)
   ◎ Nancy's a simultaneous interpreter.

44 「テレビタレント」

   (リンダはテレビタレントです)
   Linda's a ◎ Ⓐ TV personality.
   　　　　　 × Ⓑ TV talent.
   [注意] ある辞典にⒷが出ているが全く使われていない。

45 「テレビの総合司会者」

   (リズはテレビの総合司会者です)
   Liz's a ☆ Ⓐ TV anchorwoman.
   　　　　 ◎ Ⓑ TV anchor [anchorman].

46 「店員」

(a) **コンビニ・スーパーのように店員が買物客を説得する必要のない店**
   (ボブはコンビニで店員として働いています)
   Bob works at a convenience store as a ◎ Ⓐ cashier.
   　　　　　　　　　　　　　　　　　　　　 ○ Ⓑ clerk.

(b) デパートの婦人服売場，宝石店など店員が買物客を説得する必要のある店
　●単数のとき
(ナンシーは店員としてメイシーに勤めています)
Nancy works at Macy's as a
　　☆ Ⓐ salesperson.
　　△ Ⓑ salesman ［saleswoman, salesclerk］.
［注意］Ⓑの salesclerk はデパートで買物客に説得が求められていないセール(大売出し)のような所でしか使えない。
　●複数のとき
(ナンシーとリズは店員としてメイシーに勤めています)
Nancy and Liz're working at Macy's as
　　☆ Ⓐ salespeople.
　　○ Ⓑ salesclerks.
　　△ Ⓒ salesmen ［saleswomen, salespersons］.

(c) ガソリンスタンドの店員
(ジムはガソリンスタンドの店員です)
Jim's ◎ Ⓐ a gas station attendant.
　　　○ Ⓑ attendant at a gas station.
　　　△ Ⓒ a filling station attendant.

47 「電気技師」
(ダンは電気技師です)
Dan's an ◎ Ⓐ electrician.
　　　　　 ○ Ⓑ electric engineer.

48 「時計の修理士」
(ナンシーは時計の修理士です)
Nancy's a ◎ Ⓐ watch repairman.
　　　　　 × Ⓑ watch repairwoman.
［注意］女性でもⒶである。

49 「取締役理事」
(父は取締役理事なんです)
My father's ☆ Ⓐ a board member.
　　　　　　 ☆ Ⓑ on the board.
　　　　　　 ◎ Ⓒ on the board of directors.

　　　　　◎ Ⓓ a member of the board of directors.
　　　　　○ Ⓔ a member of the board.
[注意] アメリカでは「取締役理事」は普通大株主で会社の政策決定をし会長の上にいる。また会長が社長を選ぶ。従ってアメリカの会長，社長は日本と違う。

50 「トリマー」
（ナンシーは犬のトリマーなんです）
Nancy's a ☆ Ⓐ dog groomer.
　　　　　◎ Ⓑ groomer for dogs.
　　　　　○ Ⓒ dogs' groomer.
　　　　　△ Ⓓ groomer of dogs.

51 「庭師（植木屋）」
（ボブは庭師です）
Bob's a ◎ Ⓐ gardener.
　　　× Ⓑ garden designer ［landscape gardener］.
[注意] ⒷがⒶと共に辞典に出ているが，Ⓐと同じ意味では使われていない。

52 「パイロット見習い」
（ビルはパイロット見習いなんです）
Bill's ☆ Ⓐ being trained as a pilot.
　　　☆ Ⓑ training ［studying］ to be a pilot.
　　　◎ Ⓒ training as a pilot.
　　　◎ Ⓓ in pilot training.
　　　○ Ⓔ a pilot-in-training ［a pilot trainee］.
[注意] ⒷⒸⒺはパイロット養成所へ行っている場合と空軍に入っている「パイロット見習い」の意味がある。どちらであるかは文脈で決める。ⒶⒹは空軍に入っているニュアンスが特に強い。

53 「パソコン接続［取付］業者」
（彼女はパソコン接続業者なんです）
☆ Ⓐ She sets up computer networks.
◎ Ⓑ She's a network specialist.
◎ Ⓒ She's an IT guy.
○ Ⓓ She builds computer networks.
[注意] Ⓒ女性でも woman, girl でなく guy を使う。

54「パソコンの修理士」
(彼女はパソコンの修理士なんです)
☆ Ⓐ She fixes computers.
◎ Ⓑ She's a computer maintenance tech.
○ Ⓒ She's a computer repairman.
○ Ⓓ She's a computer maintenance technician.
○ Ⓔ She repairs computers.
○ Ⓕ She's a computer trouble shooter.

55「飛行機の修理士」
(ビルは飛行機の修理士なんです)
Bill's ◎ Ⓐ an airplane mechanic.
　　　 ○ Ⓑ a plane mechanic.

56「ピアノの調律師」
(ビルはピアノの調律師です)
◎ Bill's a piano tuner.
［注意］辞典に tuner for pianos, tuner が出ているが使われていない。

57「秘書」
(a)　**重役の秘書**
(リンダは重役の秘書です)
◎ Linda's an executive secretary.

(b)　**社長の秘書**
(リズは社長の秘書です)
Liz's the ◎ Ⓐ CEO's [boss's] secretary.
　　　　　 ○ Ⓑ President's secretary.
［注意］Ⓐの the boss's secretary は場面により社長以外，つまり「上司の秘書」の意味でもよく使われている。

(c)　**一般的に述べる場合**
(リンダは秘書です)
Linda's ◎ Ⓐ an administrative secretary.
　　　　 ▽ Ⓑ a secretary.
［注意］辞典では secretary＝「秘書」と出ている。しかし1970年頃から sec-

retary は「事務員」，つまり事務所で事務の仕事をしていて，特別の肩書きがない女性たちを第三者に聞こえよくするために，それ以前までよく使われていた clerk-typist に取って代わって広く使われるようになった。従って「社長の秘書」= the CEO's secretary，「部長の秘書」= the General Manager's secretary，「ブラウン氏の秘書」= Mr. Brown's secretary と特定な人の「秘書」を述べるとき，または She's a good secretary.（彼女は有能な秘書です）と形容詞が先行するとき以外は，secretary は「事務員」の意味で使われることが多い

58 「美容師見習い」
(リンダは美容師見習いなんです)
Linda's
- ☆ Ⓐ training [studying to be a beautician] at a beauty shop.
- ◎ Ⓑ being trained [studying] at a beauty shop.
- ○ Ⓒ in beautician training.
- △ Ⓓ a beautician-in-training [a cosmetician-in-training].
- △ Ⓔ a beautician trainee.

59 「弁護士」
(a) **客観的に述べる場合**
(ジムは弁護士です)
◎ Jim's a lawyer.

(b) **上品な響きを出す場合**
(ジムは弁護士です)
◎ Jim's an attorney.

(c) **否定的なニュアンスで述べる場合**
(ジムは弁護士です)
Jim's ◎ Ⓐ an ambulance chaser.
　　　△ Ⓑ a shyster.
[注意] Ⓐは交通事故・職場・アパート・店内などでのけがの事故を扱う弁護士を揶揄して述べるときに使われている。Ⓑは「悪徳弁護士」というニュアンスで使われている。

60 「編集主幹」
(彼は編集主幹です)

He's ◎ Ⓐ the chief editor.
　　◎ Ⓑ the editor-in-chief.
　　○ Ⓒ the head editor.

61 「編集長」
(a) **社内で述べる場合**
　　(ボブは編集長です)
　　Bob's the ◎ Ⓐ chief editor.
　　　　　　　○ Ⓑ editor-in-chief.

(b) **社外で述べる場合**
　　(ボブは編集長です)
　　Bob's ◎ Ⓐ a chief-editor.
　　　　　○ Ⓑ an editor-in-chief.

62 「(ホテルの) フロント」
(スティーヴはヒルトンのフロントで働いているんです)
☆ Ⓐ Steve works at the front desk of the Hilton.
◎ Ⓑ Steve's a front desk clerk at the Hilton.
○ Ⓒ Steve works behind the front desk of the Hilton.
○ Ⓓ Steve's a clerk at the front desk of the Hilton.

63 「(ホテル内で客の荷物を運ぶ) ベルボーイ」
(ジムはベルボーイとしてヒルトンに勤めています)
Jim works for the Hilton as a ◎ Ⓐ bellboy [bellhop].
　　　　　　　　　　　　　　　　○ Ⓑ porter.

64 「ベルボーイの責任者」
(ディヴィッドはベルボーイの責任者なんです)
David's ☆ Ⓐ the bell captain.
　　　　◎ Ⓑ in charge of the bellboys.
　　　　◎ Ⓒ the supervisor [head] of the bellboys.

65 「ボーイ長」
(ブライアンはボーイ長です)
Brian's the ◎ Ⓐ maitre d'hotel.
　　　　　　◎ Ⓑ headwaiter [host].

第3章　職業に関する表現

[注意] Ⓐは高級レストランのボーイ長を言う。給仕はせずに，お客をテーブルへ案内するのが仕事。Ⓑの headwaiter は普通のレストランのボーイ長を言い，お客をテーブルに案内して給仕もする。host はコーヒーショップなどのボーイ長で，テーブルにお客を案内するが，給仕はしない。

66 「ボディーガード」
（ジムは社長のボディーガードです）
Jim's the ◎ Ⓐ boss's body guard.
　　　　　△ Ⓑ boss's guard.

67 「ホテルの予約カウンター」
（スティーヴはホテルの予約カウンターで働いています）
☆ Ⓐ Steve works at the hotel reservation desk.
◎ Ⓑ Steve works behind the hotel reservation desk.
◎ Ⓒ Steve's a reservation clerk at the hotel.
○ Ⓓ Steve works at [behind] the hotel reservation counter.

68 「薬剤師」
（サリーは薬剤師です）
Sally's a ◎ Ⓐ pharmacist.
　　　　　○ Ⓑ chemist.
　　　　　▽ Ⓒ druggist.
　　　　　× Ⓓ pharmaceutist [dispenser].
[注意] 辞典にⒹが出ているが使われていない。

69 「融資の係」
(a) 2人以上いる場合
（ボブは融資の係として銀行に勤めています）
Bob ☆ Ⓐ works for a bank as a loan officer.
　　 ◎ Ⓑ is in charge of loans at a bank.
　　 ◎ Ⓒ works [is] in loans at a bank.
　　 ○ Ⓓ is in the Loan Department at a bank.

(b) 1人の場合
（融資の係の人は誰ですか）
◎ Ⓐ Who do I see about a loan?
◎ Ⓑ Who's the loan officer?

[47]

◎ ⓒ Who's (the person) in charge of loans?
◎ ⓓ Who's in loans?

70「融資の責任者」
(融資の責任者はどなたなのですか)
☆ Ⓐ Who's the head loan officer?
☆ Ⓑ Who heads Loans?
◎ ⓒ Who's the head ［in charge］ of Loans?
○ ⓓ Who's the head ［in charge］ of the Loan Department?
○ Ⓔ Who heads the Loan Department?
△ Ⓕ Who's the top ［chief］ loan officer?

71「予約係の責任者」
(ボブは予約係の責任者なんです)
☆ Ⓐ Bob's in charge of reservations ［the reservation desk］.
◎ Ⓑ Bob heads reservations.
◎ ⓒ Bob's the head of reservations ［the reservation desk］.

72「ラジオタレント」
(リンダはラジオタレントです)
Linda's a ◎ Ⓐ radio personality.
　　　　　× Ⓑ radio talent.

73「領事」
(あの方は駐日イギリス領事です)
That's the ◎ Ⓐ British Consul to Japan.
　　　　　○ Ⓑ British Consul in ［at］ Japan.

74「旅行業者」
(リンダは旅行業者です)
◎ Linda's a travel agent.
［注意］traveling agent を紹介している辞典があるが使われていない。

75「レストランの客席への案内係」
(彼女はレストランの客席への案内係です)
She's a ☆ Ⓐ hostess at a restaurant.
　　　　☆ Ⓑ restaurant hostess.

第3章　職業に関する表現

　　　　◎ ⓒ host at a restaurant.
　　　　○ ⓓ restaurant host.
[注意] ⓒの host は hostess に対する男性用語であるが女性にも非常によく使われている。これもアメリカが男性社会であることを裏書きしている一例。

76 「(新聞の) 論説委員」
（彼は論説委員です）
He's an　☆ Ⓐ editorial writer.
　　　　　 ○ Ⓑ editorialist.

第4章 会社に関する表現

1 「会社」
(a) 小さい［大きい］会社の場合
(私は小さい［大きい］会社をマンハッタンに持っています)
I have a small [big] ☆ Ⓐ business in Manhattan.
　　　　　　　　　　　◎ Ⓑ company ...
　　　　　　　　　　　○ Ⓒ firm ...
　　　　　　　　　　　△ Ⓓ outfit ...

(b) ホワイトカラーの会社の場合
(彼は大きな会社に勤めています)
◎ He works for a big firm.
［注意］firm はブルーカラーの会社には使われていない。

(c) 法人組織になっている会社であることを明示する場合
(彼は大手の会社に勤めています)
◎ He works for a major corporation.
［注意］company, firm, business, house, outfit いずれも「会社」の意味で広く使われているが，法人組織になっているか否かについては言及されていない。

(d) くだけた調子で述べる場合
(彼は大きな会社に勤めています)
◎ He works for a big outfit.
［注意］outfit は広く使えるが常にくだけた響きで述べたいときに広く使われ

第4章　会社に関する表現

(e) **場所として述べる場合**
（私は彼女と会社で知り合ったんです）
I met her ◎ Ⓐ at work ［at the office, on the job］.
　　　　　× Ⓑ at the company.

(f) **形容詞的に使われる場合**
●会社の規則
（会社の規則に従わなければなりません）
◎ You have to follow the company ［company's］ rules ［regulations］.
●会社のレストラン
（私は普通，会社のレストランで昼食を食べます）
I usually eat lunch at the ◎ Ⓐ company restaurant.
　　　　　　　　　　　　△ Ⓑ company's restaurant.

2 「株式会社にする」
（うちは来月会社を株式会社にする予定です）
We're going to ◎ Ⓐ incorporate our company next month.
　　　　　　　○ Ⓑ make our company incorporated ...
［注意］辞典に make our company a public company ［a public limited company］が出ているが使われていない。

3 「本社」
（本社はどこにあるのですか）
◎ Ⓐ Where's your head ［main］ office?
◎ Ⓑ Where are your headquarters?
○ Ⓒ Where's your headquarters?

4 「子会社」
（アンダスン製薬会社はうちの子会社のひとつです）
Anderson Drug Company's one of our ☆ Ⓐ subsidiaries.
　　　　　　　　　　　　　　　　　◎ Ⓑ subsidiary companies.

5 「合弁会社」
（リンダは日仏合弁会社に勤めているんです）

[51]

Linda works for a ☆ Ⓐ joint Japanese-French company.
　　　　　　　　　◎ Ⓑ joint Japanese-French firm.
　　　　　　　　　○ Ⓒ joint Japanese-French business.
　　　　　　　　　△ Ⓓ joint Japanese-French outfit.
　　　　　　　　　△ Ⓔ Franco-Japanese company [outfit].

［注意］辞典に Japanese-French joint company が出ているが日本語に惑わされた語順で使われていない。

6 「挨拶カード会社」
(ホールマークは挨拶カード会社です)
Hall Mark's a ◎ Ⓐ greeting card company.
　　　　　　　○ Ⓑ greeting card business [outfit].
　　　　　　　○ Ⓒ card company.
　　　　　　　△ Ⓓ card business [greeting card firm].

7 「アパート管理会社」
(ビルはアパート管理会社に勤めているんです)
Bill works for ☆ Ⓐ a company that manages apartments.
　　　　　　　◎ Ⓑ a company that manages apartment buildings.
　　　　　　　◎ Ⓒ an apartment management company.
　　　　　　　○ Ⓓ an apartment building management company.

8 「医療器具リース会社」
(リンダは大きな医療器具リース会社に勤めています)
Linda works for a big
　　☆ Ⓐ company that leases medical equipment.
　　☆ Ⓑ medical equipment leasing company.
　　◎ Ⓒ outfit [firm, service] that leases medical equipment.
　　◎ Ⓓ medical equipment leasing service.
　　○ Ⓔ medical equipment leasing business [outfit].

9 「医療品会社」
(ブライアンは医療品会社に勤めています)
Brian works for a
　　☆ Ⓐ medical supply company.
　　◎ Ⓑ medical supply maker [manufacturer, business].
　　○ Ⓒ medical supply outfit [manufacturing company].

△ Ⓓ medical supply making company ［outfit］.
　　　△ Ⓔ medical supply manufacturing outfit.
　［注意］Brian works for ◎ Ⓐ Anderson medical supply company.
　　　　　　　　　× Ⓑ Anderson medical supply maker
　　　　　　　　　　　［manufacturer］.
　maker, manufacturer は「製造者」という人を表す語なので会社名を明示するときは使えない。これは他の業種の会社にも同様のことが言える。

10 「印刷会社」

(a) 小規模の場合
　（リンダは印刷会社に勤めています）
　Linda works for a ☆ Ⓐ printshop.
　　　　　　　　　　 ◎ Ⓑ printing shop.
　　　　　　　　　　 ○ Ⓒ printer's.
　［注意］多くの辞典に printing office が紹介されているが規模に関係なく使われていない。

(b) 中規模の場合
　（リンダは印刷会社に勤めています）
　Linda works for a ◎ Ⓐ printing company ［printer's］.
　　　　　　　　　　 ○ Ⓑ printing shop.
　　　　　　　　　　 △ Ⓒ printing firm.

(c) 大規模の場合
　（リンダは印刷会社に勤めています）
　Linda works for a ☆ Ⓐ printing company.
　　　　　　　　　　 ◎ Ⓑ printing firm.
　　　　　　　　　　 ○ Ⓒ printer's.

11 「インターネット会社」

　（ナンシーはインターネット会社に勤めています）
　Nancy works for an ☆ Ⓐ internet start-up.
　　　　　　　　　　　 ◎ Ⓑ internet company.
　　　　　　　　　　　 ○ Ⓒ internet business ［outfit］.
　　　　　　　　　　　 △ Ⓓ internet firm.
　［注意］インターネット、バイオテクノロジー、携帯電話のような新分野の会社にはⒶの start-up がよく使われている。

12 「インターネットサービス会社」
(彼はインターネットサービス会社に勤めているんです)
He works for ☆ Ⓐ an internet (service) provider.
◎ Ⓑ an online (service) provider ［an ISP］.
○ Ⓒ a net (service) provider.
○ Ⓓ an internet service company.
△ Ⓔ an internet service business ［outfit］.

13 「インターネット接続会社」
(ナンシーはインターネット接続会社に勤めています)
Nancy works for a ☆ Ⓐ service that sets up computers.
◎ Ⓑ company that sets up computers.
○ Ⓒ business ［outfit］ that sets up computers.
○ Ⓓ computer setup service.
△ Ⓔ computer setup outfit.

14 「パソコンメーカー」
(リズは大きなパソコンメーカーに勤めています)
Liz works for a big
☆ Ⓐ computer maker ［company, manufacturer］.
◎ Ⓑ computer manufacturing company.
○ Ⓒ computer firm ［outfit, manufacturing outfit］.
○ Ⓓ computer making company ［outfit］.

15 「コンピューター修理会社」
(リズはコンピューター修理会社に勤めています)
Liz works for a
◎ Ⓐ computer repair shop ［service］.
○ Ⓑ computer service company ［outfit］.
○ Ⓒ computer fixing shop ［business, house, outfit］.
△ Ⓓ computer fixing company ［service］.

［注意］Ⓐの computer repair shop とⒸ computer fixing shop はユーザーが修理所へ持っていく。他は修理会社がユーザーの所へ来ることもあればその反対のこともある。

第4章　会社に関する表現

16 「ウイスキー会社」
（リズはウイスキー会社に勤めています）
Liz works for a
　　◎ Ⓐ whiskey company [maker].
　　△ Ⓑ whiskey manufacturer [manufacturing company].
[注意] 日本のサントリー，アサヒは各種のアルコールを製造している。しかしアメリカの会社はウイスキー，ジン，ワイン会社は1種類しか製造していない。

17 「運送会社」
(a) **勤めていることを述べる場合**
（ナンシーは運送会社に勤めています）
Nancy works for a ☆ Ⓐ moving company.
　　　　　　　　　◎ Ⓑ mover.
　　　　　　　　　○ Ⓒ moving service.
　　　　　　　　　△ Ⓓ moving business [outfit].

(b) **会社の所有・経営・売買を述べる場合**
（ナンシーは運送会社を持っているんです）
Nancy owns a ◎ Ⓐ moving company.
　　　　　　　△ Ⓑ moving business.

18 「運動器具の会社」
（ブライアンは運動器具の会社に勤めているんです）
Brian works for an ☆ Ⓐ exercise equipment maker [company].
　　　　　　　　　◎ Ⓑ exercise equipment manufacturer.
　　　　　　　　　○ Ⓒ exercise equipment business [outfit].
　　　　　　　　　△ Ⓓ exercise equipment firm.

19 「エアコン取付け会社」
（ビルはエアコン取付け会社に勤めているんです）
Bill works for
　☆ Ⓐ an air-conditioning installation company.
　◎ Ⓑ an air-conditioning installation business.
　○ Ⓒ an air-conditioning installation outfit [service, firm].
　○ Ⓓ a company [business, outfit, service, firm] that sets up air-conditioners.

20 「会社・商店売買仲介会社」
（ビルは会社・商店売買仲介会社に勤めています）
Bill works for a
  ◎ Ⓐ business broker.
  ○ Ⓑ business brokerage firm ［service, company, outfit］.

21 「不動産会社」
（ビルは不動産会社に勤めています）
Bill works for a ☆ Ⓐ real estate agency.
     ◎ Ⓑ realty.
     ◎ Ⓒ realtor.

22 「解体会社」
（ビルは大きな解体会社に勤めているんです）
Bill works for a big
  ☆ Ⓐ building demolisher ［demolition company］.
  ◎ Ⓑ building demolishing company.
  ○ Ⓒ building demolishing service.
  ○ Ⓓ building demolition outfit ［business, firm］.
  △ Ⓔ building demolishing outfit.
  △ Ⓕ building wrecker.

23 「化学会社」
（リズは化学会社に勤めています）
Liz works for a
  ☆ Ⓐ chemical company.
  ☆ Ⓑ company that makes chemical products.
  ◎ Ⓒ business that makes chemical products.
  ◎ Ⓓ chemical manufacturing company ［firm］.
  ○ Ⓔ chemical business ［maker, manufacturer］.
  ○ Ⓕ chemical products making company ［business］.
  ○ Ⓖ chemical manufacturing outfit ［business］.

24 「貸し衣装会社」
（リンダは貸し衣装会社に勤めているんです）
Linda works for a
  ☆ Ⓐ company that rents clothes.

第4章　会社に関する表現

◎ Ⓑ clothes rental company.
○ Ⓒ clothes rental business [service, outfit].
○ Ⓓ business [service, outfit] that rents clothes.

25 「カメラ会社」
（ビルはカメラ会社に勤めているんです）
Bill works for a
　☆ Ⓐ camera company.
　◎ Ⓑ company [business] that makes cameras.
　○ Ⓒ camera business [maker, manufacturer].
　○ Ⓓ camera manufacturing company.
　○ Ⓔ company [business] that manufactures cameras.
　○ Ⓕ firm [outfit] that makes cameras.
　△ Ⓖ camera making company [business, outfit, firm].
　△ Ⓗ camera manufacturing business.

26 「ガラス会社」
（ナンシーはガラス会社に勤めています）
Nancy works for a ☆ Ⓐ glass company.
　　　　　　　　　 ◎ Ⓑ glass manufacturer.
　　　　　　　　　 ○ Ⓒ glass maker [manufacturing company].

27 「貴金属会社」
（リンダは貴金属会社に勤めているんです）
Linda works for a ☆ Ⓐ jewelry company [business].
　　　　　　　　　 ◎ Ⓑ jewelry firm.
　　　　　　　　　 △ Ⓒ jewelry outfit.

28 「金属会社」
（リズは金属会社に勤めています）
Liz works for a ☆ Ⓐ company that makes metal products.
　　　　　　　　◎ Ⓑ business that makes metal products.
　　　　　　　　○ Ⓒ outfit that makes metal products.
　　　　　　　　○ Ⓓ company that manufactures metal products.
　　　　　　　　× Ⓔ metal company.
［注意］Ⓔはアメリカの地域により使用頻度が大きく異なるので使わないほうがよい。

29「クツのメーカー」
（リンダは大きなクツのメーカーに勤めています）
Linda works for a big ☆ Ⓐ shoe company.
◎ Ⓑ shoe manufacturer.
○ Ⓒ shoe manufacturing company [outfit].
○ Ⓓ shoe maker [outfit].
○ Ⓔ shoe making outfit.

30「車のリース会社」
（ナンシーは大きい車のリース会社に勤めているんです）
Nancy works for a big
　☆ Ⓐ car leasing company.
　◎ Ⓑ car leasing service.
　◎ Ⓒ company [outfit, business, service] that leases cars.
　○ Ⓓ car leasing business [outfit].

31「車のレンタル会社」
（リズは大きな車のレンタル会社に勤めているんです）
Liz works for a big
　☆ Ⓐ car rental company.
　◎ Ⓑ car rental service.
　◎ Ⓒ outfit that rents cars.
　○ Ⓓ car rental business [outfit].
　○ Ⓔ company [service, business] that rents cars.

32「クレジットカード会社」
（ナンシーはクレジットカード会社に勤めています）
Nancy works for a ☆ Ⓐ credit card company.
○ Ⓑ credit card firm [outfit].
○ Ⓒ credit card issuer [issuing company].
△ Ⓓ credit card service.
△ Ⓔ credit card issuing service [outfit].
　［注意］辞典に card issuing firm が出ているが使われていない。

33「経営コンサルタント会社」
（リズは大きな経営コンサルタント会社に勤めています）

Liz works for a big ☆ Ⓐ business consulting firm.
　　　　　　　　　☆ Ⓑ business consultant.
　　　　　　　　　◎ Ⓒ business consulting company.
　　　　　　　　　○ Ⓓ business consulting service [outfit].

34 「携帯電話会社」
（ブライアンは携帯電話会社に勤めているんです）
Brian works for a ☆ Ⓐ cellphone company.
　　　　　　　　◎ Ⓑ cellphone service.
　　　　　　　　○ Ⓒ cellphone outfit [business].
　　　　　　　　○ Ⓓ cellular phone company.
　　　　　　　　△ Ⓔ cellular phone outfit.
　　　　　　　　△ Ⓕ mobile phone outfit [business].
　　　　　　　　△ Ⓖ cellphone [cellular phone] carrier.

35 「警備会社」
（マイクは大きな警備会社に勤めているんです）
Mike works for a big ◎ Ⓐ security company [service, agency].
　　　　　　　　　　○ Ⓑ security firm [outfit].
　　　　　　　　　　△ Ⓒ security business.

36 「化粧品会社」
（ナンシーは化粧品会社に勤めています）
Nancy works for a
　◎ Ⓐ cosmetics [make-up] company.
　◎ Ⓑ company that makes cosmetics.
　○ Ⓒ cosmetics outfit [business, firm].
　○ Ⓓ business [outfit, firm] that makes [manufactures] cosmetics.
　△ Ⓔ cosmetics maker [manufacturer].
[注意] cosmetics の代わりに cosmetic company としてもよく使われ，company 以外の単語にも単数形の cosmetic＋名詞は使われているが複数形のほうがより使われている。

37 「建設会社」
（ナンシーは建設会社に勤めています）
Nancy works for a ☆ Ⓐ construction company.

◎ Ⓑ construction firm.
○ Ⓒ construction business [outfit].

38 「工務店」
(リンダは工務店に勤めています)
Linda works for a ☆ Ⓐ general contractor.
◎ Ⓑ contractor.
○ Ⓒ general construction company.

39 「ゼネコン」
(リンダはゼネコンに勤めているんです)
Linda works for a ◎ Ⓐ big [major] general contractor.
◎ Ⓑ general contractor.
[注意] Ⓑも非常によく使われているが「工務店」の意味もあるのであいまいになる。

40 「航空会社」
(a) **漠然と述べる場合**
(リズは大手の航空会社に勤めています)
Liz works for a major ◎ Ⓐ airline.
○ Ⓑ airline company.
× Ⓒ airways [airlines].

(b) **会社名として述べる場合**
(リズは英国航空に勤めています)
◎ Liz works for British Airways.
[注意] airline, airways のどちらを使うかは各々の会社によって異なる。

41 「ゴミ回収会社」
(ボブは大きなゴミ回収会社に勤めています)
Bob works for a big
☆ Ⓐ garbage collection service.
◎ Ⓑ garbage collection company [business, firm].
◎ Ⓒ garbage company [service].
○ Ⓓ garbage collection outfit.
○ Ⓔ garbage business [outfit].

42 「室内装飾会社」

第4章　会社に関する表現

(ビルは大きな室内装飾会社に勤めています)
Bill works for a big ☆ Ⓐ interior design company.
　　　　　　　　　　◎ Ⓑ interior design service [business].
　　　　　　　　　　○ Ⓒ interior design outfit [firm].

43 「事務機器製造会社」
(リンダは事務機器製造会社に勤めています)
Linda works for an
　　☆ Ⓐ office supply manufacturing company.
　　◎ Ⓑ office supply manufacturer.
　　○ Ⓒ office supply maker.
　　× Ⓓ office supply producing [production] company.
[注意] 辞典にⒹが出ているが使われていない。

44 「事務用品会社」
(彼は事務用品会社に勤めているんです)
He works for an ◎ Ⓐ office supply company.
　　　　　　　　○ Ⓑ office supplies company.
　　　　　　　　○ Ⓒ office supply outfit.

45 「出版社」
(リンダは出版社に勤めています)
Linda works for a ☆ Ⓐ publishing company.
　　　　　　　　　◎ Ⓑ publishing house [firm, business, outfit].

46 「証券会社」
(a) **小さい会社**
(上の階に証券会社があります)
There's a ◎ Ⓐ stockbroker upstairs.
　　　　　◎ Ⓑ stockbroker's office ...

(b) **大きな会社**
(キャロルは証券会社に勤めています)
Carol works for a
　　☆ Ⓐ (stock) brokerage firm.
　　☆ Ⓑ stockbroker.
　　◎ Ⓒ securities firm.

[61]

◎ Ⓓ brokerage service.
　　　○ Ⓔ trading company [outfit, firm, service].
　　　○ Ⓕ stockbroker's [stock trader's] office.
　　　○ Ⓖ (stock) brokerage company [outfit, house].
　　　△ Ⓗ trader's firm [stock trader].
　[注意] (1) 辞典に trader's company [service], trader's securities company [house], stockbroking office が出ているが使われていない。
　(2) 辞典に trading company [firm] ＝「貿易会社」と出ているが誤り。「貿易会社」の項を参照されたい。

47 「消費者金融会社」
(彼は大きな消費者金融会社に勤めているんです)
He works for a ☆ Ⓐ consumer credit service [company].
　　　　　　　　◎ Ⓑ consumer loan service.
　　　　　　　　○ Ⓒ consumer loan company.
　　　　　　　　○ Ⓓ consumer credit outfit.
　　　　　　　　△ Ⓔ consumer loan business.
　　　　　　　　△ Ⓕ consumer loan [credit] firm.

48 「ジン会社」
(リズはジン会社に勤めています)
Liz works for a ◎ Ⓐ gin company [maker].
　　　　　　　　△ Ⓑ gin manufacturer [manufacturing company].

49 「水道会社」
(ビルは大きな水道会社に勤めています)
Bill works for a big ◎ Ⓐ plumbing company.
　　　　　　　　　　○ Ⓑ plumbing service [outfit].
　　　　　　　　　　○ Ⓒ plumber.

50 「製菓会社」
(ナンシーは製菓会社に勤めています)
Nancy works for a ☆ Ⓐ candy company [maker].
　　　　　　　　　◎ Ⓑ candy manufacturer.
　　　　　　　　　○ Ⓒ candy business.
　　　　　　　　　○ Ⓓ candy manufacturing [making] firm.
　　　　　　　　　△ Ⓔ candy outfit.

第4章　会社に関する表現

51「清掃会社」
（リンダはビルの清掃会社に勤めているんです）
Linda works for a
　☆ Ⓐ janitorial service.
　◎ Ⓑ cleaning service for buildings.
　◎ Ⓒ building cleaning service.
　◎ Ⓓ service ［outfit, company, business］ that cleans buildings.
　◎ Ⓔ janitorial business.
　○ Ⓕ janitorial company.
　○ Ⓖ cleaning outfit for buildings.
　○ Ⓗ building cleaning outfit.
　△ Ⓘ janitorial outfit.

52「製本会社」
（ビルは製本会社に勤めているんです）
Bill works for a ☆ Ⓐ book binding company.
　　　　　　　　　◎ Ⓑ book binder.
　　　　　　　　　○ Ⓒ book binding business ［outfit］.
　　　　　　　　　△ Ⓓ book binding service ［firm］.

53「製薬会社」
（ナンシーは製薬会社に勤めているんです）
Nancy works for a ☆ Ⓐ drug company ［maker］.
　　　　　　　　　 ◎ Ⓑ drug manufacturer.
　　　　　　　　　 ◎ Ⓒ company that makes medicine.
　　　　　　　　　 ◎ Ⓓ pharmaceutical company.
　　　　　　　　　 ○ Ⓔ medicine company.
　　　　　　　　　 ○ Ⓕ pharmaceutical outfit.

54「セメント会社」
（リンダはセメント会社に勤めています）
Linda works for a
　☆ Ⓐ cement company.
　◎ Ⓑ cement maker.
　◎ Ⓒ company that makes cement.
　○ Ⓓ cement making ［manufacturing］ company.

○ Ⓔ cement business ［outfit］.
○ Ⓕ company that manufactures cement.
○ Ⓖ business that makes cement.
△ Ⓗ outfit that makes cement.

55 「繊維会社」
（リズは繊維会社に勤めています）
Liz works for a ☆ Ⓐ textile company.
◎ Ⓑ company that makes textiles.
◎ Ⓒ textile maker.
○ Ⓓ textile outfit ［firm］.
○ Ⓔ business ［firm］ that makes textiles.
△ Ⓕ textile manufacturer ［making company］.

56 「洗車会社」
（夫は洗車会社を持っているんです）
My husband owns a ☆ Ⓐ car washing business ［service］.
◎ Ⓑ car washing company.
○ Ⓒ car washing outfit.

57 「造園会社」
（ビルは大きな造園会社に勤めています）
Bill works for a big ☆ Ⓐ landscaper.
◎ Ⓑ landscape gardener.
◎ Ⓒ landscape architect ［designer］.
◎ Ⓓ landscape design company.
○ Ⓔ landscape design business.
△ Ⓕ landscape design service ［firm］.

［注意］Ⓑは庭の手入れ、ⒸⒹⒺⒻはデザインを設計、Ⓐは手入れと設計の両方に使われている。

58 「測量会社」
（スティーヴは測量会社に勤めているんです）
Steve works for a ☆ Ⓐ surveying ［land survey］ company.
☆ Ⓑ land surveyor.
◎ Ⓒ land surveying company.
○ Ⓓ land surveying business.

　　　　　△ Ⓔ land surveying service [firm, outfit].
　　　　　△ Ⓕ surveying service [business, firm, outfit].

59「タクシー会社」
　（ナンシーはタクシー会社に勤めています）
　Nancy works for a ☆ Ⓐ cab company.
　　　　　　　◎ Ⓑ taxi company [service, business].
　　　　　　　○ Ⓒ cab service.

60「宅配会社」
　（ビルは宅配会社に勤めているんです）
　Bill works for a ☆ Ⓐ courier.
　　　　　　　◎ Ⓑ package delivery service [company].
　　　　　　　○ Ⓒ package delivery business [outfit].
　　　　　　　△ Ⓓ package delivery firm.

61「炭酸飲料会社」
　（リンダは炭酸飲料会社に勤めているんです）
　Linda works for a
　　☆ Ⓐ soda [soft drink] company.
　　◎ Ⓑ soft drink outfit.
　　○ Ⓒ soda business.
　　○ Ⓓ soft drink manufacturing [making] outfit.
　　△ Ⓔ soda (manufacturing) outfit.
　　△ Ⓕ soda drink making outfit.
　［注意］soft drink は日本語の「ソフトドリンク」と下記の点で違う。日本語ではアルコールが入っていない飲物を「ソフトドリンク」と呼んでいる。従ってトマトジュースなどもそのひとつである。しかし英語では糖分が入っている飲物はすべて soft drink と呼んでいる。soft drink は炭酸が入っているものもいないものもある。

62「調査会社」
　（スティーヴは調査会社に勤めているんです）
　Steve works for a
　　☆ Ⓐ survey company.
　　◎ Ⓑ company that does surveys.
　　○ Ⓒ survey business [service].

    △ Ⓓ survey firm [outfit].
    △ Ⓔ business [service, outfit, firm] that does surveys.

63 「通信社」
（リズは通信社に勤めています）
Liz works for a ☆ Ⓐ news agency.
                ◎ Ⓑ news service.
                ○ Ⓒ news outfit [company].
                △ Ⓓ news firm.

64 「通訳会社」
（彼は大きな通訳会社に勤めています）
He works for a big ☆ Ⓐ interpreting service [company].
                  ◎ Ⓑ interpretation service.
                  ○ Ⓒ interpretation company.
                  ○ Ⓓ interpreting business [firm, outfit].
                  ○ Ⓔ translating outfit.
                  △ Ⓕ interpretation outfit.
                  △ Ⓖ translation outfit.

65 「ディーエム会社」
（ビルはディーエム会社に勤めているんです）
Bill works for a ☆ Ⓐ direct mail company.
                ◎ Ⓑ direct mailer.
                ○ Ⓒ direct mail service [outfit, business, firm].
                △ Ⓓ direct mail mailer.

66 「鉄道会社」
（リンダは鉄道会社に勤めています）
Linda works for a ◎ Ⓐ railroad company.
                 × Ⓑ railway company.

67 「テレアポ会社」
（リンダは大きなテレアポ会社に勤めています）
Linda works for a big
    ◎ Ⓐ telemarketing company.
    ○ Ⓑ telemarketing firm [business, service, outfit].

　　　　○ Ⓒ telemarketer.

68 「電気会社」
（ナンシーは電気会社に勤めています）
　◎ Nancy works for an appliance company.

69 「電子会社」
（リズは大手の電子会社に勤めているんです）
　Liz works for ☆ Ⓐ a big electronics company.
　　　　　　　　◎ Ⓑ a big electronics maker [manufacturer].
　　　　　　　　○ Ⓒ an electronics giant.
　　　　　　　　○ Ⓓ a big electronics firm [business, outfit].

70 「電力会社」
（リンダは電力会社に勤めています）
　◎ Linda works for a power [an electric] company.
[注意] power [electric] は company 以外の business, outfit などは使われていない。

71 「電話取付け会社」
（ビルは電話取付け会社に勤めているんです）
　Bill works for a ☆ Ⓐ company that sets up telephone systems.
　　　　　　　　　◎ Ⓑ business [outfit, service] that ...
　　　　　　　　　○ Ⓒ firm that ...
[注意] telephone systems の代わりに telephones としても非常によく使われている。

72 「時計会社」
（リンダは時計会社に勤めています）
　Linda works for a ☆ Ⓐ watch company [maker].
　　　　　　　　　　◎ Ⓑ watch manufacturer.
　　　　　　　　　　△ Ⓒ watch firm.

73 「(左官会社の意味での) 塗装会社」
（ビルは大きな塗装会社に勤めているんです）
　Bill works for a big ◎ Ⓐ plastering company.
　　　　　　　　　　　 ○ Ⓑ plastering service [outfit, business].

[67]

△ ⓒ plastering plasterer.

74 「ペンキ屋」
(彼はペンキ屋に勤めているんです)
He works for a ☆ Ⓐ painter.
◎ Ⓑ painting company [service].
○ ⓒ painting outfit.

[注意] Ⓑの painting company が1番大きいニュアンスがあり，painting service は大，中，小のいずれにも使われている。Ⓐは中，または小規模。ⓒは大，中，小。

75 「看板屋」
(彼は看板屋に勤めているんです)
He works for a ◎ Ⓐ sign maker.
◎ Ⓑ sign making company.
○ ⓒ sign making business [service].
○ Ⓓ sign painter.
○ Ⓔ sign maker's shop.

[注意] 看板屋としての規模はⒶⒹは中，または小，Ⓑは大，または中，ⓒは大中小，Ⓔは小に使われている。

76 「取次業者（会社）」
(XYZ は LMN 会社の唯一の取次業者です)
XYZ's ☆ Ⓐ the only distributor for LMN.
◎ Ⓑ the sole distributor ...
○ ⓒ the exclusive distributor ...
○ Ⓓ the only distributing company ...
○ Ⓔ the only distributive dealer ...
△ Ⓕ the only distributive company ...

77 「問屋」
(リズは生地の問屋に勤めています)
Liz works for a fabric ◎ Ⓐ distributor.
◎ Ⓑ wholesale company [store].

[注意] (1) いずれも「問屋」「卸売り会社」の意味だが次のような違いがある。英和，和英辞典のいずれも「問屋」「卸売り会社」＝wholesale store とのみ考えている印象を受ける。しかし，米国の wholesale store [com-

[68]

第4章　会社に関する表現

pany]は「量販店」にあたる。distributorとは1つのメーカーの製品を専門に扱う会社（Sony distributor）と多数の会社の製品を扱う場合の両方がある。
(2) 関連のある語としてsupplierがある。これは複数のメーカーの製品を小売店や個人消費者へではなく，学校・病院・レストランなどへ売る「納入業者」を指すことが多い。また注文する側が述べるときは「仕入れ先」と訳す。

78「乳製品会社」
（ナンシーは乳製品会社に勤めています）
Nancy works for a ☆ Ⓐ dairy company.
　　　　　　　　　☆ Ⓑ company that makes dairy products.
　　　　　　　　　◎ Ⓒ business that makes dairy products.
　　　　　　　　　◎ Ⓓ dairy business.
　　　　　　　　　○ Ⓔ dairy outfit.

79「農機具製作会社」
（ブライアンは農機具製作会社に勤めています）
Brian works for a ☆ Ⓐ farm equipment company.
　　　　　　　　　◎ Ⓑ farm equipment maker [manufacturer].
　　　　　　　　　◎ Ⓒ farm equipment manufacturing company.
　　　　　　　　　○ Ⓓ farm equipment business.
　　　　　　　　　○ Ⓔ farm equipment manufacturing outfit.
　　　　　　　　　△ Ⓕ farm equipment making company [outfit].

80「ハイテク会社」
（リンダは大きなハイテク会社に勤めています）
Linda works for a big ☆ Ⓐ high-tech company.
　　　　　　　　　　　◎ Ⓑ high-tech business.
　　　　　　　　　　　○ Ⓒ high-tech firm.
　　　　　　　　　　　△ Ⓓ high-tech outfit.

81「廃品回収会社」
（ボブは廃品回収会社に勤めているんです）
Bob works for a ◎ Ⓐ scrap collection company [service].
　　　　　　　　○ Ⓑ scrap collection business [outfit].

82「派遣会社」
　　（リンダは派遣会社に勤めています）
　　Linda works for a ◎ Ⓐ temp agency.
　　　　　　　　　　　○ Ⓑ temporary employment agency.
　　　　　　　　　　　× Ⓒ temp agent ［temporary agency］.

83「ヘアダイ会社」
　　（夫はヘアダイ会社に勤めています）
　　My husband works for a
　　　　☆ Ⓐ company that makes hair dye.
　　　　◎ Ⓑ hair dye company.
　　　　◎ Ⓒ business ［outfit, maker］ that makes hair dye.
　　　　○ Ⓓ hair dye business ［manufacturer］.
　　　　△ Ⓔ hair dye outfit ［firm］.

84「貿易会社」
　　（彼は貿易会社に勤めているんです）
　　He works for an ◎ Ⓐ import and export company.
　　　　　　　　　　○ Ⓑ importing and exporting company ［outfit］.
　　　　　　　　　　△ Ⓒ importing and exporting firm.
　　　　　　　　　　△ Ⓓ importer/exporter.
　　［注意］辞典に a trading company が出ているが使われていない。但し「証券会社」の意味ではよく使われている。

85「保険会社」
　　（リンダは保険会社に勤めているんです）
　　Linda works for an ◎ Ⓐ insurance company.
　　　　　　　　　　　○ Ⓑ insurance firm ［business, outfit］.
　　　　　　　　　　　△ Ⓒ insurance house.

86「保険引受会社（業者）」
　　（リズは保険引受会社〈業者〉に勤めているんです）
　　Liz works for an ◎ Ⓐ underwriter.
　　　　　　　　　　○ Ⓑ insurer ［underwriting outfit］.

87「モデル派遣会社（プロダクション）」
　　（スティーヴは大きなモデル派遣会社に勤めています）

Steve works for a big ☆ Ⓐ modeling agency.
　　　　　　　　　　　○ Ⓑ modeling agent [company, service].
　　　　　　　　　　　△ Ⓒ modeling firm [outfit].

88 「有線テレビ会社」
（リンダは有線テレビ会社に勤めています）
Linda works for a ☆ Ⓐ cable television company.
　　　　　　　　　◎ Ⓑ cable television service.
　　　　　　　　　○ Ⓒ cable television business [outfit].
　　　　　　　　　△ Ⓓ cable television firm.

89 「輸送会社」
（リズはフランスの輸送会社に勤めています）
Liz works for a French ◎ Ⓐ shipping [transport] company.
　　　　　　　　　　　 ○ Ⓑ transportation company.
［注意］(1) Ⓐは国内，海外の両方。
(2) Ⓐの shipping company は「船会社」とどの辞典にも出ているが誤り。船だけでなく飛行機，トラック，電車による輸送会社の意味で広く使われている。
(3) Ⓑは本来，乗客のための「運輸会社」であるが，アメリカ人の間で広く誤用されている。

90 「汽（客）船会社」
（私の父は大きい汽（客）船会社に勤めているんです）
My father works ◎ Ⓐ on a big ocean liner.
　　　　　　　　 ○ Ⓑ for a big passenger line.
　　　　　　　　 △ Ⓒ on a big passenger liner.
　　　　　　　　 △ Ⓓ for a big ocean line.

91 「遊覧船会社」
（私の父は大きな遊覧船会社に勤めているんです）
My father works ☆ Ⓐ for a big cruise line.
　　　　　　　　 ◎ Ⓑ on a big cruise liner.
　　　　　　　　 ○ Ⓒ for a big passenger line.
　　　　　　　　 △ Ⓓ on a big passenger liner.

92「船（船舶）会社」
(私の父は大きな船〈船舶〉会社に勤めています)
My father works for a big ☆ Ⓐ maritime shipping company.
　　　　　　　　　　　　　◎ Ⓑ maritime company.
　　　　　　　　　　　　　◎ Ⓒ ocean shipping line.
　　　　　　　　　　　　　○ Ⓓ ocean shipping company.

93「(駐車違反) レッカー移動会社」
(ビルはレッカー移動会社に勤めているんです)
Bill works for a ◎ Ⓐ towing service [company].
　　　　　　　　　○ Ⓑ towing business.
　　　　　　　　　○ Ⓒ tow-truck service [company].
　　　　　　　　　△ Ⓓ tow-truck business [outfit].
　　　　　　　　　△ Ⓔ towing outfit.

第5章
代理店・事務所に関する表現

1「会計事務所」
　（リンダは会計事務所に勤めています）
　Lind works for a ◎ Ⓐ CPA.
　　　　　　　　　　○ Ⓑ CPA office ［firm］.
　［注意］(1) ⒷのCPA firmは大きい事務所，CPA officeは小さい事務所，Ⓐは大きくても小さくても使える。
　(2) Linda works for ◎ Ⓐ Anderson CPA Office.
　　　　　　　　　　 ◎ Ⓑ Anderson CPA Firm.
　　　　　　　　　　 × Ⓒ Anderson CPA.
　ⒸのCPAは人を表す語なのでAndersonのような人名，会社名を明示するときは重複するので使えない。これは他の事務所，代理店にも同様のことが言える。

2「経理事務所」
　（リンダは経理事務所に勤めています）
　Linda works for an ◎ Ⓐ accounting firm.
　　　　　　　　　　 ○ Ⓑ accounting office.
　［注意］Ⓐは大きい事務所，Ⓑは小さい事務所。

3「税務会計事務所」
　（ナンシーは税務会計事務所に勤めています）
　Nancy works for ◎ Ⓐ a tax specialist ［accountant］.
　　　　　　　　　 ◎ Ⓑ an accountant.
　　　　　　　　　 △ Ⓒ a tax service ［accounting firm］.

4 「法律事務所」
　　（リンダは法律事務所に勤めています）
　　Linda works for a ◎ Ⓐ law firm.
　　　　　　　　　　　　○ Ⓑ law office.
　　　　　　　　　　　　△ Ⓒ lawyer's office.
　　[注意] Ⓐは大きい事務所，ⒷⒸは小さい事務所。

5 「設計事務所」
(a) **規模が小さい場合**
　　（リンダは設計事務所に勤めています）
　　Linda works ◎ Ⓐ for an architect.
　　　　　　　　◎ Ⓑ for an architectural office.
　　　　　　　　△ Ⓒ at an architect's office.

(b) **規模が大きい場合**
　　（リンダは設計事務所に勤めています）
　　Linda works for an ◎ Ⓐ architectural firm.
　　　　　　　　　　　 ◎ Ⓑ architect.
　　　　　　　　　　　 △ Ⓒ architectural company [office].

6 「保険の代理店」
　　（角を曲がった所に火災保険の代理店があります）
　　There's a fire ◎ Ⓐ insurance agency around the corner.
　　　　　　　　　 ○ Ⓑ insurance agent ...

7 「旅行代理店」
　　（ナンシーは旅行代理店に勤めています）
　　Nancy works for a ◎ Ⓐ travel agency [agent].
　　　　　　　　　　　△ Ⓑ travel company.
　　[注意] Ⓐの travel agent は小さい町ではときどきしか使われていない。

8 「総代理店」
　　（どこの会社がファイザーの日本総代理店なのですか）
　　◎ Ⓐ Who's the exclusive [sole] agent in Japan for Pfizer?
　　◎ Ⓑ What's the exclusive [sole] agency ...?
　　[注意] Pfizer はアメリカの製薬会社。

9 「販売代理店」
(角に LMN 会社の販売代理店があります)
There's a ◎ Ⓐ sales agent for LMN Company on the corner.
　　　　　○ Ⓑ selling agent ［sales agency］...

10 「広告代理店」
(アメリカ銀行の裏に広告代理店があります)
There's an ◎ Ⓐ ad agency behind Bank of America.
　　　　　○ Ⓑ advertising agency ...
　　　　　△ Ⓒ ad agent ［advertisement agency］...

11 「興信所」
(a) 企業の成績を調べる
(リンダは興信所に勤めています)
Linda works for a
　　◎ Ⓐ corporate performance-rating agency.
　　○ Ⓑ business ［company］ performance-rating agency.
　　△ Ⓒ corporate ［business, company］ performance-rating agent.

(b) 個人のクレジットカードの支払いを調べる
(リンダは興信所に勤めています)
Linda works for a ◎ Ⓐ credit-rating ［credit］ agency.
　　　　　　　　△ Ⓑ credit-rating ［credit］ agent.

(c) 個人の素行調査
(リンダは興信所に勤めています)
Linda works for a ◎ Ⓐ private detective agency.
　　　　　　　　◎ Ⓑ PI.

12 「芸能プロダクション」
(角に芸能プロダクションがあります)
There's a ☆ Ⓐ talent agency on the corner.
　　　　　◎ Ⓑ talent agent ...
　　　　　△ Ⓒ talent service ...

13 「編集プロダクション」

(リンダは編集プロダクションに勤めています)

Linda works for an ☆ Ⓐ editing company.
　　　　　　　　　◎ Ⓑ editing firm.
　　　　　　　　　○ Ⓒ editing service [business, house, outfit].
　　　　　　　　　△ Ⓓ editing agency.

第6章 工場に関する表現

1 「医療器具工場」
(デイヴィットは医療器具工場で働いているんです)
David works at a ☆ Ⓐ factory that makes medical equipment.
　　　　　　　　　◎ Ⓑ medical equipment factory.
　　　　　　　　　○ Ⓒ medical equipment plant.
　　　　　　　　　○ Ⓓ plant that makes medical equipment.
　　　　　　　　　△ Ⓔ medical machine factory.

[注意] コンピューター，電子，テレビ，カメラ，医療，車，製薬のような高度な技術，設備を必要とする分野の工場では plant は factory と違って最新式であるというニュアンスがある。

2 「医療品工場」
(ビルは医療品工場で働いているんです)
Bill works at a ☆ Ⓐ medical supply factory.
　　　　　　　　◎ Ⓑ factory that makes medical supply.
　　　　　　　　○ Ⓒ medical supply plant.
　　　　　　　　○ Ⓓ plant that makes medical supply.

3 「印刷工場」
(a) **新聞・本・雑誌**
(ブライアンは印刷工場で働いています)
Brian works at a ☆ Ⓐ printing press.
　　　　　　　　　◎ Ⓑ printer's.
　　　　　　　　　○ Ⓒ printing (press) company.

                    × Ⓓ printing shop.

(b)　**チラシ**
　　（ブライアンは印刷工場で働いています）
　　Brian works at a ◎ Ⓐ printing [print] shop.
　　　　　　　　　　○ Ⓑ printing company.
　　　　　　　　　　△ Ⓒ printing house.

[4] 「ウイスキー工場」
　　（ブライアンはウイスキー工場で働いています）
　　Brian works at a ◎ Ⓐ whiskey distillery.
　　　　　　　　　　○ Ⓑ whiskey factory.
　　　　　　　　　　△ Ⓒ whiskey plant [mill].

[5] 「運動器具工場」
　　（ブライアンは運動器具工場で働いているんです）
　　Brian works at an ◎ Ⓐ exercise machine factory.
　　　　　　　　　　 ○ Ⓑ exercise machine making factory.
　　　　　　　　　　 ○ Ⓒ exercise machine (manufacturing) plant.
　　　　　　　　　　 △ Ⓓ exercise machine manufacturing factory.
　　　　　　　　　　 △ Ⓔ exercise machine making plant.

[6] 「カーテン工場」
　　（ボブはカーテン工場で働いているんです）
　　Bob works in a ☆ Ⓐ curtain factory.
　　　　　　　　　◎ Ⓑ curtain mill.
　　　　　　　　　○ Ⓒ curtain plant.

[7] 「カーペット工場」
　　（ブライアンはカーペット工場で働いているんです）
　　Brian works in a ☆ Ⓐ carpet mill.
　　　　　　　　　　◎ Ⓑ carpet factory [plant].

[8] 「家電工場」
　　（ブライアンは家電工場で働いています）
　　Brian works at an ☆ Ⓐ appliance factory.
　　　　　　　　　　 ◎ Ⓑ appliance manufacturing plant [factory].

第6章 工場に関する表現

　　　　　◎ ⓒ appliance assembly plant［factory］.
　　　　　○ ⓓ appliance making factory［plant］.
　　　　　○ ⓔ appliance plant.

9 「カメラ工場」
（スティーヴはカメラ工場で働いているんです）
Steve works at a ☆ ⓐ factory that makes cameras.
　　　　　◎ ⓑ camera factory.
　　　　　○ ⓒ camera plant.
　　　　　○ ⓓ factory that manufactures cameras.
　　　　　△ ⓔ camera making［manufacturing］plant.

10 「化学繊維工場」
（ジムは化学繊維工場で働いています）
Jim works at a ☆ ⓐ synthetic fabric factory.
　　　　　◎ ⓑ synthetic fabric plant.
　　　　　◎ ⓒ synthetics factory［plant］.
　　　　　△ ⓓ synthetic fiber plant［factory, mill］.

11 「ガラス工場」
（ブライアンはガラス工場で働いています）
Brian works at a ◎ ⓐ glass factory.
　　　　　▽ ⓑ glassworks［glass house］.
［注意］辞典に glass foundry［plant］が出ているが使われていない。

12 「皮製品工場」
（ジムは皮製品工場で働いています）
Jim works at a ☆ ⓐ factory that makes leather goods［products］.
　　　　　◎ ⓑ plant that makes leather goods［products］.
　　　　　○ ⓒ leather-goods［leather products］factory.
　　　　　○ ⓓ factory that makes leather merchandise.

13 「缶詰工場」
（ボブは缶詰工場で働いています）
Bob works at a ◎ ⓐ cannery.
　　　　　○ ⓑ canning factory.
　　　　　△ ⓒ canned food factory.

▽ Ⓓ canning plant ［canned food plant］.

14 「クツ下製造工場」
（ジムはクツ下製造工場で働いています）
Jim works at a ☆ Ⓐ factory that makes socks.
　　　　　　　◎ Ⓑ sock factory.
　　　　　　　○ Ⓒ factory that manufactures socks.
　　　　　　　○ Ⓓ sock making factory.
　　　　　　　△ Ⓔ sock manufacturing factory.

15 「軍需工場」
（ブライアンは軍需工場で働いています）
◎ Brian works in a munitions factory ［plant］.

16 「コーヒー工場」
（ボブはコーヒー工場で働いているんです）
Bob works at a ☆ Ⓐ coffee factory.
　　　　　　　◎ Ⓑ coffee plant.
　　　　　　　○ Ⓒ coffee mill.

17 「ゴム工場」
（ジムはゴム工場で働いています）
Jim works at a ◎ Ⓐ rubber factory.
　　　　　　× Ⓑ rubber plant ［mill］.

18 「コンピューター工場」
（ブライアンはコンピューター工場で働いています）
Brian works at a
　　☆ Ⓐ computer factory.
　　◎ Ⓑ computer assembly plant ［factory］.
　　◎ Ⓒ computer manufacturing plant.
　　○ Ⓓ computer manufacturing ［making］ factory.
　　○ Ⓔ computer (making) plant.

19 「自動車組立て工場」
（ブライアンは自動車組立て工場で働いています）
Brian works at ◎ Ⓐ an auto assembly plant ［factory］.

　　　　　　△ Ⓑ an auto assembly facility.
　　　　　　△ Ⓒ a car assembly plant ［facility］.

20「自動車工場」
　　（ボブは自動車工場で働いています）
　　Bob works at an ◎ Ⓐ auto ［a car］ plant.
　　　　　　　　　○ Ⓑ auto ［a car］ factory.

21「ジン工場」
　　（ブライアンはジン工場で働いています）
　　Brian works at a ◎ Ⓐ gin distillery.
　　　　　　　　　○ Ⓑ gin factory.
　　　　　　　　　△ Ⓒ gin plant ［mill］.

22「スーツ（ドレス）縫製工場」
　　（ジムはスーツ〈ドレス〉縫製工場で働いているんです）
　　Jim works in a ◎ Ⓐ suit factory.
　　　　　　　　○ Ⓑ suit mill.
　　　　　　　　△ Ⓒ suit plant.

23「製菓工場」
　　（ブライアンは製菓工場で働いています）
　　Brian works at a ☆ Ⓐ candy factory ［maker］.
　　　　　　　　　◎ Ⓑ candy making factory ［plant］.
　　　　　　　　　○ Ⓒ candy manufacturing plant.

24「製紙工場」
　　（ジムは製紙工場で働いています）
　　Jim works at a ◎ Ⓐ paper mill.
　　　　　　　　○ Ⓑ paper factory.
　　　　　　　　× Ⓒ paper facility.

25「製粉工場」
　　（ブライアンは製粉工場で働いています）
　　Brian works at a ◎ Ⓐ flour mill.
　　　　　　　　　▽ Ⓑ flour factory ［plant］.
　　　　　　　　　× Ⓒ flour facility.

26 「製薬工場」
(ジムは製薬工場で働いています)
Jim works at a ◎ Ⓐ drug manufacturing plant.
　　　　　　　○ Ⓑ drug manufacturing factory.
　　　　　　　○ Ⓒ drug making plant ［factory］.

27 「石けん工場」
(スティーヴは石けん工場で働いているんです)
Steve works at a ◎ Ⓐ soap factory.
　　　　　　　 ◎ Ⓑ factory that makes soap.
　　　　　　　 ○ Ⓒ soap plant.
　　　　　　　 ○ Ⓓ factory that manufactures soap.

28 「セメント工場」
(ブライアンはセメント工場で働いています)
◎ Brian works at a cement factory ［plant］.

29 「繊維工場」
(ボブは繊維工場で働いています)
Bob works at a ☆ Ⓐ textile mill.
　　　　　　　◎ Ⓑ textile factory.
　　　　　　　○ Ⓒ textile plant.
　　　　　　　× Ⓓ textile facility.

30 「鉄鋼工場」
(ジムは鉄鋼工場で働いています)
Jim works at a ◎ Ⓐ steel mill.
　　　　　　　○ Ⓑ steel plant ［factory］.
［注意］Ⓑはアメリカの地域によって使用頻度は大きく異なる。Ⓐは地域に関係なく非常によく使われている。

31 「テレビ工場」
(スティーヴはテレビ工場で働いているんです)
Steve works at a ☆ Ⓐ factory that makes TVs.
　　　　　　　 ◎ Ⓑ TV factory.
　　　　　　　 ○ Ⓒ plant that makes TVs.

第6章 工場に関する表現

　　　　　　　　○ Ⓓ factory that manufactures TVs.
　　　　　　　　△ Ⓔ TV making [manufacturing] factory.

32 「電子工場」
(ブライアンは大手の電子工場に勤めています)
Brian works at a big ☆ Ⓐ electronics factory.
　　　　　　　　　　◎ Ⓑ electronics plant [manufacturer].
　　　　　　　　　　◎ Ⓒ electronics assembly factory [plant].
　　　　　　　　　　◎ Ⓓ electronics manufacturing plant.
　　　　　　　　　　○ Ⓔ electronics manufacturing factory.
　　　　　　　　　　△ Ⓕ electronics making plant [factory].

33 「時計工場」
(ブライアンは時計工場で働いています)
Brian works at a ☆ Ⓐ watch factory.
　　　　　　　　◎ Ⓑ watch making factory [plant].
　　　　　　　　○ Ⓒ watch manufacturing [assembling] plant.

34 「農機具工場」
(ディヴッドは農機具工場で働いているんです)
David works at a ◎ Ⓐ farm equipment [machine] factory.
　　　　　　　　△ Ⓑ farm equipment [machine] plant.

35 「ビール工場」
(ブライアンはビール工場で働いています)
Brian works at a ☆ Ⓐ beer brewery.
　　　　　　　　◎ Ⓑ beer bottling plant.
　　　　　　　　○ Ⓒ beer (bottling) factory.

36 「びん詰工場」
(ボブはびん詰工場で働いています)
Bob works at a ◎ Ⓐ bottling plant.
　　　　　　　○ Ⓑ bottling factory.
　　　　　　　△ Ⓒ bottling facility.

37 「ヘアダイ工場」
(夫はヘアダイ工場で働いているんです)

My husband works at a ☆ Ⓐ hair dye factory.
　　　　　　　　　　　◎ Ⓑ hair dye plant.
　　　　　　　　　　　△ Ⓒ hair dye making factory ［plant］.

38 「縫製工場」
(ボブは縫製工場で働いているんです)
Bob works at a ☆ Ⓐ clothing factory.
　　　　　　　　◎ Ⓑ clothes manufacturing plant.
　　　　　　　　○ Ⓒ clothes (manufacturing) factory.
　　　　　　　　○ Ⓓ clothes making factory ［plant］.

39 「木綿工場」
(ジムは木綿工場で働いています)
Jim works at a ◎ Ⓐ cotton mill.
　　　　　　　　× Ⓑ cotton factory ［plant］.

40 「羊毛工場」
(ボブは羊毛工場で働いているんです)
Bob works in a ☆ Ⓐ wool mill.
　　　　　　　　◎ Ⓑ woolen mill ［wool factory］.
　　　　　　　　○ Ⓒ woolen factory.
　　　　　　　　△ Ⓓ wool ［woolen］ plant.

41 「リサイクル工場」
(ジムはリサイクル工場で働いています)
Jim works in a ◎ Ⓐ recycling plant.
　　　　　　　　○ Ⓑ recycling mill.
　　　　　　　　× Ⓒ recycling factory.

第7章

…部に関する表現

1 「営業部」
（ティムは営業部で働いています）
Tim works in ◎ Ⓐ Sales.
　　　　　　　○ Ⓑ the Sales Department.
　　　　　　　△ Ⓒ the Sales Division.
[注意]（1）Ⓐを紹介している辞典がないが1番よく使われている。
（2）Ⓒは非常に大きな会社以外では使われていない。

2 「海外事業部」
（グレッグは海外事業部で働いています）
Greg works in ☆ Ⓐ Overseas Operations.
　　　　　　　 ◎ Ⓑ the Overseas Operations Department.
　　　　　　　 ○ Ⓒ the Overseas Business Department.

3 「開発部」
（ダンは開発部で働いています）
Dan works in ◎ Ⓐ R & D.
　　　　　　　○ Ⓑ the R & D Department.
　　　　　　　○ Ⓒ Research and Development.
　　　　　　　○ Ⓓ the Research and Development Department.

4 「監査部」
（ティムは監査部で働いています）
Tim works in ◎ Ⓐ Auditing.

　　　　　　○ Ⓑ the Auditing Department.

5 「企画部」
　　（グレッグは企画部で働いています）
　　Greg works in ◎ Ⓐ Planning.
　　　　　　　　○ Ⓑ the Planning Department.
　　　　　　　　△ Ⓒ the Planning Division.

6 「技術部」
(a) **お客様と接触する**
　　（ダンは技術部で働いています）
　　Dan works in ◎ Ⓐ Tech Support.
　　　　　　　　○ Ⓑ the Tech Support Department.

(b) **お客様と接触しない**
　　（ダンは技術部で働いているんです）
　　Dan works in ◎ Ⓐ Tech.
　　　　　　　　○ Ⓑ the Tech Department.

7 「経理部」
　　（ティムは経理部で働いています）
　　Tim works in ◎ Ⓐ Accounting.
　　　　　　　　○ Ⓑ the Accounting Department.
　　　　　　　　× Ⓒ the General Accounting Department.

8 「購買部」
　　（グレッグは購買部で働いています）
　　Greg works in ◎ Ⓐ Purchasing.
　　　　　　　　○ Ⓑ the Purchasing Department.
　　　　　　　　× Ⓒ Buying [the Buying Department].

9 「広報部」
　　（ダンは広報部で働いています）
　　Dan works in ◎ Ⓐ PR [Public Relations].
　　　　　　　　○ Ⓑ the Public Relations Department.
　　　　　　　　△ Ⓒ the Public Relations Division.
　　［注意］(1) 辞典に ... at the Public Relations Division. があるが使われて

第7章 …部に関する表現

　いない。
(2) ⓒだけを紹介している辞典が多いが，非常に大きな会社以外では使われていない。

10 「財務部」
　（ティムは財務部で働いています）
　Tim works in ◎ Ⓐ Finance.
　　　　　　　　○ Ⓑ the Finance Department.

11 「資金運用部」
　（グレッグは資金運用部で働いています）
　Greg works in
　　　☆ Ⓐ Fund Management.
　　　◎ Ⓑ Fund Administration.
　　　○ ⓒ the Fund Management ［Administration］ Department.

12 「市場調査部」
　（グレッグは市場調査部で働いています）
　◎ Greg works in Marketing ［the Marketing Department］.
　［注意］ある辞典で「営業部」に the Marketing Department を紹介しているが「市場調査部」の意味でしか使われていない。

13 「情報部」
　（ダンは情報部で働いています）
　Dan works in
　　　☆ Ⓐ Data Management.
　　　◎ Ⓑ Information ［Management］.
　　　○ ⓒ the Data ［the Information］ Management Department.
　　　○ Ⓓ Info Management.

14 「審査部」
　（ダンは審査部で働いています）
　Dan works in ◎ Ⓐ Credit.
　　　　　　　　○ Ⓑ the Credit Department.
　　　　　　　　△ ⓒ Crediting.

[87]

15 「人事部」
　　　（ティムは人事部で働いています）
　　Tim works in　☆ Ⓐ Human Resources.
　　　　　　　　　◎ Ⓑ Personnel.
　　　　　　　　　○ Ⓒ HR ［the Human Resources Department］.
　　　　　　　　　○ Ⓓ the Personnel Department.
　　［**注意**］ⒶⒸは大きな会社で使われる傾向がある。

16 「生産部」
　　　（グレッグは生産部で働いています）
　　Greg works in ◎ Ⓐ Production.
　　　　　　　　　○ Ⓑ the Production Department.
　　　　　　　　　× Ⓒ Producing.

17 「製造部」
　　　（グレッグは製造部で働いているんです）
　　Greg works in ◎ Ⓐ Manufacturing.
　　　　　　　　　○ Ⓑ the Manufacturing Department.

18 「総務（庶務）部」
　　　（ダンは総務部で働いています）
　　Dan works in ◎ Ⓐ General Affairs.
　　　　　　　　　○ Ⓑ the General Affairs Department.

19 「能力開発部」
　　　（ティムは能力開発部で働いています）
　　Tim works in ◎ Ⓐ Personnel Development.
　　　　　　　　　○ Ⓑ the Personnel Development Department.

20 「派遣部」
　　　（グレッグは派遣部で働いています）
　　Greg works in ◎ Ⓐ Dispatching.
　　　　　　　　　○ Ⓑ the Dispatching Department.

21 「発送部」
　　　（ダンは発送部で働いています）
　　Dan works in ◎ Ⓐ Shipping.

第 7 章　…部に関する表現

　　　　○ Ⓑ the Shipping [Dispatching] Department.
　　　　○ Ⓒ Dispatcing.

22 「販売管理部」
（ダンは販売管理部で働いています）
Dan works in
　　◎ Ⓐ Sales Management.
　　○ Ⓑ the Sales Management [Administration] Department.
　　○ Ⓒ Sales Administration.

23 「販売促進部」
（ティムは販売促進部で働いています）
Tim works in ◎ Ⓐ Sales Promotion.
　　　　　　○ Ⓑ the Sales Promotion Department.

24 「文書部」
（グレッグは文書部で働いています）
Greg works in ◎ Ⓐ Legal.
　　　　　　○ Ⓑ the Legal Department.

25 「輸入部」
（ダンは輸入部で働いています）
Dan works in ◎ Ⓐ Importing.
　　　　　　○ Ⓑ Imports [the Import Department].

26 「流通部」
(a) **新聞・雑誌**
（グレッグは流通部で働いているんです）
Greg works in ◎ Ⓐ Circulation.
　　　　　　○ Ⓑ the Circulation Department.

(b) **新聞・雑誌以外**
（グレッグは流通部で働いています）
Greg works in ◎ Ⓐ Distribution.
　　　　　　○ Ⓑ the Distribution Department.

27 「労務部」
　　（グレッグは労務部で働いています）
　　Greg works in　☆　Ⓐ Labor.
　　　　　　　　　◎　Ⓑ Labor Relations.
　　　　　　　　　○ . Ⓒ the Labor Relations Department.

第8章

勤務に関する表現

1 「求人情報誌」
（うちの会社は求人情報誌に出ています）
◎ Our company's listed in the help-wanted magazine.
[注意] 辞典に the personnel-wanted magazine が出ているがまれ。

2 「就職説明会」
（うちの会社は昨日就職説明会を開いたんです）
Our company had ☆ Ⓐ a job fair yesterday.
　　　　　　　　◎ Ⓑ a recruiting fair ...
　　　　　　　　○ Ⓒ an employment fair ...
　　　　　　　　△ Ⓓ a hiring fair ...
[注意] 辞典に explanatory meeting for the potential employee が出ているが使われていない。

3 「人材銀行」
（ビルは人材銀行に勤めているんです）
Bill works for
　☆ Ⓐ a headhunter.
　☆ Ⓑ a headhunting firm [company].
　◎ Ⓒ a headhunting service [agency].
　○ Ⓓ a headhunting outfit [agent].
　○ Ⓔ an executive search company [service].
　○ Ⓕ an executive scout service.
　△ Ⓖ an executive search firm [business].

[91]

△ Ⓗ an executive scout company ［business, outfit, firm］.
［注意］Ⓐ～Ⓗまで管理職対象である。

4 「職業紹介所」
（スティーヴは職業紹介所に勤めています）
Steve works for an ☆ Ⓐ employment agency.
　　　　　　　　　◎ Ⓑ employment service.
　　　　　　　　　○ Ⓒ employment business ［company, outfit］.
　　　　　　　　　△ Ⓓ employment firm.

5 「就職で苦労している」
（私は今就職で苦労しているんです）
I'm having ☆ Ⓐ trouble getting ［finding］ a job right now.
　　　　　　◎ Ⓑ a problem getting ［finding］ a job ...
　　　　　　◎ Ⓒ a hard ［a tough］ time getting a job ...
　　　　　　○ Ⓓ difficulty getting a job ...

6 「就職することが難しい」
（景気が悪いから今就職することは難しいんです）
☆ Ⓐ Getting ［Finding］ a job's tough right now because
◎ Ⓑ Finding work's ...
○ Ⓒ Getting work's ...
△ Ⓓ Getting ［Finding］ employment's ...
△ Ⓔ Getting employed's ...
the economy's bad.
［注意］辞典に becoming employed, getting ［finding］ a place, obtaining ［securing］ work が出ているが使われていない。

7 「労働条件」
（私はここで働くことに興味はあるのですが条件が合わないんです）
I'm interested in working here but I can't agree to the
　　☆ Ⓐ (job) terms.
　　◎ Ⓑ terms of the job.
　　× Ⓒ working conditions.
　　× Ⓓ work conditions.
［注意］英和, 和英辞典に労働条件としてⒸが紹介されているが, 全く意味が違う。ⒸⒹは「職場環境」という意味。

8 「仕事を紹介する」

（お仕事を紹介しましょうか）
Do you want me to ☆ Ⓐ get [find] you a job?
　　　　　　　　　 ◎ Ⓑ get [find] a job for you?
　　　　　　　　　 ○ Ⓒ find work for you?
　　　　　　　　　 ○ Ⓓ set [fix] you up with a job?

[注意] get, set, fix には「紹介する」というニュアンスがある。find は元来の意味には「紹介する」という意味はない。しかし混用され，同じように使われている。

9 「仕事」

(a) **ブルーカラー・臨時の仕事の場合**
（ビルは仕事を探しています）
◎ Bill's looking for work [a job].

(b) **ホワイトカラーの場合**
（ビルは仕事を探しています）
Bill's looking for ◎ Ⓐ a job.
　　　　　　　　　△ Ⓑ work.

(c) **医師・弁護士・大学の教授の場合**
（ビルは仕事を探しています）
Bill's looking for ◎ Ⓐ a position.
　　　　　　　　　○ Ⓑ a job.
　　　　　　　　　△ Ⓒ work.

(d) **専門職の場合**
（ビルは放送業界での仕事を探しています）
Bill's looking for ◎ Ⓐ a career in broadcasting.
　　　　　　　　　○ Ⓑ a job in ...
　　　　　　　　　△ Ⓒ work in ...

[注意] Ⓐの career は「一生の仕事」というニュアンスがある。

(e) **重役の場合**
（ビルは管理職の仕事を探しています）
Bill's looking for ◎ Ⓐ a position [job] in management.

　　　　　△ Ⓑ work in ...

(f) 「一生の職業」という意味で大学生などが言う場合
　　（ビルはまだ仕事を決めていません）
　　Bill hasn't decided on his ◎ Ⓐ career yet.
　　　　　　　　　　　　　　△ Ⓑ profession ...

(g) 保険・出版・新聞・株式市場・不動産・広告業の場合
　　（主人は広告の仕事をしています）
　　◎ My husband's in the advertising industry ［game, business］.

10 「空席」
　　（経理に空席が2つあります）
　　Accounting has two ☆ Ⓐ openings.
　　　　　　　　　　　 ◎ Ⓑ jobs open.
　　　　　　　　　　　 ○ Ⓒ vacancies ［jobs available］.

11 「もちろん」
(a) 丁寧に言う場合
　　（面接官：明日最終面接に来ることができますか）
　　Interviewer: Can you come for a final interview tomorrow?
　　（応募者：もちろんです）
　　Applicant: ☆ Ⓐ Certainly.
　　　　　　　 ◎ Ⓑ Of course ［Definitely］.
　　　　　　　 ◎ Ⓒ I certainly can.
　　　　　　　 ○ Ⓓ Sure (I can).
　　　　　　　 ○ Ⓔ I sure can.
　　　　　　　 ▽ Ⓕ Certainly I can.
　　［注意］大企業の面接など丁寧さが求められているときはCertainly.はSure.よりよく使われている。

(b) 少しくだけて言う場合
　　（面接官：金曜から働けますか）
　　Interviewer: Can you start working Friday?
　　（応募者：もちろんです）
　　Applicant: ◎ Ⓐ Sure ［Definitely］.
　　　　　　　 ◎ Ⓑ Sure I can ［I sure can］.

第8章　勤務に関する表現

　　　　　◎ ⓒ You bet.
[注意] コーヒーショップのアルバイトの面接など。

(c) 親しい友人同士の場合
（トム：僕たちが校庭でテニスをした昔の日々を覚えているかい）
Tom: Do you remember the old days when we played tennis in the schoolyard?
（デイヴィッド：もちろんさ）
David: ◎ Ⓐ Of course [Sure].
　　　　◎ Ⓑ You bet [betcha].
　　　　◎ ⓒ Sure I do [I sure do].
　　　　▽ Ⓓ You bet your boots [life].
[注意] (1) Ⓓが辞典に出ているがまれにしか使われていない。
(2) ⒷのYou betcha.は中年以上の人の間では非常によく使われているが，年代が若くなるにつれて使用頻度は下がる。

12 「雇う」
（XYZ銀行はたぶん私を雇うでしょう）
XYZ Bank'll probably ◎ Ⓐ hire me.
　　　　　　　　　　　◎ Ⓑ give me the job.
　　　　　　　　　　　○ ⓒ take me.

13 「雇ってもらえる」
（私は条件を全部満たせます。私を雇ってもらえますか）
I meet all the requirements. ☆ Ⓐ Do I get the job?
　　　　　　　　　　　　　　◎ Ⓑ Can you give me the job?
　　　　　　　　　　　　　　◎ ⓒ Can you hire me?
　　　　　　　　　　　　　　○ Ⓓ Can you take me?
　　　　　　　　　　　　　　△ Ⓔ Can I get the job?
　　　　　　　　　　　　　　△ Ⓕ Can you employ me?
　　　　　　　　　　　　　　△ Ⓖ Can you take me on?

14 「就職する」
(a) 高い地位
（彼は2カ月前にこの支店に就職したんです）
He ☆ Ⓐ got a job [started working] at this branch two months ago.
　　◎ Ⓑ took over [got a position at, landed a job at] this

　　　　　branch ...
　　○ Ⓒ started heading this branch ...
　　○ Ⓓ joined this branch ...
　　▽ Ⓔ found employment at this branch ...
　　× Ⓕ got work ［found a job］at this branch ...
［注意］(1) 辞典にⒻが出ているが使われていない。
(2) Ⓔは堅い文章英語ではよく使われている。
(3) あこがれの会社に就職して興奮しているときはⒷの land a job が1番よく使われている。

(b) 高くない地位
(彼はラッセル証券に警備員として就職しました)
He ◎ Ⓐ got ［found］ a job at Russel Securities Firm as a security guard.
　　◎ Ⓑ got work ...
　　○ Ⓒ found work ...
　　× Ⓓ got a position ［found employment, landed a job］...

15 「入社する」
(a) 平社員
(ビルはこの会社にいつ入社したのですか)
When did Bill ☆ Ⓐ start working for ［at］ this company?
　　　　　　　☆ Ⓑ get ［find］ a job at this ...?
　　　　　　　◎ Ⓒ land a job at this ...?
　　　　　　　▽ Ⓓ join this ...?
　　　　　　　▽ Ⓔ find employment at this ...?
　　　　　　　× Ⓕ enter this ...?
［注意］辞典にはⒹⒺⒻしか出ていないが，よく使われるのはⒶⒷⒸ。

(b) 役員・管理職
(社長はいつこの会社に入ったのですか)
When did the CEO ☆ Ⓐ take over this company?
　　　　　　　　 ☆ Ⓑ start leading ［heading］ this ...?
　　　　　　　　 ◎ Ⓒ get the position at this ...?
　　　　　　　　 ◎ Ⓓ join ［start working for］ this ...?
　　　　　　　　 × Ⓔ enter this ...?

16 「新入社員」

（うちの会社は昨日新入社員の歓迎会を開いたんです）
Our company had a welcoming party for
 ☆ Ⓐ new people [employees] yesterday.
 ◎ Ⓑ newly-hired people [employees] ...
 ○ Ⓒ newly-hired [new] staff ...
 ○ Ⓓ recruits ...

17 「研修」

（うちは新入社員の研修を１週間開きます）
We're going to
 ◎ Ⓐ give the new employees in-house skills training for a week.
 ◎ Ⓑ give the new employees a week-long skills training program [session].
 ◎ Ⓒ give the new employees an in-house skills training program [session] for a week.
 ◎ Ⓓ have a week-long in-house skills training program [session] for the new employees.

18 「出勤する」

(a) **時間が逼迫している場合**
（上司が出勤したらすぐあなたにお電話させます）
Right after the boss
 ◎ Ⓐ walks through [in] the door, I'll have him call you.
 ◎ Ⓑ gets in [arrives, comes to work, gets here], ...
 ○ Ⓒ walks in [reports to work, comes in], ...

[注意] ⒶとⒷの gets in，Ⓒの walks in は「彼が帰宅したらすぐ電話させます」の意味でもよく使われている。

(b) **習慣的なこと**
（上司は毎朝何時に出勤するのですか）
What time does your boss
 ◎ Ⓐ get to work every morning?
 ○ Ⓑ arrive at [report to, go to] work ...?
 × Ⓒ walk through [in] the door ...?

(c) ちょうど出勤してきた場合
　　●出勤時間にぎりぎりというニュアンスのとき
　（上司はちょうど出勤してきたところです）
　　◎ Ⓐ The boss just walked through [in] the door.
　　◎ Ⓑ The boss just came through the door.
　　◎ Ⓒ The boss just walked in.
　　◎ Ⓓ The boss's just walked through the door.
　　○ Ⓔ The boss's just walked in the door.
　　○ Ⓕ The boss's just come through [in] the door.
　　●時間がぎりぎりというニュアンスがないとき
　（上司はちょうど出勤してきたところです）
　　☆ Ⓐ The boss just got here.
　　☆ Ⓑ The boss just got to work.
　　◎ Ⓒ The boss's just gotten here.
　　○ Ⓓ The boss's just gotten to work.
　　○ Ⓔ The boss just reported to work.
　　△ Ⓕ The boss's just reported to work.
　　△ Ⓖ The boss just arrived at work.
　　△ Ⓗ The boss's just arrived at work.

(d) 出勤しているか否かを尋ねる場合
　　●話し手・聞き手とも会社の中にいる
　（支配人は出勤していますか）
　Is the manager ◎ Ⓐ in [here, around]?
　　　　　　　　◎ Ⓑ in the office?
　　　　　　　　◎ Ⓒ available?
　　●電話で問い合わせている
　（支配人は出勤していますか）
　Is the manager ◎ Ⓐ in [there, around]?
　　　　　　　　◎ Ⓑ in [at] the office?
　　　　　　　　◎ Ⓒ available?

19 「タイムレコーダー」
(a)（出勤して）押すと述べる場合
　（出勤したら必ずタイムコレコーダーを押して下さい）
　Be sure to ☆ Ⓐ punch in when you get to work.
　　　　　　◎ Ⓑ punch the clock when ...

(b) （退社するときに）押すと述べる場合
　　（退社するときは必ずタイムレコーダーを押して下さい）
　　Be sure to ☆ Ⓐ punch out when you leave the office.
　　　　　　　　◎ Ⓑ clock out when ...
　　　　　　　　△ Ⓒ punch the time clock when ...
　　[注意] 辞典に punch the time recorder が出ているが使われていない。

(c) 機械を述べる場合
　　（うちは新しいタイムレコーダーを買わなければならないね）
　　We have to buy a new ☆ Ⓐ clock.
　　　　　　　　　　　　　◎ Ⓑ time clock.
　　　　　　　　　　　　　× Ⓒ time recorder.

20 「退社する」

　　（リンダは何時に退社しましたか）
　　What time did Linda ☆ Ⓐ go home?
　　　　　　　　　　　　◎ Ⓑ leave work?
　　　　　　　　　　　　◎ Ⓒ leave the office?
　　　　　　　　　　　　△ Ⓓ leave her work?
　　[注意] Ⓒは事務職にしか使えないが，ⒶⒷⒹはデパート・工場・事務所など職種を問わず広く使われている。

21 「勤務」

(a) 時間帯
　　（ポールはⒶ朝の，Ⓑ昼の，Ⓒ午後の，Ⓓ夜の，Ⓔ昼夜の，Ⓕ深夜の勤務で働いています）
　　Paul works ◎ Ⓐ the morning shift.
　　　　　　　 ◎ Ⓑ the day shift.
　　　　　　　 ◎ Ⓒ the afternoon shift.
　　　　　　　 ◎ Ⓓ the night shift.
　　　　　　　 ◎ Ⓔ the day and night shift.
　　　　　　　 ◎ Ⓕ the graveyard shift.
　　[注意] (1) Paul works on the ... のように on を付けた表現はⒶ〜Ⓕいずれもときどき使われる程度。
　　(2) Ⓐ〜Ⓕいずれも始業時間が2つ以上あれば a morning shift のように the ではなく a を付けた形も使われている。これは会社のシステムによる。

(b) 体系
   (ポールはⓐフレックス勤務で，Ⓑフレックスで，Ⓒ1日置きに2部交替勤務で，Ⓓ半夜勤で，Ⓔ分割勤務で働いています)
   Paul works ◎ Ⓐ a flex shift.
   　　　　　　◎ Ⓑ flex time.
   　　　　　　◎ Ⓒ a double shift every other day.
   　　　　　　◎ Ⓓ a swing shift.
   　　　　　　◎ Ⓔ a split shift.
   [注意] (1) Ⓐ〜Ⓔいずれも勤務時間が2つ以上ある。従って数えられるので the ではなく a を使う。但しⒷは a は不要である。
   (2) Ⓒは普通16時間勤務になる。
   (3) Ⓓは午後3時頃から真夜中までの勤務になる。
   (4) Ⓔは午前，午後のように勤務時間を2つ以上に分ける就労システム。

22 「在宅勤務」
(ブライアンは在宅勤務なんです)
◎ Ⓐ Brian works from home.
○ Ⓑ Brian's a stay-at-home worker [a telecommuter].
△ Ⓒ Brian's a teleworker [a stay-at-home employee].

23 「事務職」
(a) 現在
   (私は事務職についています)
   ☆ Ⓐ I have a desk job.
   ◎ Ⓑ I work at [in] the office.
   ○ Ⓒ I have an office job.
   ○ Ⓓ My job's desk work.
   [注意] 辞典に I have desk [office] work. が出ているが使われていない。

(b) 未来
   (来週から私は事務職に変わるんです)
   I'm going to ☆ Ⓐ get a desk job next week.
   　　　　　　 ◎ Ⓑ work in [at] the office ...
   　　　　　　 ○ Ⓒ get an office job ...

24 「忙しい」

第 8 章　勤務に関する表現

(a) **動詞を従えるとき**
（ボブは司法試験の準備で忙しいんです）
Bob's busy ☆ Ⓐ getting ready for the bar.
　　　　　　▽ Ⓑ in getting ready ...
　　　　　　× Ⓒ to get ready ...
[注意] Ⓑが辞典に出ているがまれ。

(b) **名詞を従えるとき**
（ボブは今仕事で忙しいんです）
Bob's busy ◎ Ⓐ working now.
　　　　　　○ Ⓑ with [at] his work now.
[注意] Ⓐは名詞を従えていないが，動詞がある限りⒶの型が1番よく使われている。

(c) **スケジュール**
（ボブは今日1日中スケジュールが忙しいんです）
Bob's ☆ Ⓐ really booked all day today.
　　　◎ Ⓑ schedule's really full all day today.
　　　◎ Ⓒ schedule's really booked (up) all day today.
　　　◎ Ⓓ really tied up all day today.
　　　○ Ⓔ really booked up all day today.
　　　○ Ⓕ time's really limited all day today.

(d) **忙殺される**
（ボブは仕事で忙しいんです）
Bob's ◎ Ⓐ swamped with (his) work.
　　　◎ Ⓑ swamped at his job.
　　　◎ Ⓒ snowed under with (his) work.
　　　◎ Ⓓ up to his elbows with (his) work.
　　　◎ Ⓔ up to his elbows [neck] in work.
　　　◎ Ⓕ pressed with (his) work.
　　　◎ Ⓖ pressed at work.
[注意] ⒶⒷⒸが1番忙殺度が強いというニュアンスがある。ⒹⒺが次に強い。

(e) **殺人的な**
（ボブは殺人的なスケジュールなんです）
Bob's on a ◎ Ⓐ killer [very tight] schedule.

[101]

▽ Ⓑ killing schedule.
　　[注意]Ⓑが辞典に出ているがまれ。

(f)　てんてこ舞い
　　(先週はてんてこ舞いでした)
　　Last week was ◎ Ⓐ hectic [crazy].
　　　　　　　　 ◎ Ⓑ extremely busy.
　　　　　　　　 ◎ Ⓒ awfully [terribly] busy.
　　[注意]てんてこ舞いの度合いではⒶが1番強いというニュアンスがある。2番目はⒷ，3番目はⒸ。

(g)　手が離せない
　　(彼女は今，手が離せないんです)
　　◎ Ⓐ She's tied up at the moment.
　　◎ Ⓑ She can't get away right now.
　　◎ Ⓒ Her hands're full right now.

25 「あくせく働く」
　　(彼は毎日あくせく働いています)
　　He ☆ Ⓐ works like a slave every day.
　　　　◎ Ⓑ works like a dog ...
　　[注意]Ⓐのほうが Ⓑ より強いニュアンスがある。

26 「がむしゃらに働く」
　　(ビルは毎日がむしゃらに働いています)
　　Bill ☆ Ⓐ works like his head off every day.
　　　　 ◎ Ⓑ works like his tail [ass] off ...
　　　　 ◎ Ⓒ works like crazy ...
　　　　 ◎ Ⓓ works like his butt ...
　　　　 ○ Ⓔ works like mad ...

27 「仕事中毒」
(a)　否定的に述べる場合
　　(彼は仕事中毒なんです)
　　He's ◎ Ⓐ a workaholic.
　　　　 ◎ Ⓑ working too hard [much].
　　　　 ◎ Ⓒ married to his work.

△ Ⓓ addicted to (his) work.
［注意］Ⓑは穏やかなトーンで言えば客観的な述べ方になる。

(b) **冗談として述べる場合**
　　（彼は仕事中毒なんです）
　　He's ◎ Ⓐ married to his work.
　　　　　 ◎ Ⓑ a workaholic.

28 「評価する」
(a) **過大評価する場合**
　　（あなたは私を過大評価しています）
　　You're ☆ Ⓐ giving me too much credit.
　　　　　　◎ Ⓑ thinking too much［highly］of me.
　　　　　　△ Ⓒ overrating me.
［注意］Ⓐは「やった仕事」などに対しても使われている。

(b) **過小評価する場合**
　　（会社は私を評価してくれないので辞めるんです）
　　☆ Ⓐ The company doesn't appreciate me, so I'm going to quit.
　　◎ Ⓑ The company doesn't value me, so ...
　　○ Ⓒ The company doesn't rate［value］me the way it should, so ...
　　△ Ⓓ The company undervalues［underrates］me, so ...
　　△ Ⓔ I'm underappreciated［underrated, undervalued］by the company, so ...

29 「年功序列」
　　（うちの会社では昇進は年功序列なんです）
　　Promotion in our company's based on
　　　　☆ Ⓐ how long you've been working here.
　　　　◎ Ⓑ seniority.
　　　　○ Ⓒ your seniority.
　　　　△ Ⓓ the seniority system.
［注意］辞典に long service, the seniority rule が出ているが使われてもまれ。

30 「実力」
　　（この会社での昇進は全く実力次第です）

Promotion in this company's entirely based on
- ☆ Ⓐ merit.
- ◎ Ⓑ your capability.
- ◎ Ⓒ (your) job performance.
- ○ Ⓓ the merit system.
- × Ⓔ the capability system.

31 「統率力を見せる」

(統率力を見せてくれた後，会社はあなたを昇進させますよ)

After you
- ◎ Ⓐ show your leadership skills ［qualities, abilities, ability］,
- ◎ Ⓑ demonstrate your leadership skills ［qualities, abilities, ability］,
- ◎ Ⓒ prove your leadership skills ［qualities, abilities, ability］,
- × Ⓓ have your leadership skills ［qualities, abilities, ability］,

the management'll promote you.

32 「昇進する」

(a) 「そろそろ昇進していい頃だ」というニュアンスの場合

(ビルはそろそろ昇進していい頃だね)
- ◎ Ⓐ It's (about) time Bill's promoted.
- ○ Ⓑ Bill's due for a promotion.

(b) （昇進が発表された後）昇進することになっている

(ビルは昇進する予定です)

Bill's
- ☆ Ⓐ going to be ［get］ promoted.
- ◎ Ⓑ due to be ［get］ promoted.
- ○ Ⓒ scheduled to be ［get］ promoted.
- △ Ⓓ (slated) to be promoted.

［注意］ⒶⒹは「発表された」響きがあるがⒷⒸは「発表された」ときでも「発表されていない」ときでも使われている。

(c) 昇進が発表されていない場合

(ビルは昇進するはずです)
- ☆ Ⓐ Bill's supposed to be ［get］ promoted.
- ☆ Ⓑ Bill should be ［get］ promoted.
- ◎ Ⓒ Bill's expected to be ［get］ promoted.

◎ ⓓ Bill deserves to be [get] promoted.
[注意] ⒷⒹは発表されていないニュアンスがあるのに対して，Ⓐは発表されていてもいなくても使われている。Ⓒは発表されていないニュアンスのほうがずっと強い。

(d) **昇進する地位を明示する場合**
● 非常に低い地位からのとき
(ジムは早晩管理職に昇進します)
◎ Jim'll work his way up [make it up] to management sooner or later.

● 平社員からのとき
(ジムは早晩管理職に昇進します)
◎ Jim'll work up [move up, make it up] to management sooner or later.

● 支配人と平社員の中間のとき
(ジムは早晩管理職に昇進します)
Jim'll ◎ Ⓐ be [get] promoted to management sooner or later.
　　　　○ Ⓑ advance to management sooner or later.

(e) **すごく昇進したとき**
(マイクはすごく昇進したんです)
Mike ☆ Ⓐ got a big promotion.
　　　☆ Ⓑ really got promoted [was really promoted].
　　　◎ Ⓒ got a huge promotion.
　　　○ Ⓓ really got moved up.
　　　○ Ⓔ got a big step-up.

33 「出世」
(a) **事実だけを述べる場合**
(ビルは出世が速いんです)
Bill's ☆ Ⓐ on the fast track.
　　　◎ Ⓑ in the fast lane.
　　　○ Ⓒ on the quick path.
　　　△ Ⓓ on the fast path.
[注意] Ⓑは生活スタイルをほめるときに使うのが正しいが近年はⒶの意味で

[105]

も非常によく使われている。

(b) **比較して述べる場合**
（ビルは私より出世が速いんです）
Bill's ☆ Ⓐ on a faster track than me.
　　　◎ Ⓑ in a faster lane than me.
　　　○ Ⓒ on a quicker path than me.

34 「裸一貫」
（ビルは裸一貫で始めて出世したんです）
Bill ☆ Ⓐ started with nothing and made his way in the world.
　　☆ Ⓑ worked his way up from the bottom.
　　◎ Ⓒ started with nothing and made his way in life.
　　◎ Ⓓ made his way from the bottom.
　　◎ Ⓔ pulled himself up by his own boot-straps.

35 「出世頭」
（ビルは大学時代の級友の出世頭なんです）
Bill's ☆ Ⓐ the most successful of his classmates in college.
　　　◎ Ⓑ done the best of any of ...
　　　◎ Ⓒ gone further in life than any of ...

36 「降格」
（マイクは降格になったんです）
Mike ☆ Ⓐ got demoted.
　　◎ Ⓑ was demoted.
　　○ Ⓒ was moved down.

37 「すごい降格」
（ポールはすごく降格したんです）
Paul ☆ Ⓐ got a big demotion.
　　☆ Ⓑ really got demoted ［was really demoted］.
　　◎ Ⓒ really got moved down ［was really moved down］.
　　○ Ⓓ got a big step-down.
［注意］アメリカでは降格したら辞めるのであまりこのことは話題にならない。

38 「窓際族」

(成績が私よりいい若い社員が大勢いるので私は窓際族の感じがします)
I feel like I'm ☆ Ⓐ not needed because there are a
　　　　　　　　☆ Ⓑ unnecessary ...
　　　　　　　　◎ Ⓒ a fifth wheel ...
　　　　　　　　○ Ⓓ redundant ...
lot of young employees who're doing better than me.

39 「さぼる」

(ナンシーはいつもインターネットでさぼっているんです)
Nancy's always ◎ Ⓐ fooling around on the 'Net.
　　　　　　　　◎ Ⓑ goofing off ...
　　　　　　　　○ Ⓒ wasting time ...
［注意］辞典に blow off around ［on］，goof off around が出ているが使われていない。

40 「昇進が遅い」

(デイヴィッドはすごく昇進が遅いんです)
◎ Ⓐ David's getting ［being］ promoted really slow.
◎ Ⓑ David isn't getting ［being］ promoted very fast.
○ Ⓒ David's rising in the company really slow.

41 「転勤になる」

(ジムはピッツバーグ支店に転勤になるでしょう)
Jim'll be ☆ Ⓐ moved to the Pittsburgh branch.
　　　　　◎ Ⓑ transferred ［sent］ ...
　　　　　○ Ⓒ assigned ［relocated］ ...
　　　　　△ Ⓓ shifted ...
［注意］Ⓒはかしこまった響きがあるが，ビジネスの世界ではⒶⒷと同じようによく使われている。

42 「週休2日制」

(うちの会社は週休2日制です)
Our company's ◎ Ⓐ using a five-day workweek.
　　　　　　　 ○ Ⓑ on a five-day workweek (system).
　　　　　　　 ○ Ⓒ using a five-day workweek system.

43 「隔週5日制」

(うちの会社は隔週5日制です)
Our
- ☆ Ⓐ company uses a system where we work every other Saturday.
- ☆ Ⓑ company uses a system where every other Saturday's a work day.
- ◎ Ⓒ company's on a system where every other Saturday's a work day.
- ◎ Ⓓ company's on a system where we work every other Saturday.

44 「休暇」
(a) 一般の人
(ブライアンは休暇を取っています)
Brian's ◎ Ⓐ on [taking a] vacation.
　　　　○ Ⓑ taking his vacation.
　　　　○ Ⓒ vacationing.

(b) 軍人・公務員・医師・看護婦
(ブライアンは休暇を取っています)
Brian's ◎ Ⓐ on [taking] leave.
　　　　○ Ⓑ on vacation.
　　　　○ Ⓒ taking a vacation.

[注意] (1) Ⓐは数日間の休暇，数時間の休憩にも使われている。
(2) Ⓐは「許可を取った休暇」というときに使われるのに対してⒷⒸには「許可」というニュアンスがない。従ってⒷⒸは職業に関係なく広く使われている。

45 「祭日」
(明日は祭日です)
Tomorrow's a ◎ Ⓐ holiday.
　　　　　　 △ Ⓑ Federal [legal, national] holiday.

[注意] 多くの辞典に public holiday が出ているが使われていない。

46 「代休」
(日曜日働いたから明日は彼の代休なんです)
Tomorrow's his ◎ Ⓐ day-off because he worked Sunday.
　　　　　　　 ○ Ⓑ comp day ...
　　　　　　　 × Ⓒ compensatory day-off [time-off] ...

第8章　勤務に関する表現

[注意] 辞典に©が出ているが使われていない。

47 「有給休暇」
（1年にあなたは何日有給休暇があるのですか）
How many ◎ Ⓐ paid-days-off a year do you have?
　　　　　× Ⓑ paid-holidays ...?
[注意] Ⓑはアメリカ南部ではときどき使われている。

48 「アルバイトをする」
(a) 他に定職を持っている人の場合
（主人はアルバイトで警備員をしています）
My ☆ Ⓐ husband has another job [a second job] as a security guard.
　◎ Ⓑ husband's working another job [a second job] ...
　◎ Ⓒ husband works another job [a second job] ...
　◎ Ⓓ husband has another job on the side ...
　○ Ⓔ husband has a job on the side ...
　○ Ⓕ husband's moonlighting ...
　△ Ⓖ husband moonlights ...
[注意] ⒻⒼは昼間に定職を持っている人が夜にアルバイトをするときの表現。夜に定職を持っている人が昼間にアルバイトをする場合には使われていない。

(b) 主婦・学生が昼間にアルバイトをする場合
（ビルのお母さんは彼が大学に行けるようにアルバイトをしています）
Bill's ◎ Ⓐ mother works part time so he can go to college.
　◎ Ⓑ mother's working part time ...
　◎ Ⓒ mother has a part time job ...
　△ Ⓓ mother has a job part time ...

49 「定着率」
(a) 「定着率が高い」と述べる場合
（うちの会社は社員の定着率が高い）
Our ◎ Ⓐ company has a low employee turnover rate.
　○ Ⓑ company has loyal employees.
　△ Ⓒ company's employees stay for a long time.

(b) 「定着率が悪い」と述べる場合

(うちの会社は社員の定着率が悪い)
Our company has a high ◎ Ⓐ employee turnover rate.
　　　　　　　　　　　　　○ Ⓑ turnover rate of its employees.

50 「辞める」
(a) 普通の人
(ビルは仕事を辞めます)
Bill's going to ◎ Ⓐ quit his job.
　　　　　　　△ Ⓑ leave work [his job].
　　　　　　　× Ⓒ leave his work [place].
　　　　　　　× Ⓓ quit his place.
[注意] 辞典にⒸⒹが出ているが使われていない。

(b) 部長・社長など高い地位の人
(生産部長はたぶん辞めるでしょう)
The Production Manager'll probably
　　◎ Ⓐ quit his job.
　　◎ Ⓑ resign [step down].
　　◎ Ⓒ resign (from) his position.
　　○ Ⓓ step down from his position.
　　○ Ⓔ quit [leave his job].
　　△ Ⓕ leave his position.

(c) 長官・首相など高い地位の公職の人
(財務長官はたぶん辞めるでしょう)
The Secretary of the Treasury'll probably
　　☆ Ⓐ resign [step down].
　　◎ Ⓑ resign his post [position].
　　◎ Ⓒ step down from his post [position].
　　○ Ⓓ resign from his office.
　　○ Ⓔ leave his post [quit his job].
　　○ Ⓕ step down from his office [job].

51 「首になる」
(a) 社員に落度があった場合
(ブライアンは昨日首になったんです)
Brian ◎ Ⓐ was fired yesterday.

　　　　× Ⓑ got the grand bounce.
　　[注意] 辞典にⒷが出ているが使われていない。

(b) 社員に全く責任がなく会社の都合でリストラされた場合
　　（ブライアンは昨日首になったんです）
　　Brian ◎ Ⓐ was ［got］ laid off yesterday.
　　　　　 ◎ Ⓑ was dismissed ...
　　[注意] Ⓑは20%位社員に責任があるという響きもある。

(c) 社員に責任があったときと会社の都合でリストラされた場合
　　（ブライアンは昨日首になったんです）
　　Brian ○ Ⓐ was axed yesterday.
　　　　　 ○ Ⓑ got a ［his］ pink slip ...
　　　　　 ○ Ⓒ got his walking papers ...
　　　　　 △ Ⓓ was sacked ［booted out］ ...
　　　　　 △ Ⓔ got the boot ...

52 「（解雇される意味での）ひまを出される」
　　（ブライアンは昨日ひまを出されたんです）
　　☆ Ⓐ They let Brian go yesterday.
　　◎ Ⓑ Brian was let go ...

53 「解任される」
　　（社長は解任されるだろう）
　　The CEO'll be ◎ Ⓐ tossed ［thrown］ out of his post.
　　　　　　　　 ◎ Ⓑ fired ［removed, dismissed］ from ...
　　　　　　　　 ◎ Ⓒ relieved of ...
　　　　　　　　 △ Ⓓ discharged from ...
　　[注意]「解任される」語調の厳しさはⒶが1番強く，Ⓑの fired が2番，Ⓑの removed, dismissed とⒸⒹはほぼ同じで3番。

54 「総辞職する」
　　（経営陣はたぶん総辞職するでしょう）
　　The management'll probably ◎ Ⓐ resign as a group.
　　　　　　　　　　　　　　　 ◎ Ⓑ resign collectively.
　　　　　　　　　　　　　　　 ○ Ⓒ resign en masse.
　　　　　　　　　　　　　　　 ○ Ⓓ resign as a body.

55「失業者が増える」
　　（失業は来年増えるでしょう）
　　The unemployment'll ◎ Ⓐ be ［get］ worse next year.
　　　　　　　　　　　　　○ Ⓑ increase ［rise, worsen, go up］ next ...
　　　　　　　　　　　　　○ Ⓒ become worse next ...
　　　　　　　　　　　　　× Ⓓ be aggravated next ...
　　　　　　　　　　　　　× Ⓔ degenerate ［deteriorate］ next ...

56「失業率が悪化する」
　　（失業率は今年の秋もっと悪化するでしょう）
　　The unemployment rate'll ◎ Ⓐ get higher this fall.
　　　　　　　　　　　　　　◎ Ⓑ go up more ...
　　　　　　　　　　　　　　○ Ⓒ go up further ...
　　　　　　　　　　　　　　○ Ⓓ rise further ［more］ ...
　　　　　　　　　　　　　　△ Ⓔ increase further ...
　　　　　　　　　　　　　　△ Ⓕ be worse ...
　　　　　　　　　　　　　　△ Ⓖ be ［become］ higher ...

57「仕事を転々とする」
　　（ブライアンは仕事を転々としているんです）
　　☆ Ⓐ Brian goes from job to job.
　　☆ Ⓑ Brian keeps changing jobs.
　　◎ Ⓒ Brian keeps on changing jobs.
　　◎ Ⓓ Brian keeps hopping from job to job.
　　○ Ⓔ Brian's hopping ［moving, switching］ from job to job.

第9章 職場に関する表現

1 「あごで使う」
(a) 第三者のことを述べる場合
(新しい支配人は部下をあごで使うんです)
The new manager ◎ Ⓐ bosses [orders] his people [staff] around.
　　　　　　　　　 ◎ Ⓑ is bossy.

(b) 聞き手に述べる場合
(私たちをあごで使わないで下さい)
Please don't ☆ Ⓐ boss [order] us around.
　　　　　　 ◎ Ⓑ be bossy.
　　　　　　 ○ Ⓒ be bossy to us.

2 「指図される」
(私はロンに指図されたくないんです)
I don't want ☆ Ⓐ to take orders from Ron.
　　　　　　☆ Ⓑ Ron to order me around.
　　　　　　◎ Ⓒ Ron to boss me around.
　　　　　　◎ Ⓓ to be ordered around by Ron.
　　　　　　○ Ⓔ to be bossed around by Ron.
　　　　　　○ Ⓕ to take directions from Ron.
　　　　　　△ Ⓖ to be ordered by Ron.
　　　　　　△ Ⓗ Ron to order me.

3 「用件」
   (秘書：ご用件は何ですか)
   Secretary: May I ask you ◎ Ⓐ what it is regarding?
   　　　　　　　　　　　　 ◎ Ⓑ what your business is regarding?
   　　　　　　　　　　　　 ○ Ⓒ what's the nature of your business?
   　　　　　　　　　　　　 △ Ⓓ what it is about?
   　　　　　　　　　　　　 △ Ⓔ what your business is about?

4 「会社案内」
   (会社案内をいただけますか)
   Can I have your ◎ Ⓐ company fact sheet?
   　　　　　　　　△ Ⓑ company overview [profile]?
   [注意] 辞典に company backgrounder が出ているが使われていない。

5 「伝言」
(a) 伝言をするか否かを尋ねる場合
   (伝言がありますか)
   ☆ Ⓐ Can I take a message?
   ☆ Ⓑ Would you like to leave a message?
   ◎ Ⓒ Is there any message?
   ◎ Ⓓ Would you like to leave a message with me?
   △ Ⓔ Can I ask a message?
   [注意] Can I have a message? が辞典に出ているが使われていない。

(b) 伝言があることを述べる場合
   (スミスさんからあなたに伝言がありますよ)
   ◎ Ⓐ I have a message for you from Mr. Smith.
   ◎ Ⓑ You have a message from Mr. Smith.
   ◎ Ⓒ There's a message for you from Mr. Smith.

(c) 誰かが伝言を残していったことを述べる場合
   (ブラウンさんがあなたに伝言していきました)
   ◎ Ⓐ Mr. Brown left a message with me.
   ○ Ⓑ Mr. Brown left a message with me for you.

6 「客」
   (〈電話で〉上司は話せないんだ，お客がいるんだよ)

第9章　職場に関する表現

The boss can't talk to you. He has ☆ Ⓐ a client.
　　　　　　　　　　　　　　　　　◎ Ⓑ a customer.
　　　　　　　　　　　　　　　　　△ Ⓒ a guest.
　　　　　　　　　　　　　　　　　× Ⓓ company.

[注意] Ⓓの company は職場ではなく家庭のようなリラックスした場所では非常によく使われている。

7 「出て行く」

(a) **一般的に述べる場合**
（ブライアンは30分位前に事務所を出て行きました）
Brian ◎ Ⓐ went [walked] out of his office about half an hour ago.
　　　◎ Ⓑ left ...

(b) **ちょっと出て行くと述べる場合**
（上司はちょっと事務所を出て行きました）
The boss
　　◎ Ⓐ stepped out of his office.
　　◎ Ⓑ stepped away from his desk.
　　◎ Ⓒ walked out of his office for a minute.
　　◎ Ⓓ just wallked away from his desk.
　　◎ Ⓔ just walked away from his desk for a moment [a second, a sec].
　　◎ Ⓕ went out of his office for a minute [a moment].
　　◎ Ⓖ went out of his office for a second [a sec].
　　○ Ⓗ left his office for a minute [a moment].
　　△ Ⓘ left his office for a second [a sec].

(c) **怒って出て行くと述べる場合**
（支配人は怒って事務所を出て行きました）
The manager
　　☆ Ⓐ stormed out of his office.
　　◎ Ⓑ bolted [stomped, flew] out of his office in a rage.
　　◎ Ⓒ bolted out of his office in a huff.
　　○ Ⓓ stomped [flew] out of his office in a huff.
　　○ Ⓔ ran out of his office in a rage [a huff].
　　△ Ⓕ bolted out of his office in anger.

[注意] Ⓕの in anger は上記の他の動詞にも使えるが，ときどき使われる程

度。

8 「出て来る」
(a) 建物から
(私はリンダがXYZ銀行から出て来るのを見ました)
I saw Linda ◎ Ⓐ leaving XYZ Bank.
　　　　　　 ◎ Ⓑ coming out of ...
　　　　　　 △ Ⓒ coming out (from) ...

(b) 入口・裏口から
(私はブライアンが裏口から出て来るのを見ました)
I saw Brian ◎ Ⓐ coming out through the backdoor.
　　　　　　 ◎ Ⓑ coming out ...
　　　　　　 ○ Ⓒ leaving out ...
　　　　　　 △ Ⓓ coming out of ...
　　　　　　 ▽ Ⓔ leaving ...
　　　　　　 ▽ Ⓕ coming out from [by, at] ...

(c) 駅の東口・西口・南口・北口から
(私はブライアンとジムが東口から出て来るのを見ました)
I saw Brian and Jim ☆ Ⓐ leaving [coming out] the east exit.
　　　　　　　　　　 ◎ Ⓑ coming out of [through] ...
　　　　　　　　　　 ○ Ⓒ coming out from ...
　　　　　　　　　　 △ Ⓓ coming out by [at] ...

9 「片付ける」
(これらのファイルを片付けましょうか)
◎ Do you want me to put these files away [back]?

10 「もう少し」
(a) 売上げのノルマ・目標達成に近い人を励ます場合
(営業部長：もう少しだね)
Sales General Manager: You're ☆ Ⓐ almost there.
　　　　　　　　　　　　　　　 ◎ Ⓑ just about there.
　　　　　　　　　　　　　　　 ○ Ⓒ on the right track.
　　　　　　　　　　　　　　　 ○ Ⓓ nearly [practically] there.
　　　　　　　　　　　　　　　 × Ⓔ virtually [all but] there.

(b) 仕事が終了したか否かの質問に対して
（もう少しです）
☆ Ⓐ Almost.
◎ Ⓑ Just about.
◎ Ⓒ I'm just about done [through, finished].
◎ Ⓓ I'm almost done [there, finished].
○ Ⓔ I'm just about [almost] wrapped up [there].
○ Ⓕ I'm nearly there [done, wrapped up, through, finished].
○ Ⓖ I'm almost through.

11 「創立記念日」
（5月20日はうちの会社の創立記念日なんです）
May 20th's ☆ Ⓐ our company's anniversary.
　　　　　　◎ Ⓑ the anniversary of our company.
　　　　　　○ Ⓒ the anniversary of our company's establishment.
　　　　　　△ Ⓓ the anniversary of our company's founding.

12 「ごみ」
(a) 事務所
（ビルの事務所はいつもごみがたくさんあります）
Bill's office always has a lot of ☆ Ⓐ trash.
　　　　　　　　　　　　　　　　◎ Ⓑ garbage.
　　　　　　　　　　　　　　　　× Ⓒ refuse [rubbish].

[注意] (1) どの辞典でも garbage は「台所の生ごみ」として紹介されているがアメリカ英語の慣用を歪曲している。
(2)「台所の生ごみ」を述べるときは garbage が1番よく使われ trash もよく使われている。
(3) 多くの辞典でⒸを英米の区別なしに列記しているがアメリカでは使われていない。

(b) 「ごみが散らかっている」と述べる場合
（金曜日の夜パーティーを開いたから事務所はごみが散らかっているんです）
The office is
　　◎ Ⓐ messy [trashed] because we had a party on Friday night.
　　◎ Ⓑ a mess ...
　　○ Ⓒ sleazy ...

　　　　△ Ⓓ trashy ［in a mess］...

(c) 　ごみ箱
　　（それらをごみ箱に捨てて下さい）
　　Please throw them in the ☆ Ⓐ trash.
　　　　　　　　　　　　　　◎ Ⓑ trash can ［waste basket］.
　　　　　　　　　　　　　　○ Ⓒ trash basket.
　　　　　　　　　　　　　　× Ⓓ refuse basket.

13 「電卓」
　　（あなたの電卓をお借りしてもいいですか）
　　Can I use your ◎ Ⓐ calculator?
　　　　　　　　　　○ Ⓑ pocket ［desk］ calculator?
　　[注意]（1）辞典に electronic calculator, computer が出ているが使われていない。
　　　　（2）Ⓐはサイズに関係なく使われているがⒷの pocket　calculator は小型、desk calculator は大型の違いがある。

14 「シャープペン」
　　（あなたのシャープペンを借りてもいいですか）
　　Can I use your ◎ Ⓐ mechanical pencil?
　　　　　　　　　　× Ⓑ ever-sharp pencil?
　　[注意] Ⓑが辞典に出ているが使われていない。

15 「ボールペン」
　　（あなたのボールペンを借りてもいいですか）
　　Can I use your ◎ Ⓐ ball-point pen?
　　　　　　　　　　× Ⓑ ball pen?

16 「サインペン」
　　（あなたのサインペンを借りてもいいですか）
　　Can I use your ◎ Ⓐ felt-tip pen?
　　　　　　　　　　○ Ⓑ felt tip?
　　[注意] 辞典に felt-tipped pen, felt pen が出ているが使われていない。

17 「マジックペン」
　　（あなたのマジックペンを借りてもいいですか）

Can I use your ◎ Ⓐ marker?
　　　　　　　　　　○ Ⓑ felt-tip pen?
　　　　　　　　　　△ Ⓒ a Magic Marker?
　　　　　　　　　　× Ⓓ magic pen?
　［注意］Ⓒは子供の間では非常によく使われている。

18 「保留になる」
(a) 期限を明示しない場合
（あなたの提案は保留になっています）
Your proposal's ◎ Ⓐ on hold.
　　　　　　　　○ Ⓑ on the back burner.
　　　　　　　　△ Ⓒ in limbo.

(b) 期限を明示する場合
（あなたの提案はあさってまで保留になっています）
Your proposal's ◎ Ⓐ on hold until the day after tomorrow.
　　　　　　　　○ Ⓑ on the back burner ...
　　　　　　　　○ Ⓒ being held over ...
　　　　　　　　△ Ⓓ in limbo ...

19 「(仕事を) 急ぐ」
(a) 「急がなければならない」と述べるとき
（私は急がなければならないんです）
I've got to ☆ Ⓐ hurry.
　　　　　　◎ Ⓑ go.
　　　　　　◎ Ⓒ get out of here.
　　　　　　◎ Ⓓ run [get going].
　　　　　　○ Ⓔ rush [get a move on, hustle].
　　　　　　△ Ⓕ fly.

(b) 「急いで帰らなければならない」と述べるとき
（私は急いで職場へ帰らなければならないんです）
◎ I have to hurry [rush, dash, race, fly, jet] back to work.
［注意］「急いで」のニュアンスはjet, fly が1番, race, dash, rush, hurry の順で弱くなる。

(c) 命令文で述べるとき

    (急いで下さい)
    ☆ Ⓐ Hurry up, please.
    ◎ Ⓑ Hurry, please.
    △ Ⓒ Rush [Be quick], please.
    △ Ⓓ Speed it up, please.
    ▽ Ⓔ Make haste, please.

(d) 急いで何かをやってもらうとき
    (この仕事を急いでやって下さい)
    ◎ Ⓐ Hurry with this work.
    ◎ Ⓑ Finish this work in a hurry.
    ◎ Ⓒ Hurry and finish this work.
    ◎ Ⓓ Finish this work quick.
    ◯ Ⓔ Finish this work quickly.
    ◯ Ⓕ Get through (with) this work in a hurry.
    ◯ Ⓖ Be done with this work in a hurry.
    ◯ Ⓗ Wrap this work up [Wrap up this work] in a hurry.

(e) 車を運転している人に
    ●普通に言うとき
    (急いで)
    ☆ Ⓐ Step on it.
    ◎ Ⓑ Step on the gas.
    ◯ Ⓒ Speed (it) up.
    ◯ Ⓓ Get a move on.
    ◯ Ⓔ Give it some gas.
    △ Ⓕ Hit the gas.
    △ Ⓖ Give it a gun.
    [注意] 辞典に Put on [increase] the speed. が出ているが使われていない。
    ●強く急がせたいとき
    (急いでよ)
    ◎ Ⓐ Gun it.
    ◯ Ⓑ Put the pedal on the metal.
    △ Ⓒ Give it a lot of gas.

(f) 「急いでいる」と状態を述べるとき

第 9 章　職場に関する表現

（私は急いでいるんです）
I'm in a ☆ Ⓐ big hurry.
　　　　 ◎ Ⓑ big rush.
　　　　 ○ Ⓒ huge hurry.

第10章
給料に関する表現

1 「給料」
(a) 「給料が安い」と述べる場合
　●友人間で話すとき
(ブライアン：仕事を辞めようと思っているんだ)
Brian: I'm going to quit my job.
(トム：どうして)
Tom: How come?
(ブライアン：給料が安いんだ)
Brian: ◎ Ⓐ It doesn't pay well (enough).
　　　　 ◎ Ⓑ The pay's bad.
　　　　 ○ Ⓒ They don't pay good [enough] money.
　　　　 ○ Ⓓ They pay me peanuts [chickenfeed].
　　　　 ○ Ⓔ The pay's peanuts [chickenfeed].
　●就職の面接で話すとき
(面接者：どうしてこの前の仕事を辞めたのですか)
Interviewer: I was wondering why you quit your last job.
(被面接者：給料が安かったんです)
Interviewee: ◎ Ⓐ It didn't pay well (enough).
　　　　　　 ○ Ⓑ The pay was poor [bad].

(b) 「給料がいい」と述べる場合
(ブライアンは給料のいい仕事を探しています)
Brian's looking for a ◎ Ⓐ good-paying [well-paying] job.
　　　　　　　　　　　 △ Ⓑ well-paid ...

[122]

2 「昇給してもらう」

(a) **普通に述べる場合**
(私は大きな取引をまとめたので昇給してもらったんです)
I ☆ Ⓐ got a raise because I closed the big deal.
　◎ Ⓑ got a pay raise ...
　△ Ⓒ got a salary increase [raise] ...
[注意] 辞典に I got [had] my salary raised. が出ているが使われていない。

(b) **先月, 去年の昇給を述べる場合**
(私は先月昇給してもらったんです)
I ☆ Ⓐ got a raise last month.
　☆ Ⓑ had a raise ...
　◎ Ⓒ got [had] a pay raise ...
[注意] ⒷとⒸの had は過去を示す語があるときにしか使われていない。

(c) **昇給のパーセンテージに言及する場合**
(私は20%昇給してもらったんです)
I ☆ Ⓐ got a 20% raise.
　◎ Ⓑ got a 20% pay raise.
　○ Ⓒ got a raise of 20%.

(d) **昇給すると述べる場合**
(深夜勤務で働いてくれれば昇給するよ)
We'll ☆ Ⓐ give you a raise if you work the graveyard shift.
　　◎ Ⓑ increase your salary ...
　　○ Ⓒ increase your pay ...
　　△ Ⓓ increase your paycheck ...

(e) **昇給のスピードを述べる場合**
(うちの会社は昇給が速いんです)
Our company ☆ Ⓐ raises our pay fast.
　　　◎ Ⓑ increases our pay fast.
　　　○ Ⓒ increases our paychecks fast.

(f) **昇給が遅いと述べる場合**

(うちの夫は昇給してもらえるのが遅いんです)
◎ Ⓐ My husband doesn't get raises often.
× Ⓑ My husband's slow to get a raise.

3 「皆勤手当」
(私は皆勤手当をもらったんです)
I got ◎ Ⓐ a bonus for perfect attendance.
　　　○ Ⓑ a perfect attendance bonus.

4 「通勤手当」
(通勤手当はいくらいただけるのですか)
How much ◎ Ⓐ transportation allowance can I get?
　　　　　△ Ⓑ travel allowance can I get?
[注意] Ⓑは「出張による旅費」の意味では非常によく使われている。

5 「(…割) 増し」
(a)　5 割増し
(アメリカ人：アメリカでは残業は 5 割増しです)
American: We get time and
　◎ Ⓐ a half for overtime in the United States.
　△ Ⓑ a half for overtime work in the United States.
　× Ⓒ a 50% for overtime in the United States.

(b)　2 割増し
(私たちは残業は 2 割増しです)
We get 20% more for ◎ Ⓐ overtime.
　　　　　　　　　　△ Ⓑ overtime work.

6 「手取り」
(私は手取りで年に 8 万ドル稼がなければならないんです)
◎ Ⓐ I have to clear [net] $80,000 a year.
◎ Ⓑ I have to earn [make] $80,000 after taxes ...
◎ Ⓒ My take-home-pay has to be $80,000 ...
○ Ⓓ My net-income has to be $80,000 ...
[注意] Ⓐは低い給料には使われていない。Ⓒは非常に高額な給料には使われていない。

7 「高給取り」
(ビルは高給取りなんです)
- ☆ Ⓐ Bill makes a lot of money.
- ☆ Ⓑ Bill's a highly-paid man.
- ◎ Ⓒ Bill has a really big paycheck.
- ○ Ⓓ Bill makes [earns] big bucks.
- ○ Ⓔ Bill earns a lot of money.
- ○ Ⓕ Bill's a high-paid man.

[注意] ⒶⒹは会社員とは限らない。

8 「かなり（いい収入）」
(息子はかなりいい収入があります)

My son has ◎ Ⓐ a pretty good income.
　　　　　◎ Ⓑ a fairly good …
　　　　　○ Ⓒ a comfortable …
　　　　　△ Ⓓ a sizable [handsome, respectable] …
　　　　　△ Ⓔ a considerable …
　　　　　▽ Ⓕ a rather good …

[注意] Ⓐが1番収入が多いという響きがある。ⒸⒺは2番，ⒹⒻは3番，1番少ないのはⒷ。

9 「賃金凍結」
(組合は1年間の賃金凍結を受け入れたんです)

The union accepted a one-year ◎ Ⓐ pay freeze.
　　　　　　　　　　　　　　　○ Ⓑ salary freeze.
　　　　　　　　　　　　　　　○ Ⓒ wage freeze.

[注意] Ⓐはホワイトカラー，ブルーカラーの両方に使われている。Ⓑはホワイトカラー，Ⓒはブルーカラーに使い分けられている。

10 「減給」
(a) **給料をカットする**
(会社は私が取引を失ったので給料をカットしたんです)

The company ◎ Ⓐ cut my pay because I lost the deal.
　　　　　　○ Ⓑ cut my salary [paycheck] …
　　　　　　○ Ⓒ reduced my pay …

(b) 給料をカットされる

(私は取引を失ったので給料をカットされたんです)

I ◎ Ⓐ had my pay cut because I lost the deal.
　◎ Ⓑ got a pay cut ...
　○ Ⓒ got a salary cut ...
　△ Ⓓ got a pay reduction ...

11 「未払い給料」

(会社は社員に6カ月の未払い給料があるんです)

The company owes its employees ☆ Ⓐ six months' back pay.
　　　　　　　　　　　　　　　　◎ Ⓑ six months' unpaid salary.
　　　　　　　　　　　　　　　　○ Ⓒ six months' back salary.

[注意] 辞典に This company still has a huge amount of back pay [pay in arrear]. が出ているが使われていない。

第11章

経営に関する表現

1 「何時まで」
(このお店は日曜日何時まで開いているのですか)
◎ Ⓐ How late is this [your] store open on Sundays?
◎ Ⓑ How late are you open ...?
○ Ⓒ When do you close ...?
○ Ⓓ When [What time] does this store close ...?
△ Ⓔ Until what time are you open ...?
△ Ⓕ Until what time is this store open ...?

[注意]「何時まで」は常に How late ...? のほうが Until what time ...? よりもよく使われている。How late can you stay here?（何時までここにいられますか），How late can I call you tonight?（今晩何時までお電話してもいいですか）

2 「置いている」
(a) 店を主語にして述べる場合
(角を曲がったところの店はイタリア食品を置いています)
The store around the corner ☆ Ⓐ has [sells] Italian food.
　　　　　　　　　　　　　　 ◎ Ⓑ carries ...
　　　　　　　　　　　　　　 ○ Ⓒ stocks ...
　　　　　　　　　　　　　　 ○ Ⓓ has Italian food in stock.

(b) 社員（**They**）を主語にして述べる場合
(角を曲がったところの店はイタリア食品を置いています)
They ☆ Ⓐ have [sell] Italian food at the store around the corner.

    ◎ Ⓑ carry Italian food ...
    ○ Ⓒ stock Italian food ...
    ○ Ⓓ have Italian food in stock ...

3 「小規模で」
(息子はビジネスを小規模で始めたんです)
My son started ◎ Ⓐ his business on a small scale.
             ◎ Ⓑ out small.
             △ Ⓒ his business in a small way.

4 「設立する」
(いつあなたの会社は設立されたのですか)
When ◎ Ⓐ was your company started [established, founded]?
     ◎ Ⓑ was your company formed [set up]?
     ◎ Ⓒ did your company start [form]?

[注意] (1) start, form は大きな会社（但し巨大企業を除く），小さい会社の両方に使われている。
(2) set up は小さい会社にしか使われていない。
(3) establish, found は小さい会社にも使われているが，主として大会社に使われている。

5 「法人組織になっている」
(ハリスンさん：ゴードンの会社は法人組織になっているのですか)
Mr. Harrison: ◎ Is Gordon's company incorporated?

6 「運転資金」
(多くの会社は貸ししぶりのため運転資金不足で苦しんでいます)
Many companies're suffering from the lack of
    ☆ Ⓐ working capital because of the credit squeeze.
    ◎ Ⓑ operating capital ...
    ○ Ⓒ working funds ...
    △ Ⓓ operating funds ...

7 「売り出す」
(a) 新製品を発表するだけでなく市場に出すというニュアンスの場合
(うちの会社は今年の9月新しい車を売り出します)
Our company'll

第11章　経営に関する表現

　　◎ Ⓐ release [introduce, launch] a new car this September.
　　◎ Ⓑ come out with ...
　　◎ Ⓒ bring out ...
　　[注意] 従来の車を改良して新しい型の車を「売り出す」というときに使われる。

(b) 消費者をあっと驚かせる従来にない新製品を発表して売り出すというニュアンスの場合
　　（うちの会社は水で走る新しい車を売り出します）
　　Our company'll ◎ Ⓐ reveal [unveil] a new car that runs on water.
　　　　　　　　　 × Ⓑ disclose ...

(c) 新製品を市場に出すというニュアンスの場合
　　（うちの会社は今年の９月新しい車を売り出します）
　　Our company'll ◎ Ⓐ market a new car this September.
　　　　　　　　　 ◎ Ⓑ put [place] a new car on the market ...
　　　　　　　　　 ◎ Ⓒ put up this car for sale ...
　　　　　　　　　 ◎ Ⓓ put this car up for sale ...
　　　　　　　　　 ◎ Ⓔ offer [place] this car on the market ...
　　　　　　　　　 ◎ Ⓕ put this car on sale ...
　　[注意] Ⓐは売り出すための「広告を大々的にする」というニュアンスがあるのに対して、Ⓑは「売る準備ができている」というニュアンスが強い。ⒸⒹⒺⒻは新しい車にも古い車にも使われている点に注意。またⒻは値下げして売るというときに使われている。

(d) どこの国の市場で売り出すかを明示する場合
　　（うちの新型はアメリカの市場で来週売り出されます）
　　Our new model will ☆ Ⓐ be available on the American market next week.
　　　　　　　　　　　 ◎ Ⓑ be on the American market ...
　　　　　　　　　　　 ◎ Ⓒ hit the American market ...
　　　　　　　　　　　 ◎ Ⓓ hit the stores in America ...
　　　　　　　　　　　 ◎ Ⓔ go on sale in America ...
　　　　　　　　　　　 ◎ Ⓕ be in stores [be sold] in America ...
　　　　　　　　　　　 ◎ Ⓖ be sold on the American market ...

(e) 売りに出すものが主語の場合
(このビルは早晩売りに出されるでしょう)
This building'll ◎ Ⓐ be (placed) on the market sooner or later.
　　　　　　　　　◎ Ⓑ be (put up) for sale sooner or later.

(f) 売りに出すものが目的語の場合
(LMN会社は早晩工場を売りに出すでしょう)
LMN Company'll ◎ Ⓐ sell its mill sooner or later.
　　　　　　　　　◎ Ⓑ put its mill up for sale sooner or later.
　　　　　　　　　◎ Ⓒ put its mill on the market sooner or later.

8 「はやっている」

(a) 店
(下のレストランははやっています)
The restaurant downstairs
　　◎ Ⓐ is doing well.
　　◎ Ⓑ has a lot of business.
　　◎ Ⓒ is doing a good [a lot of] business.
　　◎ Ⓓ is successful [busy].
　　○ Ⓔ is doing good business.
　　△ Ⓕ is flourishing [thriving].

(b) 法律事務所
(この法律事務所ははやっています)
This law firm ☆ Ⓐ has a lot of clients.
　　　　　　　　◎ Ⓑ has a large clientele [practice].
　　　　　　　　△ Ⓒ has a big practice.

(c) 経理事務所
(この経理事務所ははやっています)
This accounting firm ◎ Ⓐ has a lot of clients.
　　　　　　　　　　　◎ Ⓑ has a large clientele.
　　　　　　　　　　　△ Ⓒ has a large practice.

[注意] Ⓒは法律事務所には非常によく使われているが、経理事務所にはときどきしか使われていない。

第11章　経営に関する表現

9　「(会社の) 成績はいい」
　　(この会社の成績はいいんです)
　　This ☆ Ⓐ company's doing well.
　　　　　◎ Ⓑ company's doing a good [a lot of] business.
　　　　　◎ Ⓒ company has a lot of business.
　　　　　○ Ⓓ company's doing good business.
　　　　　○ Ⓔ company('s) performance's good.

10　「回転がいい」
　　(うちのすぐ上のレストランは回転がいい)
　　The restaurant right above us
　　　☆ Ⓐ gets customers in and out really fast.
　　　◎ Ⓑ gets customers in and out very fast.
　　　◎ Ⓒ gets customers in and out really quick.
　　　◎ Ⓓ has a high customer turnover rate.
　　　○ Ⓔ has customers in and out really fast [quickly].
　　　△ Ⓕ has customers in and out very fast.
　　　△ Ⓖ has customers in and out really quick [quickly].
　　　△ Ⓗ has a high turnover rate of (its) customers.
　　　× Ⓘ has a high turnover rate.
　　[注意] 辞典に①が出ているがこの意味では使われていない。「従業員の定着率が悪い」という意味でならよく使われている。

11　「(会社が) 伸びている」
(a)　普通に述べる場合
　　(XYZ会社は伸びています)
　　XYZ Company's ◎ Ⓐ on its way up.
　　　　　　　　　◎ Ⓑ growing.
　　　　　　　　　○ Ⓒ expanding [up and coming].
　　　　　　　　　○ Ⓓ getting big.
　　　　　　　　　△ Ⓔ rising [on the rise].

(b)　強調して述べる場合
　　(XYZ会社は非常に伸びています)
　　XYZ Company's ◎ Ⓐ really on its way up.
　　　　　　　　　◎ Ⓑ really growing [expanding].
　　　　　　　　　◎ Ⓒ really up and coming.

◎ Ⓓ really getting big.
[注意] really の代わりに fast を文尾に置いても使用頻度はほぼ同じ。

12 「(売り上げが) 持ち直す」
(うちの売上げはまもなく持ち直すでしょう)
Our sales'll ☆ Ⓐ bounce back soon.
　　　　　　◎ Ⓑ recover soon.
　　　　　　◎ Ⓒ jump back up soon.
　　　　　　◎ Ⓓ go back up soon.
[注意] ⒶⒸがⒷⒹより強い響きがある。

13 「(会社の成績が) 下り坂」
(XYZ会社は最近下り坂なんです)
XYZ Company's ☆ Ⓐ in decline these days.
　　　　　　　☆ Ⓑ on the [its] way down ...
　　　　　　　○ Ⓒ in a [on the, going into a] decline ...

14 「(会社の経営が) 立ち直る」
(XYZ会社は立ち直ってきています)
XYZ Company's ☆ Ⓐ on its [the] way back up.
　　　　　　　☆ Ⓑ making a comeback.
　　　　　　　◎ Ⓒ having [coming] a comeback.
　　　　　　　◎ Ⓓ on its way up again.
　　　　　　　○ Ⓔ coming to life again.
　　　　　　　○ Ⓕ staying a comeback.
　　　　　　　△ Ⓖ having a renaissance [rebirth].

15 「注文」
(a) 「注文する」と述べる場合
(小麦粉ときな粉を注文してくれますか)
Will you ☆ Ⓐ order flour and soybean flour?
　　　　　◎ Ⓑ place an order for flour and soybean flour?
　　　　　○ Ⓒ put in an order for ...
　　　　　△ Ⓓ give an order for ...
[注意] ⒷⒸは複数形もよく使われているが単数形のほうがずっとよく使われている。

第11章　経営に関する表現

(b) 注文を明示する場合
（子牛の肉と牛肉を仕入先に注文してくれますか）
Will you ☆ Ⓐ order veal and beef from the supplier?
　　　　 ◎ Ⓑ place an order for veal and beef with the supplier?
　　　　 ○ Ⓒ put in an order for veal and beef with the supplier?
　　　　 ○ Ⓓ place an order with the supplier for veal and beef?
　　　　 △ Ⓔ put in an order with the supplier for veal and beef?
［注意］ⒷⒸⒹは orders と複数形もよく使われているが単数形のほうがよく使われている。

(c) 「注文してある」状態を述べる場合
（それはブルーク問屋に注文してあります）
☆ Ⓐ That's on order from Brook Distributor.
◎ Ⓑ That's being orderd from ...
◎ Ⓒ We've already ordered that from ...

16 「注文が本当にじゃんじゃん入ってきている」

(a) 製品を明示しないで述べる場合
（注文が本当にじゃんじゃん入ってきています）
◎ Ⓐ Orders're really pouring in.
◎ Ⓑ We're really flooded with orders.
△ Ⓒ Orders're really flying [rushing] in.
△ Ⓓ We're snowed with orders.
［注意］辞典に We have a pressure of orders. We're submerged with [snowed by] orders. が出ているが使われていない。

(b) 製品を明示して述べる場合
（これらの新製品の注文が本当にじゃんじゃん入ってきています）
◎ Ⓐ Orders're really pouring [flooding] in for these new products.
◎ Ⓑ Orders for these new products're really pouring [flooding] in.
○ Ⓒ Orders're really flying [rushing] in for these new products.

(c) 注文がものすごく入っている状態
（これらの新製品はものすごく注文があるんです）
We have ☆ Ⓐ tons of orders for these new products.
　　　　　 ◎ Ⓑ piles [a pile] of orders ...
　　　　　 ○ Ⓒ a flood [rush] of orders ...

17 「(値段を) 下げる」

(a) **大幅に下げる場合**
(この土地の値段を大幅に下げなければならないな)
We have to
　　☆ Ⓐ lower [cut] the price on this land drastically [a lot].
　　◎ Ⓑ bring down the price on this land a lot.
　　◎ Ⓒ slash the price on this land.
　　○ Ⓓ reduce the price on this land drastically [a lot].

(b) **普通に下げる場合**
(この土地の値段を下げなければならないね)
We have to ☆ Ⓐ drop the price on this land.
　　　　　　◎ Ⓑ lower [bring down] the price on this land.
　　　　　　○ Ⓒ cut [reduce] the price on this land.
　　　　　　○ Ⓓ lower this land's [land] price.

(c) **値下げのパーセンテージを述べる場合**
(15%値下げします)
We'll ☆ Ⓐ take 15% off the price.
　　　☆ Ⓑ take a 15% discount off the price.
　　　◎ Ⓒ give you a 15% discount.
　　　◎ Ⓓ discount 15% off the price.
　　　○ Ⓔ cut [lower, mark] 15% off the price.
　　　○ Ⓕ bring the price down 15%.

18 「合理化する」

(a) **経費の削減を意味する場合**
(うちは合理化しなければならないんです)
We've got to ◎ Ⓐ streamline our operations.
　　　　　　　× Ⓑ rationalize ...

[注意] (1) 和英辞典にはⒷが紹介されているが, 全く使われていない。Ⓐは辞典に出ていないが非常によく使われている。
(2) どの英和辞典も rationalize に「合理化する」の意味を出しているが, この語は「正当化する」の意味でしか使われていない。
(3) Ⓐの streamline は人件費, 制作費, 運搬費など, ありとあらゆる可能な費用の削減を意味している。従って人員の解雇も含まれている。

第11章　経営に関する表現

(b) 改良を意味する場合
（うちは合理化しなければならないんです）
◎ We've got to improve [work on] our operations.

19 「改装する」
(a) 大規模の場合
（今うちのレストランを改装しているところなんです）
We're
　　　◎ Ⓐ having our restaurant renovated [remodeled] right now.
　　　○ Ⓑ giving our restaurant a face-lift on the inside ...
[注意] 店内を広くするため壁などを取り払うような改装。

(b) 小規模の場合
（今うちのレストランを改装しているところなんです）
◎ We're having our restaurant fixed up right now.
[注意] ペンキなどを塗り替えたり，壁紙を張り替えたりするような改装。

(c) 店の正面だけの場合
（今うちのレストランを改装しているところなんです）
We're ◎ Ⓐ remodeling the front of our restaurant right now.
　　　　○ Ⓑ giving our restaurant a face-lift ...
　　　　○ Ⓒ renovating the front of our restaurant ...
　　　　○ Ⓓ improving our restaurant a face-lift ...
　　　　△ Ⓔ refurbishing the front of our restaurant ...

20 「見積り」
(a) 普通に述べる場合
（見積りはいつもらえますか）
When can I get your ☆ Ⓐ estimate?
　　　　　　　　　　　◎ Ⓑ quote?

(b) 概算の見積り
（概算の見積りを今日中にファックスします）
I can fax you ☆ Ⓐ a rough estimate by today.
　　　　　　　☆ Ⓑ ballpark figures ...
　　　　　　　◎ Ⓒ a ballpark [an approximate] estimate ...
　　　　　　　◎ Ⓓ a rough quote ...

        ○ Ⓔ rough numbers ...
        ○ Ⓕ approximate figures ...
        ○ Ⓖ a ballpark [an approximate] quote ...
        ○ Ⓗ a rough guesstimate ...
        △ Ⓘ ballpark [approximate] numbers ...

(c) **正確な見積り**
(正確な見積りはいついただけますか)
When can I get ☆ Ⓐ the exact quote?
        ☆ Ⓑ the detailed estimate?
        ☆ Ⓒ the itemized quote [estimate]?
        ◎ Ⓓ the detailed quote?
        ○ Ⓔ the exact estimate?

(d) **最初の見積り**
(最初の見積りはいくらだったのですか)
What ☆ Ⓐ was the original estimate?
      ◎ Ⓑ was the original quote?
      ◎ Ⓒ were the original figures [numbers]?
      △ Ⓓ was the original assessment?
[注意] 辞典に original quotation, estimation が出ているが使われていない。

(e) **最終的な見積り**
(最終的な見積りは1万ドルだったんです)
The final ☆ Ⓐ estimate was $10,000.
      ◎ Ⓑ quote was ...
      ◎ Ⓒ numbers [figures] were ...

(f) **低めの見積り**
(これは低めの見積りなんです，ですから実際の値段は少し高くなるかもしれません)
This is a ☆ Ⓐ low-end estimate, so the actual price
      ◎ Ⓑ conservative estimate, ...
might be a little higher.
[注意] 辞典に bottom [modest, low-priced] estimate が出ているが使われていない。

第11章　経営に関する表現

21 「多めに見る」
(あなたが必要と思う費用より少なくとも15%多めに見たほうがいいですよ)
You'd better ☆ Ⓐ add at least 15% more to the cost of what
　　　　　　　◎ Ⓑ figure at least 15% more into the cost of what
　　　　　　　○ Ⓒ estimate at least 15% more into the cost of what
you think you need.
[注意] Ⓐ〜Ⓒいずれも more はなくても非常によく使われている。ⒷⒸは more があると意味上重複になるが，よく使われている。

22 「予算を組む」
(新しいプロジェクトの予算を組まなければならないんです)
We need to ☆ Ⓐ budget for the new project.
　　　　　　☆ Ⓑ put together a budget for ...
　　　　　　◎ Ⓒ make [prepare] a budget for ...
　　　　　　○ Ⓓ compile [draw up] a budget for ...

23 「生産に入っている」
(a) **工場が主語の場合**
(うちの工場は生産に入っています)
☆ Ⓐ We're making that in our plant.
◎ Ⓑ We're producing that in ...
◎ Ⓒ That's being made [produced] in ...
○ Ⓓ The plant's in production in ...

(b) **製品が主語の場合**
(その新型は生産に入っています)
☆ Ⓐ We're making that new model.
◎ Ⓑ We're producing that new model.
◎ Ⓒ That new model's being made [produced].
○ Ⓓ That new model's in production.

24 「めどがつく」
(2年もかかったが，ついにプロジェクトのめどがついた)
It took as long as two years but finally
　　◎ Ⓐ we can see the [a] light at the end of the tunnel on the project.
　　◎ Ⓑ we can see the [an] end on [to] the project.

[137]

◎ ⓒ we can get close [near] to the end on the project.
○ ⓓ we're moving on toward the end on the project.
△ ⓔ we're approaching the end on the project.

25 「受注残」
（うちは受注残がたくさんあるんです）
◎ We have a big backlog [back order].
［注意］辞典に backlog of demand が出ているが使われていない。

26 「利益」
(a) **投資・株などが主語の場合**
（これに投資すればたぶんうんと利益が出るでしょう）
This investment'll most likely
　　◎ Ⓐ give you a good return.
　　◎ Ⓑ bring you a good return [profit].
　　◎ Ⓒ bring [make] a good return.
　　◎ Ⓓ make you good money.
　　◎ Ⓔ make good money for you.
　　◎ Ⓖ bring you in a good return.
　　○ Ⓗ give [make] you a good profit.
　　△ Ⓘ make a good return for you.
　　× Ⓙ give you a good gain.

(b) **ビジネス・商品が主語の場合**
（このビジネスはたぶんうんと利益が出るでしょう）
This business'll probably
　　◎ Ⓐ make you a good profit.
　　◎ Ⓑ make you good money.
　　◎ Ⓒ make good money [a good profit] for you.
　　◎ Ⓓ bring you good money [a good profit].
　　○ Ⓔ bring you in good money [a good profit].
　　○ Ⓕ bring good money [a good profit] for you.

27 「合併する」
（XYZ 証券会社は来年 ABC 証券会社と合併します）
XYZ Brokerage Firm'll
　　◎ Ⓐ merge with ABC Stockbroker next year.

　　　　◯ Ⓑ be combined with ...
　　　　△ Ⓒ join [combine, unite] with ...
　　[注意] 多くの辞典に amalgamate with が出ているが使われていない。

28 「買収する」
　　(XYZ 会社は STU 会社を買収しようとしているんです)
　　XYZ Company's tryng to
　　　　◎ Ⓐ take over [buy out] STU Company.
　　　　◯ Ⓑ get ownership of ...
　　　　◯ Ⓒ purchase [acquire] ...
　　　　△ Ⓓ buy off ...
　　[注意] Ⓐは100%または51%以上の株の取得，ⒷⒸⒹは100%の株取得を意味する。

29 「技術提携している」
　　(うちの会社は XYZ 会社と技術提携しています)
　　Our company
　　　　☆ Ⓐ shares technology with XYZ Company.
　　　　◎ Ⓑ exchanges technology ...
　　　　△ Ⓒ has a technological affiliation [alliance, link] ...
　　　　△ Ⓓ is technologically affiliated [linked] ...
　　[注意] (1) ⒸⒹは堅い文章英語では使用頻度は少し上がり普通に使われている。
(2) 辞典には非常によく使われているⒶⒷは全く出ていないで，be technically tied with，have a technical tie-up with が出ているが意味が違う。これは「名目上」という意味しかない。下記の例文で technically の意味をしっかりつかまれたい。
Our company's ☆ Ⓐ tied up with XYZ Company in name only,
　　　　　　　　◎ Ⓑ tied up with XYZ Company on paper,
　　　　　　　　◯ Ⓒ tied up with XYZ Company nominally,
　　　　　　　　◯ Ⓓ technically tied up with XYZ Company,
　　　　　　　　△ Ⓔ tied up with XYZ Company technically,
but really we have little to do with each other.
(うちの会社は XYZ 会社と名目上は提携していますが，実際にはお互いにほとんど関係がないんです)

30 「共同出資する」

(a) 小規模
（私たちはこの会社を始めるのに共同出資したんです）
We ☆ Ⓐ put our money together to start this company.
　　◎ Ⓑ went in together ...
　　○ Ⓒ combined ［pooled］ our money ...

(b) 大規模
（私たちは電気自動車を開発するために共同出資しました）
We ☆ Ⓐ went in together to develop an electric car.
　　◎ Ⓑ put our resources ...
　　◎ Ⓒ put our money together ...
　　◎ Ⓓ pooled our money ...
　　○ Ⓔ pooled our resources ...
　　△ Ⓕ combined our resources ...

31 「資金を出す（スポンサーとなる）」

（誰がこのプロジェクトの資金を出すのですか）
Who's going to ☆ Ⓐ finance this project?
　　　　　　　　◎ Ⓑ back this project?
　　　　　　　　○ Ⓒ support this project financially?
　　　　　　　　○ Ⓓ fund ［bankroll］ this project?
　　　　　　　　△ Ⓔ be the bankroll for this project?

32 「営業拠点」

（うちの営業拠点はサンフランシスコなんです）
Our ◎ Ⓐ business base is San Francisco.
　　○ Ⓑ trading base ...

33 「営業を拡大する」

（うちは営業を拡大する予定です）
We're going to
　　☆ Ⓐ diversify our operations.
　　◎ Ⓑ expand our operations into many industries.
　　◎ Ⓒ make our operations more diverse.
　　○ Ⓓ make our operations diversified.
　　△ Ⓔ make our operations multilateral ［multifaceted］.

[注意] 辞典に make one's operations multiple が出ているが使われていない。

34 「強化する」
(我々は営業スタッフを強化する予定です)
We're going to ☆ Ⓐ increase our sales staff.
　　　　　　　 ◎ Ⓑ beef up our ...
　　　　　　　 ○ Ⓒ build up [expand, strengthen, reinforce] our ...
　　　　　　　 △ Ⓓ bolster [enhance] our ...
　　　　　　　 × Ⓔ set up our ...
[注意] Ⓔが辞典に出ているが使われていない。

35 「カタログを改訂する」
(うちはカタログを改訂しなければならないんです)
We have to ◎ Ⓐ update [revise] our catalogue.
　　　　　　 ○ Ⓑ bring [make, get] our catalogue up-to-date.
[注意] Ⓐの update は「最新のものにする」という意味の「改訂する」、revise は単なる「校訂する」という意味でも使われているが update の意味でも非常によく使われている。

36 「固定費」
(御社の固定費はいくらですか)
☆ Ⓐ What're your company's fixed costs?
◎ Ⓑ What're your company's fixed expenses?
○ Ⓒ What's your company's fixed expenditure?
[注意] 辞典に standing costs [expenses] が出ているが使われていない。

37 「原価」
(a) 生産原価を尋ねる場合
(生産原価はいくらですか)
What's ☆ Ⓐ the production cost?
　　　　 ◎ Ⓑ the cost of production?

(b) 仕入れ原価
(もし2割お値引したら仕入れ原価より安くなってしまいます)
If I give you a 20% discount, it'll be lower than

☆ Ⓐ our [the] cost.
◎ Ⓑ our purchasing cost.
○ Ⓒ our purchasing price.
× Ⓓ our buying cost [price].
［注意］辞典にⒹが出ているが使われていない。

38 「原価計算」
(値段を決める前に新製品の原価計算をしなければならないんです)
We have to ☆ Ⓐ figure out the cost of our new product
　　　　　　◎ Ⓑ calculate the cost ...
　　　　　　○ Ⓒ figure the cost ...
　　　　　　○ Ⓓ make a calculation on the cost ...
before we decide on the price.

39 「合わない」
(a) 勘定
(勘定が合わないんです)
The books don't ◎ Ⓐ balance (out).
　　　　　　　　○ Ⓑ match (with each other).
　　　　　　　　△ Ⓒ jive (with each other).
　　　　　　　　△ Ⓓ mesh (with each other).
　　　　　　　　△ Ⓔ agree (with each other).

(b) 商品と送り状
(商品が送り状と合いません)
The merchandise doesn't ◎ Ⓐ match [agree with] the invoice.
　　　　　　　　　　　　○ Ⓑ jive with ...
　　　　　　　　　　　　▽ Ⓒ square [mesh, tally] with ...
［注意］Ⓒが辞典に出ているがまれ。

40 「決算」
(a) 普通に述べるとき
(御社の決算はいつなのですか)
When does your company ☆ Ⓐ close its books?
　　　　　　　　　　　　◎ Ⓑ close out its books [accounts]?
　　　　　　　　　　　　◎ Ⓒ balance its books?
　　　　　　　　　　　　○ Ⓓ balance its accounts?

○ Ⓔ settle its books ［balance］?
△ Ⓕ settle its accounts?

(b) 粉飾決算
(XYZ 会社は粉飾決算をしたんです)
XYZ Company ☆ Ⓐ overstated its books.
◎ Ⓑ overstated its accounts.
◎ Ⓒ padded its books.
○ Ⓓ inflated its books ［accounts］.
○ Ⓔ overstated its bottom line.
［注意］辞典にはⒶ〜Ⓔは出ていない。しかし window-dress its books が出ているが使われていない。

41 「粗利」
(粗利はいくらなのですか)
What's ☆ Ⓐ the gross profit?
◎ Ⓑ the profit before taxes?

42 「黒字」
(a) 会社
(うちの会社はすごい黒字なんです)
Our company's ☆ Ⓐ making a lot of money.
◎ Ⓑ making a big ［a lot of］ profit.
◎ Ⓒ really in the black.
○ Ⓓ making a big money.

(b) 会社の黒字の数字を述べる場合
(うちの会社は今年50万ドルの黒字だったんです)
Our company ☆ Ⓐ made ［showed］ a profit of $500,000 this year.
☆ Ⓑ made a $500,000 profit ...
◎ Ⓒ had a profit of $500,000 ...
◎ Ⓓ shows ［has］ a $500,000 profit ...
◎ Ⓔ is $500,000 in the black ...
○ Ⓕ ran a $500,000 profit ...
○ Ⓖ ran a profit of $500,000 ...

(c) 国の財政
（クリントン政権のときアメリカの財政は巨額な黒字だったんです）
America
　　☆ Ⓐ had a huge fiscal ［financial］ surplus while Clinton was in office.
　　◎ Ⓑ had a huge revenue surplus ...
　　○ Ⓒ was fiscally ［financially］ in the black ...
　　△ Ⓓ was in the black in its revenue ［finances］ ...
［注意］辞典に have a huge sound ［balanced］ financing が出ているが使われていない。

(d) 国の貿易黒字
（日本は巨額な貿易黒字である）
Japan has ☆ Ⓐ a huge ［big］ trade surplus.
　　　　　　◎ Ⓑ a large trade surplus.

43 「赤字」

(a) 決算書作成直後に会社の赤字の状態を述べる場合
（うちの会社は今年赤字なんです）
Our ☆ Ⓐ company showed a loss this year.
　　☆ Ⓑ company's in the red ...
　　☆ Ⓒ company's losing money ...
　　◎ Ⓓ company shows a loss ...
　　◎ Ⓔ company's showing a loss ...
　　○ Ⓕ company had a loss ...
　　△ Ⓖ company has a loss ...

(b) 会社の赤字の数字を述べる場合
（うちの会社は今年50万ドルの赤字なんです）
Our company ☆ Ⓐ showed a $500,000 loss this year.
　　　　　　　◎ Ⓑ had ［shows, has］ a $500,000 loss ...
　　　　　　　◎ Ⓒ is $500,000 in the red ...
　　　　　　　○ Ⓓ shows a loss of $500,000 ...
　　　　　　　△ Ⓔ has a loss of $500,000 ...

(c) 国の財政
（日本は財政赤字なんです）

Japan ◎ Ⓐ has a financial [fiscal] deficit.
　　　○ Ⓑ is financially [fiscally] in the red.
　　　△ Ⓒ is in the red in its revenue [finances].

44 「赤字に転落する」
(この会社はたぶん赤字に転落するでしょう)
This company'll probably ◎ Ⓐ fall [drop] into the red.
　　　　　　　　　　　　　○ Ⓑ plunge into the red.
[注意] Ⓑは急激に転落する響きがある。

45 「裏書きする」
(小切手に裏書きしてくれますか)
Can you ☆ Ⓐ sign the back of the check?
　　　　 ◎ Ⓑ endorse the check?
[注意] 辞典に vouch for the back of the check が出ているが使われていない。

46 「不渡り手形を出す」
(a) 会社
(LMN 会社は昨日不渡り手形を5枚出したんです)
LMN Company ◎ Ⓐ wrote [issued] five bad checks yesterday.
　　　　　　　○ Ⓑ bounced five checks ...
　　　　　　　▽ Ⓒ passed five drafts ...
　　　　　　　× Ⓓ wrote five rubbers [dishonored checks] ...
　　　　　　　× Ⓔ failed five checks ...
[注意] (1) 辞典にⒹⒺが出ているが使われていない。Ⓒはまれ。
(2) 辞典では「手形」＝draft，「小切手」＝check と出ているが一般の人の間では check と draft の違いは認識されていない。

(b) 個人
(ボブは昨日不渡り手形を3枚出したんです)
Bob ◎ Ⓐ wrote three bad checks yesterday.
　　 ○ Ⓑ bounced three checks ...
　　 × Ⓒ issued three bad checks ...

47 「破産する」
(a) 客観的に述べる場合

(OPQ 会社は3日前に破産したんです)
OPQ Company ◎ Ⓐ went into bankruptcy three days ago.
　　　　　　 ◎ Ⓑ went bankrupt [went broke] ...
　　　　　　 ◎ Ⓒ failed ...
　　　　　　 ○ Ⓓ folded ...
　　　　　　 △ Ⓔ folded up ...
　　　　　　 △ Ⓕ went belly-up ...
　　　　　　 ▽ Ⓖ went bust ...

(b) **会社更生の破産申請をしていることを述べる場合**
(LMN 会社は破産しているんです)
LMN Company's
　◎ Ⓐ in Chapter 11 [Chapter 13, bankruptcy].
　◎ Ⓑ filing for Chapter 11 [Chapter 13, bankruptcy].
　◎ Ⓒ insolvent.
[注意] 正しくは Chapter 11 は法人の破産，Chapter 13 は個人の破産，しかし多くのアメリカ人はこの違いを知らず混用している。

(c) **会社の清算を述べる場合**
(LMN 会社は破産しています)
LMN Company's ◎ Ⓐ in Chapter 7.
　　　　　　　 ◎ Ⓑ in bankruptcy.
　　　　　　　 ○ Ⓒ in liquidation.
　　　　　　　 ○ Ⓓ in solvency.
[注意] Ⓑは会社更生か破産かはあいまい。

48 「価格競争」
(XYZ 会社は価格競争に負けたので倒産したんです)
XYZ Company went bankrupt because it lost in
　☆ Ⓐ the price wars.
　◎ Ⓑ the price war.
　△ Ⓒ the price competition(s).
　△ Ⓓ the price-cutting race.
[注意] ⒶⒷはどの辞典にも出ていないが非常によく使われている。

49 「(信用調査機関による) 支払い能力評価」
(a) **よい場合**

(彼の支払い能力評価はいいです)
He ☆ Ⓐ has a good [high] credit rating.
　　◎ Ⓑ is a good credit risk.
　　◎ Ⓒ has good credit.
　　△ Ⓓ has high credit.
[注意] Ⓓはアメリカ人の間で「よい」「悪い」の両方の意味で使われている。

(b) 悪い場合
(彼の支払い能力評価は悪いんです)
He ☆ Ⓐ has a bad credit rating.
　　◎ Ⓑ has bad credit.
　　◎ Ⓒ is a bad credit risk.
　　◎ Ⓓ is in a lot of debt.
　　○ Ⓔ has a low credit rating.
　　△ Ⓕ has high credit.
[注意] 辞典に be in a lot of debts が出ているが使われていない。

50 「掛売りする」
(うちは掛売りをしません)
We don't ☆ Ⓐ do business on credit.
　　　　　◎ Ⓑ sell on credit.
　　　　　○ Ⓒ deal with our customers on credit.
　　　　　○ Ⓓ do credit business.

51 「委託販売」
(a) 製造会社
(うちは多くの店で家具を委託販売で売っています)
We ☆ Ⓐ sell furniture on consignment at many stores.
　　◎ Ⓑ put furniture on consignment ...

(b) 小売店
(うちは委託販売で多くのメーカーと取引しています)
◎ We're doing business with a lot of makers on a consignment basis.

52 「内金」
(内金はいくらなのですか)
What's the ☆ Ⓐ downpayment?

○ Ⓑ initial amount I have to put down?
[注意] 辞典に initial installment が出ているが使われていない。

53 「代金引換えで払う」
(代金引換えで払うことができますか)
Can I pay ☆ Ⓐ COD?
◎ Ⓑ in cash when it's delivered [on delivery]?
◎ Ⓒ in cash when you deliver it?
○ Ⓓ cash [the money] when it's delivered [on delivery]?
○ Ⓔ cash [the money] when you deliver it?

54 「未払い金」
(私たちの未払い金はいくらなのですか)
◎ Ⓐ How much do we have left to pay?
◎ Ⓑ How much more do we have left to pay?
◎ Ⓒ How much more do we have to pay?
◎ Ⓓ How much do we have to pay?
◎ Ⓔ What's our balance due [unpaid balance]?
◎ Ⓕ What's the amount due?

55 「貸倒れ」
(うちは50件以上の貸倒れがあるんです)
We have more than
  ☆ Ⓐ fifty accounts we have to write off as losses.
  ◎ Ⓑ fifty accounts we have to take as losses.
  ○ Ⓒ fifty credit losses.

56 「売掛未収金」
(うちには売掛未収金が50件以上あるんです)
We have more than fifty ☆ Ⓐ late [overdue] accounts.
                        ◎ Ⓑ delinquent accounts.
                        ◎ Ⓒ accounts that're behind [late].

57 「派遣する」
(a) 派遣している会社数のみを述べる場合
(うちは約800の会社にスタッフを派遣しています)
We ☆ Ⓐ work with roughly 800 companies.

　　　　☆ Ⓑ send staff to roughly 800 companies.
　　　　◎ Ⓒ provide roughly 800 companies with staff.
　　　　◎ Ⓓ staff roughly 800 companies.
　　　　◎ Ⓔ provide staff for [to] roughly 800 companies.
　　　　○ Ⓕ dispatch staff to roughly 800 companies.

(b)　派遣している人材の内容と会社数を述べる場合
　　（うちは通訳を約600の会社に派遣しています）
　　We ☆ Ⓐ provide roughly 600 companies with interpreters.
　　　　☆ Ⓑ send interpreters to roughly 600 companies.
　　　　◎ Ⓒ staff interpreters for roughly 600 companies.
　　　　◎ Ⓓ provide interpreters for [to] roughly 600 companies.
　　　　○ Ⓔ dispatch interpreters for roughly 600 companies.

58 「工場の設備」
（うちは工場の設備を新しいものと取り替えなければならないんです）
We have to replace
　　　☆ Ⓐ the equipment in our factory with new equipment.
　　　◎ Ⓑ the machines in our factory with new ones.
　　　◎ Ⓒ update the machinery in our factory.
　　　◎ Ⓓ update the machines in our factory with new ones.
［注意］辞典に the facilities, arrangements が出ているが使われていない。

59 「工場の設備投資」
（企業の工場の設備投資はまもなく回復するでしょう）
Corporate capital ☆ Ⓐ spending in factories'll recover soon.
　　　　　　　　　 ◎ Ⓑ investing in factories'll ...

60 「契約」
(a)　ビジネス
　　●書面に書いたもの
　　（彼らは契約を守るでしょう）
　　◎ They'll honor the contract.
　　●口頭のもの
　　（彼らは口頭の契約を破ったんです）
　　◎ They broke our verbal agreement.

(b) **賃貸借契約**
　　（家主は契約を更新するでしょう）
　　◎ The landlord'll renew the lease.

61 「正式契約書」
（これは仮契約ですからできるだけ早く正式契約書を作らなければなりませんね）
This is a temporary contract, so we have to make a
　　☆ Ⓐ permanent one as soon as possible.
　　◎ Ⓑ official ...
　　○ Ⓒ formal ...
　　△ Ⓓ solid [proper] ...

62 「口頭契約」
（私たちは口頭契約しかしなかったんです）
We only made ◎ Ⓐ a verbal agreement.
　　　　　　　　△ Ⓑ an oral agreement.

63 「契約している」
（彼はヤンキースと3年契約しているんです）
◎ He's signed [under] a three-year contract with the New York Yankees.

64 「切れる」
（賃貸契約は来年の4月に切れるんです）
The lease'll ◎ Ⓐ run out [expire, be up] next April.
　　　　　　　○ Ⓑ end ...
　　　　　　　△ Ⓒ finish [terminate, come to an end] ...
　　　　　　　▽ Ⓓ be over [history] ...
[注意] 辞典にⒹが出ているがこの文脈では使われてもまれ。

65 「念書」
（この会社から念書をもらっておいたほうがいいよ）
You'd better get ☆ Ⓐ a written guarantee [guaranty]
　　　　　　　　　　◎ Ⓑ something in writing
　　　　　　　　　　△ Ⓒ a letter with a signature of assurance
from this company.

第11章　経営に関する表現

66 「(署名が) にせもの」
(この署名はにせものかもしれない)
This signature might be ☆ Ⓐ a forgery.
　　　　　　　　　　　　 ◎ Ⓑ forged.
　　　　　　　　　　　　 ○ Ⓒ a fraud.
　　　　　　　　　　　　 ○ Ⓓ phony [bogus].
　　　　　　　　　　　　 △ Ⓔ a fake.
　　　　　　　　　　　　 △ Ⓕ fake [falsified].
　　　　　　　　　　　　 ▽ Ⓖ falsification.
　　　　　　　　　　　　 × Ⓗ sham [a rip-off].

67 「破棄する」
(a) 法律違反になる場合
(LMN会社は契約を破棄するでしょう)
LMN Company'll ◎ Ⓐ break the contract.
　　　　　　　　 △ Ⓑ breach ...

(b) 法律違反にならない場合
(LMN会社は契約を破棄するでしょう)
LMN Company'll ◎ Ⓐ break the contract.
　　　　　　　　 ○ Ⓑ cancel ...

68 「契約違反」
(XYZ会社がやっていることは契約違反です)
What XYZ Company's doing's a ◎ Ⓐ violation of the contract.
　　　　　　　　　　　　　　　 ◎ Ⓑ breach of contract.
　　　　　　　　　　　　　　　 × Ⓒ breach of the contract.
　[注意] breach of contract は決り文句で，contract に the は付かない。

69 「取引」
(a) 特定の取引
(うちはバークシャー会社と取引ができると思います)
I think we can ☆ Ⓐ make a deal with Berkshire Company.
　　　　　　　 ◎ Ⓑ do business with ...
　　　　　　　 ○ Ⓒ strike a deal with ...
　　　　　　　 △ Ⓓ swing a deal with ...

(b) 継続的な取引
　●一般の会社
（うちはランカスター会社と取引があります）
　◎ Ⓐ We're doing business ［We're dealing］ with Lancaster Company.
　◎ Ⓑ We do business ［We deal］ with ...
　●銀行
1) 会社と銀行
（うちはレヴンワース銀行と取引があります）
　☆ Ⓐ We do ［We're doing］ business with Leavenworth Bank.
　◎ Ⓑ We deal ［We're dealing］ with ...
　◎ Ⓒ We have an account with ...
　◎ Ⓓ We're banking with ...
　○ Ⓔ We bank with ...
2) 個人と銀行
（私はジャクソン銀行と取引があります）
　☆ Ⓐ I have an account with Jackson Bank.
　◎ Ⓑ I'm banking with ...
　○ Ⓒ I bank with ...
　○ Ⓓ I deal ［I'm dealing］ with ...
　△ Ⓔ I do ［I'm doing］ business with ...

70 「電子商取引」
（電子商取引は今後ますます普及するでしょう）
　☆ Ⓐ Doing business online'll be more and more popular in the future.
　☆ Ⓑ Doing business on the net'll ［Net'll, internet'll］ be ...
　◎ Ⓒ Doing business through the internet'll be ...
　◎ Ⓓ E-business'll be ...
　○ Ⓔ Doing business on the web'll be ...
　○ Ⓕ E-commerce'll ［Electric commerce'll］ be ...
　○ Ⓖ Electronic ［Internet, Online］ business'll be ...

71 「取引をまとめる」
(a) 取引の条件・契約書の交換・金銭の授受を意味する場合
　（いつ取引をまとめられますか）

第11章　経営に関する表現

When can we ◎ Ⓐ close the deal?
　　　　　　　○ Ⓑ get the deal closed?

(b) 契約書の署名・交換・金銭の授受だけを意味する場合
（いつ取引をまとめられますか）
When can we
　　◎ Ⓐ finish [complete] the transaction?
　　○ Ⓑ get through [be through, be done] with the transaction?

72 「相場」
(a) 買う場合
（3 LDK の分譲マンションの相場はいくらですか）
What's the ☆ Ⓐ going price for a 3-bedroom condo?
　　　　　　◎ Ⓑ market price for ...?
　　　　　　△ Ⓒ going [market] rate for ...?
　　　　　　△ Ⓓ current price for ...?
[注意] 辞典に going quote [quotation] が出ているがまれ。

(b) 借りる場合
（3 LDK のマンションの相場はいくらですか）
What's the ☆ Ⓐ going rate for a 3-bedroom apartment?
　　　　　　◎ Ⓑ market rate for ...?
　　　　　　○ Ⓒ going [market] rate for rent for ...?
　　　　　　△ Ⓓ going [market] rate rent for ...?

73 「支払う」
（いつ残金を支払ってくれますか）
When're you going to ◎ Ⓐ pay the balance?
　　　　　　　　　　○ Ⓑ take care of ...?
　　　　　　　　　　△ Ⓒ clear up [settle] ...?
　　　　　　　　　　× Ⓓ fix [square] ...?
[注意] Ⓓは辞典に出ているが使われていない。

74 「時間稼ぎをする」
（彼は私たちからいい条件を引き出すために時間稼ぎをしているんでしょう）
He must be ☆ Ⓐ stalling time to get better terms from us.
　　　　　　◎ Ⓑ stalling for time [buying time] ...

　　　　　　○ Ⓒ playing for time ...
[注意] 辞典に gaining time が出ているが使われていない。

75 「手を引く」
（あなたは取引から手を引いたほうがいいですよ）
You'd better ◎ Ⓐ get [back, pull] out of the deal.
　　　　　　○ Ⓑ pull the plug on ...
　　　　　　○ Ⓒ wash your hands of ...
　　　　　　△ Ⓓ withdraw from ...

76 「決裂する」
（交渉は決裂するでしょう）
The negotiations'll ☆ Ⓐ break down.
　　　　　　◎ Ⓑ fall through [apart].
　　　　　　○ Ⓒ go nowhere [fail (collapse)].
　　　　　　△ Ⓓ get nowhere [falter, go up in smoke].
　　　　　　△ Ⓓ fall by the wayside.

第12章
コンピューターに関する表現

1「最先端」
(うちのコンピューターは最先端をいっています)
Our computer's ◎ Ⓐ on the cutting edge (of technology).
　　　　　　　 ◎ Ⓑ (the) state of the art.
　　　　　　　 ◎ Ⓒ (the) top of the line.
　　　　　　　 ◎ Ⓓ the most up-to-date.
　　　　　　　 ○ Ⓔ the most sophisticated.
　　　　　　　 △ Ⓕ on the leading edge (of technology).
[注意] 元来はⒶⒷⒸⒹⒺⒻは技術と質の両方に言及しているが、技術のほうに焦点がある。Ⓒは質のことに言及しているが、両方のニュアンスがある。どちらであるかは文脈で判断する。

2「デスクトップパソコン」
(私はデスクトップパソコンを買おうと思っています)
I'm going to buy a ☆ Ⓐ desktop computer.
　　　　　　　　　 ◎ Ⓑ desktop.
　　　　　　　　　 ○ Ⓒ mini-tower [tower].
　　　　　　　　　 ○ Ⓓ mini-tower [tower] computer.

3「ノートパソコン」
(私はノートパソコンを買おうと思っています)
I'm going to buy a ☆ Ⓐ laptop [notebook].
　　　　　　　　　 ◎ Ⓑ notebook computer.
　　　　　　　　　 ○ Ⓒ laptop computer.

         ○ Ⓓ portable PC.
         △ Ⓔ laptop [notebook] PC.

4 「手の平サイズパソコン」
 (私は手の平サイズパソコンを買おうと思っています)
 I'm going to buy a ☆ Ⓐ PDA.
                  ◎ Ⓑ palm.
                  ○ Ⓒ Palm Pilot.
                  △ Ⓓ palm top.

5 「ブロードバンド」
(a) パソコンにブロードバンドが付いていると述べる場合
    (私のパソコンにはブロードバンドが付いています)
    My computer has ☆ Ⓐ broadband [DSL, cable].
                    ☆ Ⓑ a broadband [a DSL] connection.
                    ☆ Ⓒ a high-speed internet connection.
                    ◎ Ⓓ a broadband [a DSL] line.
                    ◎ Ⓔ a cable connection.
                    ◎ Ⓕ a high-speed cable (connection).
                    ○ Ⓖ a cable line.
                    ○ Ⓗ a high-speed internet connection line.
                    ○ Ⓘ a high-speed online connection.
                    △ Ⓙ an ADSL line [connection].
    [注意] (1) broadband は DSL と cable modem (cable) のこと。
    DSL は ADSL, SDSL, HDSL, IDSL, VDSL, RADSL がある。
    (2) cable は cable line から，DSL は telephone line を通したもの。以上
        のように DSL と cable は正しくは違うが，ほとんどのアメリカ人は違い
        が分かっていないので混用して使われている。

(b) ブロードバンドが付いたアパートと述べる場合
    (私たちはブロードバンドが付いているアパートを探しています)
    We're looking for an apartment with
        ☆ Ⓐ broadband.
        ☆ Ⓑ a broadband connection [line].
        ◎ Ⓒ a DSL or cable modem line [connection].
    [注意] Ⓒは broadband, DSL, cable modem の違いをはっきり知ってい
    る人の表現。ほとんどの人はブロードバンドが付いたアパートと述べるとき(a)

第12章　コンピューターに関する表現

の🅐～🅙を使うであろう。

6 「パソコンのスイッチを入れる」
（パソコンのスイッチを入れて下さい）
☆　🅐　Turn on the computer, please.
◎　🅑　Start up ...
○　🅒　Switch on ...

7 「接続する」
（ビルはメッセージが届いたとき接続されていなかったのかもしれません）
Bill might not have been ☆　🅐　on line when the message arrived.
　　　　　　　　　　　　　◎　🅑　logged on ...
　　　　　　　　　　　　　△　🅒　logged in ...
　　　　　　　　　　　　　×　🅓　accessed ...
［注意］(1) ある辞典に🅓が出ているが使われていない。
(2) 🅐はどの辞典にも出ていないが1番よく使われている。

8 「コンピューターに入力する」
（データを全部あのコンピューターに入力しなさい）
☆　🅐　Enter all the date into that computer.
◎　🅑　Enter all the date in ...
◎　🅒　Put ［Feed］ all the date into ［in］ ...
○　🅓　Input all the data into ［in］ ...

9 「サイト」
(a)　**新製品紹介**
　●ページ数が多いとき
（うちの会社は新型のサイトをインターネットに載せる予定です）
Our company's going to
　　☆　🅐　create a web site for our new version.
　　☆　🅑　create a site for our new version on the internet.
　　◎　🅒　set up a web site for our new version.
　　◎　🅓　set up a site for our new version on the internet.
　　○　🅔　put up ［make, start, build, establish］ a web site for our new version.
　　○　🅕　put up ［make, start, build, establish］ a site for our new version on the internet.

△ Ⓖ construct [produce] a web site for our new version.
　　　△ Ⓗ construct a site for our new version on the internet.
　［注意］ⒶⒸⒺⒼは文尾に on the internet，または on the net を付け加えても使用頻度は同じ。
　● 1～2ページのとき
　（うちの会社は新型のサイトをインターネットに載せる予定です）
　Our company's going to
　　　☆ Ⓐ create a web page for our new version.
　　　◎ Ⓑ set up a web page ...
　　　○ Ⓒ put up [make, start, build, establish] a web page ...
　　　△ Ⓓ produce [construct] a web page ...
　［注意］Ⓐ～Ⓓいずれも文尾に on the internet，または on the net を付け加えても使用頻度は同じ。

(b) 求人
　（うちは求人のサイトをインターネットに載せる予定です）
　We're going to
　　　☆ Ⓐ create a web site for hiring employees.
　　　☆ Ⓑ create a site for hiring employees online [on the internet, on the net].
　　　◎ Ⓒ set up a web site for hiring employees.
　　　◎ Ⓓ set up a site for hiring employees online [on the internet, on the net].
　　　○ Ⓔ put up [make, start, build, establish] a web site for hiring employees.
　　　○ Ⓕ put up [make, start, build, establish] a site for hiring employees online [on the internet, on the net].
　［注意］(1) ⒷⒹⒻの online, on the internet, on the net は on the internet が1番使用頻度が高く，online, on the net の順で下がるがいずれもよく使われている。
　(2) on the 'Net, on the 'net と書いても可。

10 「求人サイト」
　（求人サイトをクリックして下さい）
　　　☆ Ⓐ Click "Help Wanted."
　　　☆ Ⓑ Click the "Help Wanted" button.
　　　◎ Ⓒ Click on the "Help Wanted" button.

◎ Ⓓ Click on "Help Wanted."
◎ Ⓔ Click the "Help Wanted" link.
○ Ⓕ Click on the "Help Wanted" link.
△ Ⓖ Click the "Help Wanted" site.
［注意］多くの辞典に Click the "Help Wanted." が出ているが文尾に button，link，site がないときは the を使うことはできない。

11 「職業別電話帳」

(職業別電話帳をクリックして下さい)
◎ Ⓐ Click (on) "Yellow Pages."
○ Ⓑ Click (on) the "Yellow Pages" link.
○ Ⓒ Push the "Yellow Pages" button.

12 「不動産サイト」

(店舗をを探すのに不動産サイトをクリックして下さい)
Please ☆ Ⓐ click (on) "Real Estate" to look for a store space.
　　　　☆ Ⓑ click the Real Estate site to ...
　　　　◎ Ⓒ click on the Real Estate site to ...
　　　　◎ Ⓓ click (on) the Real Estate link to ...
　　　　○ Ⓔ click (on) the Real Estate button to ...

13 「お気に入り」

(a) **マイクロソフト**

(お気に入りをクリックして下さい)
Please ☆ Ⓐ click (on) Favorites.
　　　　◎ Ⓑ click the Favorite button.
　　　　○ Ⓒ click on the Favorite button.
［注意］"Favorites"，<u>Favorites</u> のように書いてもよい。

(b) **ネットスケープ**

(お気に入りをクリックして下さい)
Please ☆ Ⓐ click (on) Bookmarks.
　　　　◎ Ⓑ click the Bookmark button.
　　　　○ Ⓒ click on the Bookmark button.

14 「ネット利用者」

(ネット利用者の数は最近非常に増えています)

The number of ☆ Ⓐ Web surfers [users] has really increased lately.
　　　　　　　☆ Ⓑ internet users ...
　　　　　　　◎ Ⓒ online surfers ...
　　　　　　　△ Ⓓ online users ...
　　　　　　　△ Ⓔ net surfers [users] ...

［注意］surfer は user とは違っていろいろなサイトを時間つぶしに閲覧しているニュアンスがあるが利用しているという点で混用もされている。

15 「ネット」

(a) **ネットショッピングをする**
　　（最近私はネットショッピングをしています）
　　These days I ☆ Ⓐ shop online.
　　　　　　　 ◎ Ⓑ shop on the internet.
　　　　　　　 ◯ Ⓒ shop on the net.
　　　　　　　 △ Ⓓ do virtual shopping.
　　［注意］Ⓒは 'net, Net, 'Net とも書く。

(b) **ネットで買う**
　　（最近はほとんど何でもネットで買えます）
　　These days you can buy almost anything
　　　　☆ Ⓐ online.
　　　　◎ Ⓑ on the internet [the Net, the net].
　　　　× Ⓒ on the website.
　　［注意］Ⓑの Net は大文字でも非常によく使われている。'Net, 'net もときどき使われている。

(c) **ネットで注文が入る**
　　（ネットで注文がじゃんじゃん入ってくるんです）
　　Orders're pouring in ☆ Ⓐ online.
　　　　　　　　　　　 ◎ Ⓑ from [on] the website.
　　　　　　　　　　　 ◎ Ⓒ from the internet.
　　　　　　　　　　　 ◯ Ⓓ through the internet.
　　　　　　　　　　　 ◯ Ⓔ over [on] the net.
　　　　　　　　　　　 ◯ Ⓕ over the website.

16 「ネットで株の売買をする」
(私はネットで株の売買をしています)
I ☆ Ⓐ do online trading.
　☆ Ⓑ buy and sell stocks on the internet.
　◎ Ⓒ do trading online [on the internet].
　◎ Ⓓ do internet trading.
　○ Ⓔ buy and sell stocks online [on the net].
　○ Ⓕ do net trading [do trading on the net].

17 「検索エンジンで調べる」
(a) 検索エンジン名を特定しない場合
(検索エンジンで調べたらどうですか)
Why don't you ☆ Ⓐ use a search engine?
　　　　　　　◎ Ⓑ try searching on the internet?
　　　　　　　◎ Ⓒ do a search online [on the internet]?
　　　　　　　○ Ⓓ do a search on the net?
　　　　　　　○ Ⓔ try searching online?
　　　　　　　△ Ⓕ try searching on the net?

(b) 検索エンジンを特定する場合
(グーゴー検索エンジンで調べたらどうですか)
Why don't you ☆ Ⓐ use Google?
　　　　　　　◎ Ⓑ use Google's [Google] search engine?
　　　　　　　○ Ⓒ use Google it?
[注意] (1) 検索エンジンにはグーゴーが1番使われている。
(2) 発音はグーグルではなくグーゴー。

18 「目を通す（検索する）」
(私は毎日ネットでサイトに目を通しています)
I ☆ Ⓐ browse the internet every day.
　☆ Ⓑ browse [look at] sites on the internet ...
　◎ Ⓒ look around the internet ...
　○ Ⓓ take a look around the internet ...

19 「インターネットをあちこち見て回る」
(私は夕食後毎日インターネットをあちこち見て回っています)
I ☆ Ⓐ surf [browse around] the internet every day after dinner.

◎ Ⓑ surf the net ...
◎ Ⓒ look at [around] the internet ...
◎ Ⓓ check out the internet ...
○ Ⓔ surf on-line [online, on line] ...
○ Ⓕ take [have] a look around the internet ...

20 「誤作動」
(コンピューターに誤作動があったんです)
There was ☆ Ⓐ an error [trouble] in the computer.
　　　　　◎ Ⓑ a problem ...
　　　　　○ Ⓒ a glitch [a mistake] ...

21 「コンピューターの調子」
(コンピューターの調子がよくないんです)
◎ Ⓐ The computer's acting up.
◎ Ⓑ There's something wrong with the computer.
◎ Ⓒ There's a problem with the computer.
◎ Ⓓ The computer isn't working well.
△ Ⓔ The computer doesn't work well.
△ Ⓕ There's trouble with the computer.

22 「動く」
(このパソコンは動かない)
This computer doesn't ☆ Ⓐ work.
　　　　　　　　　◎ Ⓑ run.
　　　　　　　　　△ Ⓒ function.

23 「パソコンを消す」
(パソコンを消して下さい)
☆ Ⓐ Turn off [Shut down] the computer.
◎ Ⓑ Switch off ...

24 「コンピューターを使える」
(私はコンピューターを使えますがコンピューター通ではありません)
◎ Ⓐ I'm computer-literate, but I'm not a computer expert.
◎ Ⓑ I know how to use computers, ...
[注意] 辞典にⒶを「コンピューター通」と訳しているが誤り。

25 「コンピューター通」

(a) **主語が 3 人称の場合**
（ビルはコンピューター通です）
Bill's ◎ Ⓐ a computer genius.
　　　 ◎ Ⓑ a computer expert ［wiz］.
　　　 ◎ Ⓒ a computer pro.
　　　 ○ Ⓓ a computer guru.
　　　 △ Ⓔ computer savvy.
［注意］(1) Ⓔの savvy は形容詞なので不定冠詞の a は不要。
(2) Ⓑの wiz は年配者の間では非常によく使われている。
(3) 強さの点ではⒶが 1 番強く，Ⓑが 2 番，ⒸⒹはほぼ同じで 3 番，Ⓔは 4 番。

(b) **主語が 1 人称の場合**
（私はコンピューター通です）
I'm ◎ Ⓐ a computer expert.
　　 ○ Ⓑ a computer wiz ［guru］.
　　 △ Ⓒ computer savvy.
　　 × Ⓓ a computer genius.

(c) **会社・営業部・人事部のような場所を限定して述べる場合**
（私は会社でコンピューター通です）
I'm ☆ Ⓐ the computer expert at the office.
　　 ◎ Ⓑ the computer guru ...
　　 ○ Ⓒ the computer wiz ...
　　 △ Ⓓ the computer pro ...
　　 × Ⓔ the computer genius ［savvy］ ...

26 「マニア」

（グレッグはパソコンマニアなんです）
Greg's ☆ Ⓐ a computer geek.
　　　　 ◎ Ⓑ a computer nerd ［nut］.
　　　　 ◎ Ⓒ crazy about computers.
　　　　 ○ Ⓓ nuts for ［addicted to］ computers.
　　　　 ○ Ⓔ a computer addict.
　　　　 △ Ⓕ a computer junkie ［freak］.

27「コンピューターは苦手」
　　（彼はコンピューターは苦手なんです）
　　He ☆ Ⓐ has trouble with computers.
　　　　◎ Ⓑ has a problem [a hard time] using computers.
　　　　◎ Ⓒ has problems [trouble] using computers.
　　　　◎ Ⓓ isn't good at computers.

28「コンピューターは全く使えない」
　　（彼はコンピューターは全く使えないんです）
　　☆ Ⓐ He's no good at computers.
　　☆ Ⓑ He doesn't know anything about computers at all.
　　◎ Ⓒ He can't use computers at all.
　　○ Ⓓ He's computer-illiterate.

29「コンピューター恐怖症」
　　（彼はコンピューター恐怖症なんです）
　　☆ Ⓐ He's afraid of computers.
　　◎ Ⓑ He has a fear of computers.
　　○ Ⓒ He's a phobia of computers.
　　△ Ⓓ He has a computer phobia.
　　△ Ⓔ He's a computer phobe.
　　[**注意**] 辞典に He's a cyberphobe. が出ているが会話では使われていない。しかし堅い文章英語ではときどき使われている。

第13章 商品に関する表現

1 「目玉商品」
（これは目玉商品なんです）
This is an ☆ Ⓐ attention-getting product ［attention-getter］.
　　　　　　◎ Ⓑ attention-grabbing ［eye-catching］ product.
　　　　　　◎ Ⓒ attention-grabber.
　　　　　　〇 Ⓓ eye-grabbing product.
　　　　　　△ Ⓔ attention-catcher.

[注意] (1) 辞典に a leader, a loss leader が出ているが使われていない。しかしビジネスの世界ではまれではあるが使われている。
(2) 辞典に come-on が「目玉商品」の適訳として出ているが使われていない。但し「おとり」という意味では非常によく使われている。

2 「ドル箱」
（この商品は以前うちの会社のドル箱だったんです）
This product used to be ◎ Ⓐ a real gold mine for our company.
　　　　　　　　　　　◎ Ⓑ a money-maker ...
　　　　　　　　　　　◎ Ⓒ making our company rich.
　　　　　　　　　　　× Ⓓ a cashbox ［a money box］ ...

[注意] 多くの辞典にⒹが出ているが使われていない。

3 「必需品」
（ノートパソコンは私たちの生活で必需品です）
A laptop computer's ☆ Ⓐ indispensable for our life.
　　　　　　　　　◎ Ⓑ essential for ［in］...

◎ ⓒ necessary [a necessity] for...
◎ ⓓ a requirement in...
[注意] Ⓐが1番強い響きがある。Ⓑが2番，Ⓓが3番，Ⓒが4番。

4 「競争力のある」
（この製品は国際市場で非常に競争力がある）
This ☆ Ⓐ product's really competitive on the global market.
　　 ☆ Ⓑ product really competes ...
　　 ◎ Ⓒ product's highly [very] competitive ...
　　 ○ Ⓓ product has a really competitive edge ...
　　 △ Ⓔ product competes a lot ...

5 「売れそうな」
(a) **消費者が述べる場合**
（あの商品は飛ぶように売れそうだ）
That ◎ Ⓐ product [item] looks like it's going to sell like crazy.
　　 ◎ Ⓑ product [item] has a lot of potential.
　　 ◎ Ⓒ product [item] has (the) potential to sell like crazy.
　　 ◎ Ⓓ product [item] has what it takes to sell like crazy.
　　 △ Ⓔ merchandise looks like it's going to sell like crazy.
　　 △ Ⓕ merchandise has a lot of potential.
　　 △ Ⓖ merchandise has the potential to sell like crazy.
　　 △ Ⓗ merchandise has what it takes to sell like crazy.

(b) **業界人・ビジネスマンが述べる場合**
（あの商品は飛ぶように売れそうだ）
That ◎ Ⓐ is a highly marketable product [item].
　　 ◎ Ⓑ product [item] looks like it's going to sell like crazy.
　　 ◎ Ⓒ product [item] has a lot of potential.
　　 ◎ Ⓓ product [item] has the potential to sell like crazy.
　　 ○ Ⓔ product [item] has what it takes to sell like crazy.
　　 ○ Ⓕ merchandise looks like it's going to sell like crazy.
　　 ○ Ⓖ merchandise has a lot of potential.
　　 ○ Ⓗ merchandise has the potential to sell like crazy.
　　 ○ Ⓘ merchandise has what it takes to sell like crazy.
　　 ○ Ⓙ is highly marketable merchandise.
　　 × Ⓚ is a highly saleable product [item].

　　　　× ⓛ is highly saleable merchandise.
[注意] (1) 辞典にⓚⓛが出ているが使われていない。
(2) item は時計のような小さいものに使われている。
(3) 辞典では merchandise を集合名詞としてのみ紹介しているが，現代アメリカ英語では product の意味でよく使われている。

6 「飛ぶように売れている」

(a) **動詞で述べる場合**
　●いかなる商品でも使える
　(私の今度の本は飛ぶように売れています)
　My new book's ◎ Ⓐ selling like mad [crazy].
　　　　　　　　△ Ⓑ selling like hot cakes.
　[注意] Ⓑは1970年代まではよく使われていた。
　●棚に陳列してある商品
　(あの本は飛ぶように売れています)
　That book's ◎ Ⓐ selling like mad [crazy].
　　　　　　　○ Ⓑ flying off the shelves.
　　　　　　　△ Ⓒ selling like hot cakes.

(b) **名詞で述べる場合**
　●時計
　(あれは最近飛ぶように売れているんです)
　That watch's ☆ Ⓐ a best seller these days.
　　　　　　　◎ Ⓑ a hot seller ...
　　　　　　　◎ Ⓒ a hot product ...
　　　　　　　○ Ⓓ a hot item ...
　　　　　　　△ Ⓔ hot stuff ...
　[注意] (1) Ⓔは不定冠詞の a が不要。
　(2) ⒸⒹⒺは these days を消すと「あれは盗品だ」の意味にもなる。
　●ノートパソコン
　(このノートパソコンは最近飛ぶように売れているんです)
　This notebook computer's
　　　◎ Ⓐ a hot seller [product, item] these days.
　　　◎ Ⓑ a best seller...
　　　× Ⓒ hot stuff...
　●ハンドバッグのようなブランド物
　(このハンドバッグは最近飛ぶように売れているんです)

This purse's ◎ Ⓐ a hot item [product] these days.
　　　　　　　　◎ Ⓑ a best seller ...
　　　　　　　　○ Ⓒ a hot seller ...
　　　　　　　　▽ Ⓓ hot stuff ...
　●香水
　（あの香水は今飛ぶように売れているんです）
　◎ Ⓐ That's best-selling perfume right now.
　◎ Ⓑ That perfume's a hot product ...
　○ Ⓒ That perfume's a hot [best] seller ...
　▽ Ⓓ That perfume's hot stuff ...

7「商品の回転が速い」
　（この商品の回転は速いです）
　This product ☆ Ⓐ sells out quick [fast].
　　　　　　　 ◎ Ⓑ has a high turnover rate.
　　　　　　　 ◎ Ⓒ sells out quickly.

8「在庫がある」
　（今それは在庫があります）
　◎ Ⓐ We have that in stock [storage] now.
　◎ Ⓑ We have that on hand [shelves] now.
　◎ Ⓒ That's in stock now.
　[注意] stock と on hand は店内と倉庫，storage は倉庫を普通意味するが人により多少異なる。

9「在庫がたくさんある」
　（今それは在庫はたくさんあります）
　◎ Ⓐ We have a lot of that in stock [storage] now.
　◎ Ⓑ We have a lot of that on hand [shelves] now.
　○ Ⓒ That's in stock in large quantities now.

10「在庫が少なくなってきている」
　（今それは在庫が少なくなってきています）
　◎ Ⓐ We're running out of that now.
　◎ Ⓑ We're running low [short] on that now.
　○ Ⓒ We have a shortage of that now.

第13章　商品に関する表現

11「在庫を切らしている」
（それは今在庫を切らしています）
　◎ Ⓐ We're out of stock of that now.
　◎ Ⓑ We don't have that in our store [in stock] now.
　◎ Ⓒ That is out of stock [sold out] now.
　○ Ⓓ We're out of that now.
　○ Ⓔ We're all sold out on that now.
　○ Ⓕ We've run of stock of that now.
　△ Ⓖ That isn't in our store now.

12「在庫を切らして注文してある」
（それは在庫を切らして注文してあります）
　☆ Ⓐ That's on back order.
　◎ Ⓑ We ordered that, but it hasn't come in yet.
　○ Ⓒ We have that on back order.

13「傷がある」
（このテーブルは新しいのに傷がたくさんあります）
　☆ Ⓐ This table has a lot of scratches even though it's brandnew.
　◎ Ⓑ This table's scratched in a lot places ...
　○ Ⓒ This table's damaged in a lot of places ...

14「にせもの」
(a)　絵
　（あの絵はにせものだ）
　That picture's
　　　☆ Ⓐ a fake.
　　　◎ Ⓑ fake [a rip-off].
　　　○ Ⓒ a fraud [a phony, counterfeit, phony, imitation].
　　　△ Ⓓ bogus.

(b)　ダイヤモンド
　（あれはにせのダイヤモンドだ）
　That's
　　　☆ Ⓐ a fake diamond.
　　　◎ Ⓑ a faked diamond.
　　　◎ Ⓒ a phony [a bogus, an imitation, a counterfeit, a mock]

                diamond.
            × Ⓓ a false [a sham, a spurious] diamond.

15「国産品」
(私たちはもっと国産品を使うようにしなければならない)
We have to try to use more
    ☆ Ⓐ domestic products.
    ◎ Ⓑ domestic goods [merchandise].
    ◎ Ⓒ domestically-produced goods [merchandise].
    ○ Ⓓ domestically-made products [goods, merchandise].
    △ Ⓔ domestic [domestically-produced] stuff.

16「需要が多い」
(日本の商品は世界市場で需要が多いんです)
Japanese merchandise is ☆ Ⓐ in great demand
                        ☆ Ⓑ really [very much] in demand
                        ◎ Ⓒ highly in demand
                        ○ Ⓓ very in demand
on the global market.

17「品薄です」
(この製品は今品薄です)
This product's ☆ Ⓐ in short supply now.
              ☆ Ⓑ hard to get ...
              ◎ Ⓒ difficult to get ...
              ◎ Ⓓ hard to come by ...
              ○ Ⓔ difficult [tough] to come by ...
              ○ Ⓕ tough to get ...

18「向きである」
(あれは輸出向きです)
That's ☆ Ⓐ for export.
       ◎ Ⓑ intended [made, meant] for export.
       ○ Ⓒ targeted [geared] for export.
       ○ Ⓓ aimed at export.

19 「市場」

(a) 「市場に出ている」と述べる場合
(この新しいノートパソコンはすでに市場に出ています)
This new notebook computer's already ◎ Ⓐ on the market.
　　　　　　　　　　　　　　　　　◎ Ⓑ in stores.
　　　　　　　　　　　　　　　　　◎ Ⓒ available.
　　　　　　　　　　　　　　　　　○ Ⓓ selling.
　　　　　　　　　　　　　　　　　△ Ⓔ in the market.

(b) 「市場に出す」と述べる場合
(〈記者会見で〉リポーター：いつこの型を市場に出すのですか)
Reporter:
　☆ Ⓐ When're you going to put this new version on the market?
　◎ Ⓑ When're you going to market [offer] this new version?
　◎ Ⓒ When's this version going to be [come out] on the market?
　○ Ⓓ When's this version going to hit [come on, go on] the market?
　○ Ⓔ When're you going to place [offer] this new version on the market?

20 「市場がだぶついている」

(石油市場は今だぶついています)
　☆ Ⓐ The oil market's glutted [flooded] now.
　◎ Ⓑ The oil market has a surplus ...
　◎ Ⓒ The oil market's oversupplied ...
　○ Ⓓ The oil market has an oversupply ...
　○ Ⓔ There's a glut [a surplus, an oversupply] on the oil market ...

21 「(市場を)買い占める」

(石油市場を買い占めている会社がいくつかあるようだね)
It looks like some companies're ☆ Ⓐ cornering the oil market.
　　　　　　　　　　　　　　　◎ Ⓑ buying out ...
　　　　　　　　　　　　　　　○ Ⓒ buying up ...
　　　　　　　　　　　　　　　△ Ⓓ rigging ...

[注意] (1) ⒶⒹは買い占め行為を全体的に述べているのに対してⒷⒸは買い占め行為のプロセスを述べている。
(2) 辞典に making [establishing] a corner in oil が出ているが使われていない。

第14章

広告に関する表現

1 「広告する」
(a) **テレビ・ラジオ**
　●数種類の広告をするとき
（うちはこの商品をフォックスに大きく出す予定です）

We're going to ☆ Ⓐ advertise this merchandise on a large scale on Fox.
　　　　　　　☆ Ⓑ run ads for this merchandise on a large scale on Fox.
　　　　　　　◎ Ⓒ place ads [buy air time] for this merchandise on a large scale on Fox.
　　　　　　　◎ Ⓓ buy a lot of air time for this merchandise (on a large scale) on Fox.
　　　　　　　○ Ⓔ buy time spots for this merchandise on a large scale on Fox.
　　　　　　　○ Ⓕ buy a lot of time for this merchandise (on a large scale) on Fox.
　　　　　　　△ Ⓖ buy a lot of Fox time for this marchandise (on a large scale).
　　　　　　　△ Ⓗ buy a lot of Fox (time) spots (on a large scale).

[注意] (1) Ⓔ～Ⓗは広告業界の人たちの間では非常によく使われている。
(2) Foxはアメリカ最大のテレビ局。

●1種類の広告を何回も出すとき
（うちはNBCに広告を出す予定です）
We're going to

第14章　広告に関する表現

　　　　☆ Ⓐ put an ad on NBC.
　　　　◎ Ⓑ run an ad [buy ad time] on NBC.
　　　　◎ Ⓒ advertise on NBC.
　　　　○ Ⓓ buy advertising spot [buy time spots] on NBC.
　　　　○ Ⓔ buy air time [place an ad] on NBC.
　　　　△ Ⓕ buy a NBC (time) spot [slot].
　　　　△ Ⓖ put [run] ads on NBC.
　　　　△ Ⓗ buy advertising spots on NBC.
　　　　△ Ⓘ buy NBC (time) spots [slots].
　　　［注意］NBC は Fox, ABC, CBS の4大テレビ局のひとつ。

(b) **新聞・雑誌**
　　●数種類の広告を出すとき
　　（うちは3, 4紙の新聞に広告を出す予定です）
　　We're going to ☆ Ⓐ run ads in three or four papers.
　　　　　　　　　◎ Ⓑ put [place] ads ...
　　　　　　　　　◎ Ⓒ advertise ...
　　　　　　　　　◎ Ⓓ buy ad [some] space ...
　　　　　　　　　○ Ⓔ buy advertising space ...
　　　　　　　　　○ Ⓕ buy space [spots] ...
　　　　　　　　　○ Ⓖ buy some spots ...
　　●1種類の広告を出すとき
　　（うちはニューヨークポストに広告を出す予定です）
　　We're going to ☆ Ⓐ run an ad [ads] in *the New York Post*.
　　　　　　　　　◎ Ⓑ advertise [buy some space] ...
　　　　　　　　　◎ Ⓒ put an ad [ads] ...
　　　　　　　　　◎ Ⓓ place an ad [ads] ...
　　　　　　　　　○ Ⓔ buy space [a spot, spots] ...
　　　　　　　　　○ Ⓕ buy advertising space ...
　　［注意］*the New York Post* はニューヨークのタブロイド新聞。

2 「テレビ広告」
(a) **テレビ局名を明示しないとき**
　　（私は御社のテレビ広告を見ました）
　　I saw your company's ☆ Ⓐ ad on TV.
　　　　　　　　　　　　◎ Ⓑ TV ad.

(b) **テレビ局名を明示したとき**
　　（私はフォックステレビ局に御社が出した広告を見ました）
　　I saw your company's ◎ Ⓐ ad on Fox.
　　　　　　　　　　　　× Ⓑ Fox's ad.

3 「ラジオ広告」
（私は御社が出したラジオ広告を聞きました）
I heard your company's ☆ Ⓐ ad on the radio.
　　　　　　　　　　　◎ Ⓑ radio ad.

4 「バスの外側の壁面広告」
（私は御社のバスの外側の壁面広告を見ました）
◎ I saw your company's ad on (the side of) a bus.
[注意] ad on a bus はバスの中にも使える。

5 「バスの中の広告」
（私は御社のバスの中の広告を見ました）
I saw your company's ☆ Ⓐ ad on [inside] a bus.
　　　　　　　　　　　◎ Ⓑ ad inside of a bus.

6 「中吊り広告」
（私は御社の中吊り広告を地下鉄で見ました）
◎ I saw your campany's hanging ad on the subway.

7 「壁面広告」
（私はペン駅で御社の壁面広告を見ました）
I saw your campany's ◎ Ⓐ ad on the wall
　　　　　　　　　　 ○ Ⓑ wall ad
at Penn Station.

8 「キャッチコピー」
（彼はキャッチコピーを書くのが上手です）
He's good at writing
　　☆ Ⓐ attention-getting copy.
　　◎ Ⓑ attention-grabbing copy.
　　○ Ⓒ eye-catching [eye-grabbing] copy.
　　△ Ⓓ attention-getting [attention-grabbing] copies.

9 「効果」

(ニューヨークポストの広告の効果はありましたか)

- ☆ Ⓐ Did you get a good response from the ad in *the New York Post*?
- ☆ Ⓑ Did the ad in *the New York Post* work good?
- ◎ Ⓒ Did the ad in *the New York Post* work well?
- ○ Ⓓ Did the ad in *the New York Post* get [give] you a good response?
- ○ Ⓔ Was the ad in *the New York Post* effective?

第15章

銀行に関する表現

1「地方銀行」
（ビルは地方銀行に勤めているんです）
Bill works for a ◎ Ⓐ regional bank.
　　　　　　　× Ⓑ local bank.
　　　　　　　× Ⓒ provincial bank.
［注意］ⒷⒸが辞典に出ているが使われていない。但しⒷは「地元の」銀行としてなら非常によく使われている。

2「地元の銀行」
（ビルは地元の銀行に勤めているんです）
Bill works for a ◎ Ⓐ local bank.
　　　　　　　○ Ⓑ neighborhood bank.

3「貯蓄銀行」
（ビルは貯蓄銀行に勤めているんです）
◎ Bill works for a savings bank.

4「輸出入銀行」
（ビルは輸出入銀行に勤めているんです）
◎ Bill works for an import-export bank.
［注意］辞典に export-import bank が出ているが使われていない。

5「外国為替銀行」
（ビルは外国為替銀行に勤めているんです）

◎ Bill works for a foreign exchange bank.

6 「抵当銀行」
（ビルは抵当銀行に勤めているんです）
◎ Bill works for a mortgage bank.

7 「インターネットバンキング」
（代金を支払うのにインターネットバンキングを使うといいよ）
You should use ☆ Ⓐ internet banking to pay your bills.
　　　　　　　　 ◎ Ⓑ online banking ...
　　　　　　　　 ○ Ⓒ net [web] banking ...

8 「預金通帳」
(a) **銀行外の場合**
（私は預金通帳をなくしてしまったんです）
I've lost my ◎ Ⓐ bankbook.
　　　　　　　△ Ⓑ passbook.
　　　　　　　× Ⓒ depositbook [deposit passbook].
［注意］辞典にⒸが出ているが使われていない。Ⓑも場所によりときどき使われているがアメリカ全体で使われているとは言えない。

(b) **銀行の中の場合**
（窓口：お客様のお通帳が一杯になっています）
Teller:
☆ Ⓐ Your book's filled up.
☆ Ⓑ Your book doesn't have any more spaces [left].
◎ Ⓒ Your book has no more spaces [left].
◎ Ⓓ There's no more room in this book (left).
○ Ⓔ Your bankbook's filled up.
× Ⓕ Your passbook's filled up.

9 「口座」
（どこの銀行に口座があるのですか）
Which bank do you have ◎ Ⓐ an account at?
　　　　　　　　　　　　× Ⓑ a deposit at?
［注意］辞典にⒷが出ているが使われていない。

10 「当座預金」
(私はシカゴ銀行に当座預金があります)
I have ◎ Ⓐ a checking account at Chicago Bank.
　　　　× Ⓑ a check [current] account ...
　　　　× Ⓒ a checking [current] deposit ...
[注意] 辞典にⒷⒸが出ているが使われていない。

11 「普通預金」
(私はシカゴ銀行に普通預金があります)
I have ◎ Ⓐ a savings account at Chicago Bank.
　　　　× Ⓑ a savings deposit ...
[注意] 辞典にⒷが出ているが使われていない。

12 「口座の名義人」
(口座の名義人は誰ですか)
　☆ Ⓐ Who's the account holder?
　☆ Ⓑ What's the name on the account?
　◎ Ⓒ What's the account name?

13 「口座番号」
(口座番号は何番ですか)
What's ☆ Ⓐ the account number?
　　　　◎ Ⓑ the number on the account?

14 「架空名義口座」
(最近はどこの銀行でも架空名義口座は開けません)
You can't open an account under a
　☆ Ⓐ fake name at any bank these days.
　◎ Ⓑ false name ...
　○ Ⓒ fictitious [phony, assumed] name ...

15 「貯金する」
(a) **未来の内容**
(あなたはまさかの日に備えてお金を貯金したほうがいいですよ)
You'd better ◎ Ⓐ save money for a rainy day.
　　　　　　 ◎ Ⓑ put money away [put away money] ...
　　　　　　 ○ Ⓒ put money aside [put aside money] ...

第15章　銀行に関する表現

　　　　　△　Ⓓ　save money up ［save up money］...
　　　　　△　Ⓔ　deposit money ...
　　　　　△　Ⓕ　stash money away ［stash away money］...
　　　　　△　Ⓖ　sock away money ［sock money away］...
［注意］Ⓓには長期間という響きがある。

(b) 過去から現在まで
（私は新しい分譲マンションのために毎月１千ドル貯金をしてきています）
I've been ◎　Ⓐ　saving $1,000 every month for my new condo.
　　　　　◎　Ⓑ　putting aside $1,000 ...
　　　　　◎　Ⓒ　putting $1,000 aside ...
　　　　　△　Ⓓ　saving up $1,000 ［putting $1,000 away］...
　　　　　△　Ⓔ　putting ［stashing, socking］ away $1,000 ...

(c) 習慣的内容
（私たちは毎月銀行へ１千ドル貯金しています）
We ◎　Ⓐ　put $1,000 in the bank every month.
　　　◎　Ⓑ　deposit $1,000 ...
　　　○　Ⓒ　put $1,000 aside ...
　　　○　Ⓓ　put aside $1,000 ...
　　　△　Ⓔ　put ［stash, sock］ $1,000 away ...
　　　△　Ⓕ　put ［stash, sock］ away $1,000 ...

(d) 隠して貯金しているというニュアンスで
（アラファトは外国の多くの銀行に巨額のお金を貯金していると多くの新聞は報じている）
Many papers say Arafat's ☆　Ⓐ　hiding (away)
　　　　　　　　　　　　◎　Ⓑ　stashing (away)
　　　　　　　　　　　　○　Ⓒ　socking away
　　　　　　　　　　　　△　Ⓓ　socking ［hoarding］
a huge amount of money in a lot of banks overseas.

16 「下ろす」
（銀行から300ドル下ろしてきて下さい）
Please ☆　Ⓐ　get ［take］ $300 out of the bank.
　　　　◎　Ⓑ　get ［take］ $300 from ...
　　　　◎　Ⓒ　withdraw $300 out of ［from］ ...

[179]

17 「入金する」
(このお金を銀行に入金して下さい)
- ☆ Ⓐ Put this money in the bank, please.
- ◎ Ⓑ Deposit this money in ...
- ◎ Ⓒ Put [Deposit] this money into ...

18 「振り込む」
(明日までに500ドル当方の口座に振り込んで下さい)
- Please ☆ Ⓐ move $500 into our account by tomorrow.
- ◎ Ⓑ transfer ...

19 「現金の振り込み」
(今日うちの口座に現金の振り込みが30ありました)
- ◎ Ⓐ We got 30 (cash, money) transfers into our bank account today.
- ○ Ⓑ We got (cash, money) transfers into our bank account from 30 people today.
- ○ Ⓒ 30 people moved [transferred] money into our bank account today.

20 「自動的に振り込まれる」
(私の給料は口座に自動的に振り込まれます)
- ☆ Ⓐ My pay's automatically deposited into my account.
- ◎ Ⓑ My pay's automatically put in ...
- ◎ Ⓒ My pay's automatically transferred into ...
- ○ Ⓓ My pay's automatically deposited in [put into] ...
- ○ Ⓔ I have [get] my salary paid automatically ...
- △ Ⓕ I have my salary paid by direct deposit in ...

[注意] 辞典に I have my salary paid through the bank paid direct into my bank account. が出ているが全く使われていない。

21 「公定歩合」
(アメリカの中央銀行は数週間以内に公定歩合を上げるでしょう)
- The Fed'll raise the ☆ Ⓐ bank rate within a few weeks.
- ◎ Ⓑ official bank rate ...
- ○ Ⓒ official discount rate ...

22 「解約する」
(私は定期預金を解約しなければならないんです)
I have to ☆ Ⓐ sell the CD.
　　　　　 ◎ Ⓑ cash in ...
　　　　　 ◎ Ⓒ sell off ...
　　　　　 ○ Ⓓ cash out ...

23 「融資する」
(デトロイト銀行はうちの会社に融資するでしょう)
Detroit Bank'll
　☆ Ⓐ finance our company.
　◎ Ⓑ help our company with the money.
　◎ Ⓒ lend [loan] our company the money.
　◎ Ⓓ loan the money to our company.
　○ Ⓔ provide the money for our company.
　○ Ⓕ provide our company with the money.
　○ Ⓖ supply the money for [to] our company.
　△ Ⓗ supply our company with the money.
　× Ⓘ furnish [accommodate] the money to our company.
　× Ⓙ accommodate our company with the money.
［注意］辞典にⒾⒿが出ているが使われていない。

24 「金利」
(a)　金利を尋ねる場合
(あなたの住宅ローンの金利はいくらですか)
What's ☆ Ⓐ the interest rate on your home loan?
　　　　 ◎ Ⓑ the rate [interest] on ...
　　　　 ◎ Ⓒ the rate of interest on ...
［注意］... on your home loan. が1番よく使われているが，for もよく使われている。of はときどき使われている。

(b)　金利が高い（安い）に言及する場合
(最近金利は高い)
Interest rates're ◎ Ⓐ high these days.
　　　　　　　　 ○ Ⓑ expensive ...
［注意］辞典に Money's expensive these days. が出ているが使われていな

い。

25 「連帯保証人」
(a) 一般に
(誰があなたの家の連帯保証人になるのですか)
Who'll be the ◎ Ⓐ cosigner for your home loan?
　　　　　　　○ Ⓑ cosigner on ...?

(b) 親子など親密な間柄
(お父さん，銀行ローンを申し込むんですけど，連帯保証人になってくれますか)
We're going to apply for a bank loan. Could you
◎ Ⓐ cosign for me, Dad?
○ Ⓑ be my cosigner, ...?
× Ⓒ be my guarantor, ...?
× Ⓓ guarantee my loan, ...?
［注意］Ⓓは親子ではなくビジネスの世界ではよく使われている。

26 「連帯保証をする」
(私の1番上の兄が家のローンの連帯保証をするんです)
My oldest brother'll ◎ Ⓐ cosign for [on] my home loan.
　　　　　　　　　　○ Ⓑ cosign my ...
　　　　　　　　　　○ Ⓒ be the cosigner for my ...
　　　　　　　　　　× Ⓓ be the guarantor [guarantee] for my ...
［注意］Ⓓの guarantee は他人同士，特にビジネスピープルの間ではよく使われている。

27 「ローンの支払いが遅れている」
(a) 単に遅れていると述べる場合
(私は銀行ローンが遅れているんです)
I'm ◎ Ⓐ behind on [with, in] my bank loan.
　　◎ Ⓑ late with my ...
　　○ Ⓒ late in paying my ...
　　△ Ⓓ overdue with [in] my ...

(b) 遅れている日数・月数を述べる場合
(私たちの銀行ローンは2カ月遅れています)

Our bank loan's two months ◎ Ⓐ late [overdue].
　　　　　　　　　　　　○ Ⓑ behind.
　　　　　　　　　　　　△ Ⓒ slow.

28 「競売」
(a) 競売にかけられると述べる場合
　　（このビルはまもなく競売にかけられるでしょう）
　　This building'll ◎ Ⓐ be sold at auction soon.
　　　　　　　　　◎ Ⓑ be auctioned (off) soon.
　　　　　　　　　◎ Ⓒ be put up for auction soon.
　　　　　　　　　○ Ⓓ be put on the auction block soon.
　　　　　　　　　○ Ⓔ be sold at an auction soon.
　　　　　　　　　× Ⓕ be put up to auction soon.
　　　　　　　　　× Ⓖ be (put) on the block soon.
　　[注意] 辞典にⒻⒼが出ているが使われていない。

(b) 競売で買った（売った）と述べる場合
　　（私はこのビルを競売で買ったんです）
　　I bought this building ◎ Ⓐ at an auction.
　　　　　　　　　　　　△ Ⓑ in an auction.
　　　　　　　　　　　　△ Ⓒ at a sale by auction.
　　　　　　　　　　　　× Ⓓ at [in] a public sale.
　　　　　　　　　　　　× Ⓔ at [in] an auction sale.
　　　　　　　　　　　　× Ⓕ at a sale at auction.
　　[注意] 辞典にⒹⒺⒻが出ているが使われていない。

29 「不良債権」
　　（XYZ銀行は不良債権がたくさんあるんです）
　　XYZ Bank
　　☆ Ⓐ has a lot of bad loans.
　　◎ Ⓑ has a lot of defaulted loans.
　　○ Ⓒ has [made] a lot of loans that've been defaulted on.

30 「債権がある」
(a) 事実だけを述べる場合
　　（うちはXYZ会社に債権がある）
　　☆ Ⓐ XYZ Company owes us money.

◎ Ⓑ XYZ Company's our creditor.
　　◎ Ⓒ XYZ Company has claims on us.

(b) **債権を放棄する旨を述べる場合**
　　(うちはXYZ会社の債権を放棄せざるをえない)
　　◎ We have no other choice but to write off XYZ Company's loan.

第16章 電話に関する表現

1 「電話」

(a) 鳴っている電話に「出る」と述べる場合
　　(電話に出てちょうだい)
　　Please ☆ Ⓐ get the phone.
　　　　　　☆ Ⓑ answer the phone.
　　　　　　◎ Ⓒ pick up the phone.
　　　　　　○ Ⓓ grab the phone.
　　　　　　○ Ⓔ get [answer] the call.
　　[注意] 辞典に take the phone が出ているが使われていない。

(b) 電話をかけた先に「…のお宅ですか」と尋ねる場合
　　(ブラウンさんのお宅ですか)
　　Is this ☆ Ⓐ the Browns?
　　　　　　◎ Ⓑ the Brown residence?
　　　　　　◎ Ⓒ Mr. Brown's house?
　　　　　　○ Ⓓ Mr. Brown's residence?
　　　　　　○ Ⓔ Mr. Brown's home?
　　　　　　△ Ⓕ Mr. Brown's place?

(c) かかってきた電話に対して「…です」と述べる場合
● 家族全体を述べるとき
　　(こちらはブラウンです)
　　This is the ☆ Ⓐ Browns.
　　　　　　　　☆ Ⓑ Brown residence.

　　　　◎ ⓒ Brown's residence.
　　　　◎ ⓓ Brown's house.
　　　　○ ⓔ Brown house.
　　　　○ ⓕ Brown place.
　　　　△ ⓖ Brown home.

(d) 電話で話をしたい人を呼び出す場合
　　●丁重に述べるとき
　　（スティーヴ・スミスさんとお話できますか）
　　☆ ⓐ May I speak to Mr. Steve Smith?
　　☆ ⓑ Could I speak to ...
　　◎ ⓒ May I please speak with ...
　　◎ ⓓ Could I speak with ...
　　◎ ⓔ Could I please speak to ...
　　［注意］ⓒⓔが1番丁重さがある。
　　●普通に述べるとき
　　（スティーヴ・スミスさんとお話できますか）
　　◎ ⓐ Can I speak to Mr. Steve Smith?
　　◎ ⓑ Is Mr. Steve Smith there?
　　［注意］ⓐのほうがⓑより丁重さはある。

(e) 電話をかけてきた人の名前を尋ねる場合
　　●非常に丁重に尋ねるとき
　　（どちら様でいらっしゃいますか）
　　☆ ⓐ Can I ask who's calling, please?
　　◎ ⓑ May I ask who's calling, please?
　　○ ⓒ Could I ask who's calling, please?
　　○ ⓓ Who am I speaking to, please?
　　［注意］ⓑⓒのほうがⓐⓓよりずっと丁重に聞こえる。
　　●少し丁重に尋ねるとき
　　（どちら様ですか）
　　Who's ◎ ⓐ calling, please?
　　　　　　◎ ⓑ this, please?
　　●普通に尋ねるとき
　　（どなたですか）
　　◎ ⓐ Who?
　　◎ ⓑ Who's this?

[注意] ⒶⒷともトーン次第で非常に乱暴な尋ね方になる。

(f) 呼び出してもらうとき
　　●非常に丁重に述べるとき
　　（デイヴィッドを電話に出していただけますか）
　　Could you ◎ Ⓐ please put David on the phone, please?
　　　　　　　◎ Ⓑ please get David for me, please?
　　　　　　　◎ Ⓒ go get David for me, please?
　　●普通に述べるとき
　　（デイヴィッドを電話に出してくれますか）
　　Can [Will] you ◎ Ⓐ put David on the phone?
　　　　　　　　　◎ Ⓑ get David for me?
　　　　　　　　　◎ Ⓒ go get David for me?

(g) 電話に出た人が当人の場合
　　●丁重に述べるとき
　　（リサ：もしもし，ブライアン・メロイさんとお話したいのですが）
　　Lisa: Hello, may I speak to Mr. Brian Maloy?
　　（ブライアン：私ですが）
　　Brian: This is ☆ Ⓐ him.
　　　　　　　　　☆ Ⓑ Brian.
　　　　　　　　　◎ Ⓒ Brian Maloy.
　　　　　　　　　○ Ⓓ him speaking.
　　　　　　　　　○ Ⓔ he.
　　[注意] 丁重さはⒺが1番，Ⓑが2番，ⒶⒸは3番，Ⓓが4番。
　　●普通に述べるとき
　　（ブライアン：私ですが）
　　Brian: ◎ Ⓐ Speaking.
　　　　　○ Ⓑ This is me.
　　　　　△ Ⓒ You're talking [speaking] to him.
　　●くだけた調子で述べるとき
　　（ブライアン：私ですが）
　　Brian: ◎ Ⓐ You've got him.
　　　　　◎ Ⓑ You got him.

(h) 切らないで待ってもらいたい場合
　　●丁重に述べるとき

(ちょっとお待ちいただけますか)
Could you ◎ Ⓐ hold a minute?
　　　　　 ◎ Ⓑ hold on a minute?
　　　　　 ◎ Ⓒ wait a minute?
　　　　　 ◎ Ⓓ hold the line a minute?
●少し丁重に述べるとき
(そのままちょっと待ってくれますか)
Can you ◎ Ⓐ hold a second?
　　　　　 ◎ Ⓑ hold on a second?
　　　　　 ○ Ⓒ hold the line a second?
●普通に述べるとき
(切らないで待ってくれますか)
Can you ☆ Ⓐ hang on?
　　　　　 ◎ Ⓑ stay on?
　　　　　 ○ Ⓒ stay on the line?
　　　　　 △ Ⓓ hang on the line?

(i) 「誰々から電話です」と伝える場合
　　(ジムから電話がかかってます)
　　☆ Ⓐ You have a (phone) call from Jim.
　　◎ Ⓑ Jim's on the phone (for you).
　　◎ Ⓒ Jim wants to talk to you on the phone.
　　○ Ⓓ There's a (phone) call for you from Jim.
　　○ Ⓔ There's a telephone call from Jim.
　　○ Ⓕ Jim's calling you.
　　○ Ⓖ You're wanted on the phone by Jim.
　　[注意] ⒹⒺは事務所でなら非常によく使われているが自宅なら使用頻度は少し下がる。

(j) 電話をかけてきた人が誰であったかを尋ねる場合
　　(電話は誰だったの)
　　Who ☆ Ⓐ was that?
　　　　 ☆ Ⓑ called you?
　　　　 ☆ Ⓒ called?
　　　　 ◎ Ⓓ was that on the phone?
　　[注意] Who が先行しているときの that は the person と同じ意味になり、that のほうがずっとよく使われている。

第16章　電話に関する表現

(k) 「電話で話す」と述べる場合
　　（今晩そのことを電話で話しましょう）
　　Let's talk about it ◎ Ⓐ on the phone tonight.
　　　　　　　　　　　 ◎ Ⓑ over the phone ...
　　　　　　　　　　　 ○ Ⓒ by phone ...
　　[注意] 辞典に through the phone が出ているが使われていない。

(l) 電話をひくと述べる場合
　　（明日電話を取りつけてもらうんです）
　　I'm going to have a telephone ☆ Ⓐ hooked up tomorrow.
　　　　　　　　　　　　　　　　 ◎ Ⓑ put in ...
　　　　　　　　　　　　　　　　 ○ Ⓒ installed ...

(m) もう一度電話をかけ直すと述べる場合
　　（3時頃もう一度彼に電話します）
　　I'll ◎ Ⓐ call him back around 3:00.
　　　　◎ Ⓑ call him later ...
　　　　◎ Ⓒ call him again ...
　　　　○ Ⓓ give him another call ...
　　　　△ Ⓔ call him once more ...

(n) 番号が間違っている場合
　　（何番におかけですか）
　　What number ☆ Ⓐ did you call?
　　　　　　　　 ◎ Ⓑ did you dial?
　　　　　　　　 ○ Ⓒ are you calling?

2 「(電話を) つなぐ」

　　（彼らの電話は私につながないで下さい）
　　When they phone me, please don't
　　　　☆ Ⓐ transfer their calls to me.
　　　　◎ Ⓑ put their calls through to me.
　　　　○ Ⓒ give me their calls.
　　　　○ Ⓓ connect them to me.
　　　　△ Ⓔ connect their calls to me.

3 「(電話が) すぐつながる」
(早朝電話してくれれば私にすぐつながるはずです)
If you call me early in the morning, you should be able to
- ☆ Ⓐ get through to me right away.
- ☆ Ⓑ get me right away.
- ◎ Ⓒ reach me right away.

4 「(電話で) 誰々が話し中」
(a) 人を主語にして述べる場合
(彼は別の電話で話し中なんです)
He's ◎ Ⓐ on the other line.
　　　◎ Ⓑ on another line.
　　　◎ Ⓒ talking to someone on the other line.
　　　◎ Ⓓ talking to someone on another line.

(b) 電話機を主語にして述べる場合
(ビルの電話はまだ話し中ですか)
Is Bill's ☆ Ⓐ line still busy?
　　　　 ◎ Ⓑ phone still busy?
　　　　 △ Ⓒ telephone still busy?

(c) 話し中が長く続いていることを述べる場合
(今朝からお話し中なんです)
- ☆ Ⓐ The line's been busy since this morning.
- ◎ Ⓑ Someone's been on the phone …
- ◎ Ⓒ Someone's been on the line …

5 「(電話で) よく聞こえる」
(あなたの声はよく聞こえます)
I can hear ◎ Ⓐ your voice clearly.
　　　　　 ○ Ⓑ your voice clear.
　　　　　 ○ Ⓒ you clearly.
　　　　　 ○ Ⓓ you clear.

6 「受話器を口に近づける」
(受話器を口に近づけてくれますか)
Will you ◎ Ⓐ hold the phone [line] close [closer] to your mouth?

第16章　電話に関する表現

　　　　　○ Ⓑ speak (more) directly into the receiver ［phone］?

7 「声を大きくする」
（もっと声を大きくして話してくれますか）
Can you ◎ Ⓐ speak louder?
　　　　　◎ Ⓑ speak up?

8 「病気で欠勤する電話をかける」
（ビルは数分前に病気で欠勤する電話をかけてきました）
Bill ☆ Ⓐ called in sick a few minutes ago.
　　 ◎ Ⓑ phoned in sick ...
［注意］ある辞典に made a phone call in sick が出ているが使われていない。

9 「フリーダイヤル」
（御社にはフリーダイヤルがあるのですか）
Does your company have ☆ Ⓐ an 800 number?
　　　　　　　　　　　　　◎ Ⓑ a toll free number?
［注意］アメリカでは800の他に888，877が使われている。しかし一般の会話ではⒶかⒷで言う。

10 「(電話が) 切れていました」
（私が電話に出たら電話は切れていました）
When I picked up the phone, ◎ Ⓐ the line was dead.
　　　　　　　　　　　　　　　◎ Ⓑ there was no dial tone.
［注意］be cut off が辞典に出ているが，これは電話局が料金未払いのような理由でサービスを停止したときにしか使われていない。

第17章

投資に関する表現

1 「株」

(a) 株数を述べる場合
  (私はこの会社の株を8万株持っています)
  I have eighty thousand ◎ Ⓐ shares in this company.
  　　　　　　　　　　　　× Ⓑ stocks [interests] ...

(b) 株を持っている会社の数に言及する場合
  (私は6つの会社の株に投資しています)
  I'm investing in six different ◎ Ⓐ stocks.
  　　　　　　　　　　　　　　× Ⓑ shares [interests].

(c) 漠然とある会社の株に言及する場合
  (私はXYZ会社の株を持っています)
  I ◎ Ⓐ hold an interest in XYZ Company.
  　◎ Ⓑ have shares [stock] ...
  　○ Ⓒ hold shares [stock] ...
  　○ Ⓓ have an interest ...
  　× Ⓔ have stocks [a stock] ...
  [注意] (1) Ⓓは「興味がある」の意味でも使われている。しかし「興味がある」の意味では be interested in のほうがよく使われている。
  (2) 多くの辞典に shares はイギリス英語，stock はアメリカ英語と書いてあるが事実に反する。

2 「株式を公開する」

第17章　投資に関する表現

（うちの会社はまもなくニューヨーク株式取引所に株式を公開する予定です）
Our company's going to
　　☆ Ⓐ go public on the New York Stock Exchange soon.
　　◎ Ⓑ sell stock ［shares］ to the public on ...
　　○ Ⓒ offer ［issue］ stock ［shares］ to the public on ...
　　△ Ⓓ list stock ［shares］ on ...

3 「買い占める」
（うちの株を買い占めている会社がいくつかあるようだね）
It looks like some companies're ◎ Ⓐ buying out our stock.
　　　　　　　　　　　　　　　　○ Ⓑ buying up ...
　　　　　　　　　　　　　　　　△ Ⓒ cornering ...

4 「優良株」
（これは優良株です）
This is a ☆ Ⓐ blue chip stock.
　　　　　◎ Ⓑ blue chip.
　　　　　△ Ⓒ high-grade ［high-quality］ stock.
［注意］(1) 辞典に gilt-edged stock が出ているが使われていない。
(2) 株式市場にプロである人たちの間ではⒷはⒶよりよく使われている。

5 「花形株」
（これは花形株です）
◎ Ⓐ This is a leading stock.
○ Ⓑ This stock's a (market) leader.

6 「人気株」
（これは人気株です）
◎ This is a popular stock.
［注意］辞典に glamor ［favorite］ stock が出ているが使われていない。

7 「優先株」
（これは優先株です）
This is a ◎ Ⓐ preferred stock.
　　　　　× Ⓑ preferential share.
　　　　　× Ⓒ preference stock ［share］.
［注意］数冊の辞典にⒷⒸが出ているが使われていない。

8 「有望株」
（これは有望株です）
This is a ☆ Ⓐ stock that has promise.
　　　　　◎ Ⓑ stock that has potential.
　　　　　◎ Ⓒ stock with potential.
　　　　　◎ Ⓓ promising stock.
　　　　　○ Ⓔ stock with promise.
[注意] 辞典に a potential stock，a hopeful stock，a stock with hope が出ているが全く使われていない。

9 「推奨株」
（これは推奨株です）
☆ Ⓐ This stock's highly recommended by experts.
◎ Ⓑ This is a favored stock.
○ Ⓒ This is a highly recommended stock by experts.

10 「小型株」
（小型株に投資しないほうがいいですよ）
You'd better not invest in a ☆ Ⓐ small-cap stock.
　　　　　　　　　　　　　　◎ Ⓑ small-capitalization stock.
　　　　　　　　　　　　　　○ Ⓒ small-cap.
[注意] Ⓒは株に携わっている人たちの間では非常によく使われている。

11 「店頭株（非上場株）」
（これは店頭株です）
☆ Ⓐ This stock isn't listed.
◎ Ⓑ This stock isn't public.
○ Ⓒ This is an unlisted [an over the counter] stock.
[注意] 辞典に a counter stock が出ているが使われていない。

12 「ハイテク株」
（ハイテク株がぐーんと上がり始めるには時間がかかるでしょう）
It'll take a long time before ◎ Ⓐ high-tech stocks
　　　　　　　　　　　　　　△ Ⓑ high technology stocks
start to go up dramatically.

第17章 投資に関する表現

13「取引高の多い株」
(これは取引高の多い株です)
　◎ This is an active stock.

14「織り込み済みです」
(それはこの株価に織り込み済みです)
That's already ☆ Ⓐ included in this stock price.
　　　　　　　 ◎ Ⓑ factored into …
　　　　　　　 ○ Ⓒ digested into …
　　　　　　　 ○ Ⓓ taken into consideration［account］in …

15「大口投資家」
(彼は大口投資家です)
He's a ☆ Ⓐ high roller.
　　　　◎ Ⓑ major roller.
　　　　○ Ⓒ big (spending) investor.
　　　　○ Ⓓ high rolling investor.
　　　　△ Ⓔ large spending investor.

16「機関投資家」
(最近機関投資家がこの株を買い始めたんです)
　◎ Institutional investors've started to buy this stock recently.

17「個人投資家」
(この株は法人投資家よりも個人投資家の間で人気があります)
This stock's more popular with ◎ Ⓐ private［individual］investors
　　　　　　　　　　　　　　　 ○ Ⓑ personal investors
than corporate investors.

18「(株価が) ものすごく上がる」
(XYZの株価はものすごく上がっています)
XYZ stock's ☆ Ⓐ skyrocketing.
　　　　　　 ◎ Ⓑ soaring［going through the roof］.
　　　　　　 ◎ Ⓒ shooting up.
　　　　　　 ◎ Ⓓ going up really fast［quick］.
　　　　　　 ◎ Ⓔ going up dramatically.
　　　　　　 ○ Ⓕ taking off［jumping］really fast［quick］.

　　　　△ ⓖ rising very fast [quick].
　　　　△ ⓗ zooming [running up].
　[注意] ⒶとⒷの going through the roof が1番強く，Ⓑの soaring とⒸが2番，Ⓕが3番，残りは個人的主観で決められない。

19 「(株の) 相場」
　(IT 産業の相場は上がってきている)
　☆ Ⓐ Stock [The stock] prices for the IT industry're going up.
　◎ Ⓑ Prices [The prices] for ...
　○ Ⓒ Quotes [The quotes] for ...
　○ Ⓓ The market prices for ...

20 「上げ相場」
　(今、株式は上げ相場です)
　☆ Ⓐ The stock market's strong now.
　◎ Ⓑ This is a strong market ...
　○ Ⓒ This is a bull market ...
　○ Ⓓ We're in a bull [strong] market ...
　○ Ⓔ The stock market's on [in] an upswing ...
　△ Ⓕ The stock market's bullish ...

21 「上げ局面」
　(株式市場は上げ局面です)
　The stock market's ◎ Ⓐ in an increasing phase [stage].
　　　　　　　　　　　○ Ⓑ in a rising phase [stage].

22 「高値をつける」
　(今日 XYZ 会社はまた高値をつけました)
　Today the market price for XYZ Company
　　　☆ Ⓐ is at its high again.
　　　◎ Ⓑ has hit its high ...

23 「下げ相場」
　(今，株式は下げ相場です)
　☆ Ⓐ The stock market's weak now.
　☆ Ⓑ The market's weak ...
　◎ Ⓒ We're in a weak [bear] market ...

◎ ⓓ This is a weak market ...
○ ⓔ This is a bear market ...
△ ⓕ This is [We're in] a bearish market ...

24 「(株式市場の) 不安材料」

(いくつかの不安材料のために株式市場は下落しました)
The stock market's fallen because of some
  ◎ ⓐ bad news.
  △ ⓑ unfavorable news [factors].

25 「大量売却による株価急落」

(今日 XYZ 会社の株価が大量売却により急落しました)
☆ ⓐ There was a sell-off of XYZ Company's stock today.
○ ⓑ There was a sell-off on XYZ Company's stock ...
○ ⓒ XYZ Company's stock had a sell-off ...

26 「暴落する」

(株式市場が暴落したんです)
The stock market's
  ◎ ⓐ nosedived [taken a nosedive].
  ◎ ⓑ plunged [plummeted, tumbled, slumped, tobogganed].
  ◎ ⓒ fallen drastically [dramatically, tremendously].
  ◎ ⓓ dropped drastically [dramatically, tremendously].
  ◎ ⓔ crashed.
[注意] ⓔは「底を打った」という意味でも非常によく使われている。

27 「持ち直す」

(株式市場は数週間で持ち直すだろう)
The stock market'll
  ☆ ⓐ recover in a few weeks.
  ◎ ⓑ improve [go back up, bounce back, rebound] in ...
  ○ ⓒ pick up [come back, rally, jump back] in ...
  △ ⓓ rise back in ...
[注意] (1) ⓐと，ⓒの come back，jump back は話し手が喜んでいるニュアンスが他の表現より強い。
(2) ⓒの rally は株式市場の人の間では非常によく使われている。

28「(市場は) しっかりしている」
(株式市場はこの2カ月しっかりしています)
The stock market's been ☆ Ⓐ stable for the last two months.
　　　　　　　　　　　　◎ Ⓑ steady ...
[注意] 辞典に firm を stable と並べて紹介しているがニュアンスが違う。Ⓐ
Ⓑは浮沈が多少あるのに対して firm には浮沈がない。

29「引ける」
(ダウ平均株価は3,357.84で引けました)
The Dow-Jones average ☆ Ⓐ closed at 3,357.84.
　　　　　　　　　　　◎ Ⓑ ended [closed] the day at ...
　　　　　　　　　　　○ Ⓒ wrapped up the day at ...
　　　　　　　　　　　○ Ⓓ wrapped the day up at ...
　　　　　　　　　　　○ Ⓔ wound the day up at ...
　　　　　　　　　　　○ Ⓕ finished the day at ...
　　　　　　　　　　　○ Ⓖ finished [ended] at ...
　　　　　　　　　　　△ Ⓗ wound up the day at ...

30「高値で引ける」
(今日，株式市場は高値で引けました)
The stock market ◎ Ⓐ closed high today.
　　　　　　　　○ Ⓑ closed way up today.

31「配当」
(この株の配当はいくらだったのですか)
☆ Ⓐ What were the devidends on this stock?
◎ Ⓑ What dividends did this stock yield [produce, make, return]?
○ Ⓒ What dividends did this stock bring [give] you?

第18章 買物・店に関する表現

1 「見てまわる」
(a) 何かを探して，または時間つぶしに
(メイシーを見てまわろう)
Let's ☆ Ⓐ check out Macy's.
　　　◎ Ⓑ look around (in) ...
　　　◎ Ⓒ take a look around (in) ...
　　　◎ Ⓓ browse around in ...
　　　○ Ⓔ browse (around) ...
　　　○ Ⓕ have a look around (in) ...

(b) 時間つぶしに
(メイシーを見てまわろう)
Let's ◎ Ⓐ walk around (in) Macy's.
　　　○ Ⓑ wander around (in) ...

(c) 目的に関する含みのない場合
(ブルーミングデールの中を見てまわろう)
◎ Let's browse [look, have a look, take a look] around Bloomingdale's.

2 「用件（店で）」
(誰かご用件を伺っておりますか)
☆ Ⓐ Is someone taking care of [helping] you?
◎ Ⓑ Has someone taken care of [helped] you?

◎ Ⓒ Are you being taken care of [helped]?
◎ Ⓓ Have you been taken care of [helped]?
○ Ⓔ Have you been waited on?
○ Ⓕ Has someone waited on you?
○ Ⓖ Is someone waiting on you?
○ Ⓗ Are you being waited on?
× Ⓘ Has [Is] someone attended to you?
[注意] 辞典にⒾが出ているが使われていない。但し超高級な宝石店などでは使われている。

3 「ありますか」
(a) **色**
(客：このグレーはありますか)
Customer: ☆ Ⓐ Do you have this in gray?
　　　　　◎ Ⓑ Is this available in ...?
　　　　　◎ Ⓒ Can I get this in ...?

(b) **サイズ**
(これはもう少し大きいサイズはありますか)
☆ Ⓐ Do you have this in a larger size?
◎ Ⓑ Can I get this ...?
◎ Ⓒ Is this avaliable ...?

4 「贈答品として包装する」
(これを贈答品として包装していただけますか)
Could you ◎ Ⓐ gift-wrap this, please?
　　　　　○ Ⓑ wrap this (up) as a gift, ...?

5 「目方をごまかす」
(肉屋が目方をごまかしたのかもしれない)
☆ Ⓐ The butcher might've gyped me.
◎ Ⓑ The butcher might've ripped me off.
◎ Ⓒ I might've gotten cheated [screwed] at the meat market.
○ Ⓓ The butcher might've shorted me.
× Ⓔ The butcher might've short-weighted me.
× Ⓕ The butcher might've given me short weight.
[注意] ⒺⒻが辞典に出ているが使われていない。

6 「商品券」
(彼が商品券をくれたんです)
He gave me a ☆ Ⓐ gift certificate.
　　　　　　　◎ Ⓑ gift coupon.
　　　　　　　△ Ⓒ gift voucher.
[注意] 辞典に merchandise coupon, credit slip, exchange check [ticket] が「商品券」の意味で紹介されているが使われていない。

7 「目のこえたお客」
(あのお客さんは目がこえています)
☆ Ⓐ That customer knows his stuff.
◎ Ⓑ That's an educated customer.
○ Ⓒ That's a well-informed customer.

8 「言い値」
(言い値はいくらなのですか)
◎ Ⓐ What's the seller's (asking) price?
◎ Ⓑ How much does the seller want?

9 「電話のセールスで」
(私はこれを電話のセールスで買いました)
I bought this ☆ Ⓐ from a telemarketer.
　　　　　　　◎ Ⓑ from a telemarketing company.
　　　　　　　○ Ⓒ through a telemarketing company.
[注意] 辞典に from cold calling, from telesales が出ているが使われていない。

10 「通販で」
(私はこのコンピューターを通販で買ったんです)
I bought this computer ◎ Ⓐ by mail order.
　　　　　　　　　　　○ Ⓑ through mail order.
　　　　　　　　　　　△ Ⓒ by mail order shopping.
　　　　　　　　　　　△ Ⓓ through mail order shopping.
　　　　　　　　　　　× Ⓔ by [through] mail order system.
[注意] Ⓔが辞典に出ているが使われていない。

11 「老舗の」
(ニーマン・マーカスは老舗のデパートなんです)
Neiman Marcus
- ☆ Ⓐ has been around a long time and is still going strong.
- ◎ Ⓑ has been in business for a long time and is still going strong.
- ◎ Ⓒ is a well-established department store.
- △ Ⓓ is a department store with a long history and it's still going strong.

12 「挨拶のカード店」
(角に挨拶カード店があります)
There's a ◎ Ⓐ card store on the corner.
　　　　　○ Ⓑ greeting card store [shop] ...

13 「インターネットカフェ」
(市役所の裏にインターネットカフェがあります)
◎ Ⓐ There's a cybercafe [an internet cafe] behind city hall.

14 「運送屋」
(角を曲った所に運送屋があります)
There's a ◎ Ⓐ moving company around the corner.
　　　　　○ Ⓑ mover ...
　　　　　× Ⓒ carrier [forwarding agent] ...
[注意] Ⓒが辞典に出ているが使われていない。

15 「エステ」
(この先にエステがあります)
There's ◎ Ⓐ a (health) spa down the street.
　　　　× Ⓑ an esthetic salon [an esthetician] ...

16 「お菓子屋」
(消防署の少し先へ行った所にお菓子屋があります)
There's a ◎ Ⓐ candy store a little past the fire station.
　　　　　○ Ⓑ candy shop ...
　　　　　× Ⓒ confectionery store ...
[注意] Ⓒが辞典に出ているが今は使われていない。

17 「かぎ屋」
(証券会社から数軒先にかぎ屋があります)
There's a
 ☆ Ⓐ locksmith a few doors away from the stockbroker.
 ◎ Ⓑ key store ...
 ○ Ⓒ key shop ...

18 「家具屋」
(郵便局の隣に家具屋があります)
There's a ◎ Ⓐ furniture store next door to the post office.
    ○ Ⓑ home furnishing store ...

19 「貸し衣装屋」
(a) 男女対象
(ナンシーは貸し衣装屋に勤めているんです)
Nancy works for a ☆ Ⓐ shop [store] that rents clothes.
      ◎ Ⓑ shop [store] that rents clothing.
      ◎ Ⓒ clothing rental shop [store].
      ◎ Ⓓ formal wear shop [store].
      ○ Ⓔ clothes rental shop [store].
[注意] store のほうが shop より大きい響きがある。

(b) 女性対象
(ナンシーは貸し衣装屋に勤めているんです)
Nancy works for a ☆ Ⓐ bridal shop [store].
      ☆ Ⓑ shop [store] that rents bridal clothes.
      ◎ Ⓒ shop [store] that rents bridal clothing.

(c) 男性対象
(ジムは貸し衣装屋に勤めているんです)
Jim works for a ◎ Ⓐ tuxedo shop.
     ◎ Ⓑ tuxedo rental shop [store].
     ◎ Ⓒ shop [store] that rents tuxedoes.

20 「ガソリンスタンド」
(この高速道路の先にガソリンスタンドがあります)
There's a ◎ Ⓐ gas station down the highway.

                △ Ⓑ filling station ...

21「金物屋」
　　（角を曲った所に金物屋があります）
　　There's a ◎ Ⓐ hardware store around the corner.
　　　　　　　△ Ⓑ hardware shop ...

22「画廊」
　　●オリジナルの絵を置いている店
　　（消防署の少し手前に画廊があります）
　　◎ There's an art gallery ［a gallery］ a little before the fire station.
　　●複製の絵を置いている店
　　（消防署の少し手前に画廊があります）
　　There's a ◎ Ⓐ printshop a little before the fire station.
　　　　　　　○ Ⓑ poster store ...

23「生地屋」
　　（シアトル銀行の少し手前に生地屋があります）
　　There's a ◎ Ⓐ fabric store a little before Seattle Bank.
　　　　　　　× Ⓑ material store ...
　　　　　　　× Ⓒ dry-goods store ［shop］...

24「クリーニング屋」
　　（これらのシャツをクリーニング屋へ持って行って下さい）
　　Take these shirts to the ◎ Ⓐ cleaners, please.
　　　　　　　　　　　　　　△ Ⓑ laundry, ...
　　　　　　　　　　　　　　× Ⓒ cleaner's, ...
　　　　　　　　　　　　　　× Ⓓ laundry ［cleaning］ shop, ...
　　［注意］(1) Ⓒは辞典に出ているが使われていない。
　　　　　(2) 以前は水洗いのクリーニング屋はⒷの laundry, ドライクリーニング屋は
　　　　　　 Ⓒの cleaner's であったが，今はどちらにもⒶの cleaners が使われている。
　　　　　(3) cleners は単複同型で，複数でも cleanerses とはしない。There are
　　　　　　 some cleaners near my office. (私の事務所の近くにクリーニング屋が何
　　　　　　 軒かあります)

25「車の修理所」
　　●自動車修理所を指していることがはっきりしている場合

[204]

第18章　買物・店に関する表現

(デイヴィッドはこの近くの自動車修理所で修理工として働いています。)
◎ David works for the shop [garage] near here as a mechanic.
● ガレージと誤解される恐れがある場合
(リンダ：あら，高級車を持っているのね)
Linda: Gee that's an expensive car you have!
(ナンシー：ありがとう。でも実を言うとお父さんのなのよ。私のは今，自動車修理所に出してあるのよ)
Nancy: Oh thank you, but to tell you the truth it's my father's. Mine's in the ◎ Ⓐ shop now.
　　　　　△ Ⓑ garage ...
[注意] 上の対話でⒷの garage を使うと自宅のガレージに誤解される恐れがある。
● shop か garage かはっきりしない場合
(マリア：どこで会いましょうか)
Maria: Where should we meet?
(ジム：ブラウン自動車修理所で会おう)
Jim: Let's meet at ◎ Ⓐ Brown's Auto [Garage].
　　　　　　　　　◎ Ⓑ Brown's (Shop).
[注意] この地域をよく知らない人にはⒶが普通使われ，Ⓑは知っている者同士で使われている。

26 「車の販売店」

● 新車
(市役所の真向いに車の販売店があります)
◎ There's a car dealer [dealership] across the street from town hall.
[注意] car dealer は多くのメーカーの車を扱っている。car dealership は一社のメーカーの車しか販売していない。しかし，アメリカ人でこの違いを知っている人は少なく，混用されている。
● 中古車
(市役所の真向いに中古車の販売店があります)
There's a
　　◎ Ⓐ used car dealer [lot] across the street from town hall.
　　△ Ⓑ secondhand car dealer [lot] ...

27 「コインランドリー」

(郵便局の隣にコインランドリーがあります)
There's a ◎ Ⓐ laundromat next door to the post office.

[205]

○ Ⓑ coin laundry ...
△ Ⓒ self-service laundry ...

28 「コーヒーショップ」
（この近くにコーヒーショップがありますか）
Is there ◎ Ⓐ a coffee shop ［a diner］ near here?
　　　　× Ⓑ an eating place near here?
［注意］(1) Ⓑが辞典に出ているが使われていない。
(2) アメリカの coffee shop は日本の喫茶店とは違う。

29 「魚屋」
●スーパーの中で店員に尋ねるとき
（魚屋はどこですか）
☆ Ⓐ Where's the fish department?
◎ Ⓑ Where's the fish section?
◎ Ⓒ Where's the sea food department ［section］?
○ Ⓓ Where do you have ［keep］ the fish?
○ Ⓔ Where's the sea food?
△ Ⓕ Where's the fish?
［注意］アメリカでスーパーがある市や町では独立した魚屋はない。スーパーの中にある。
●小さい町で
（役場の真裏に魚屋があります）
There's a ☆ Ⓐ fish market right behind town hall.
　　　　　　◎ Ⓑ fish shop ［store］ ...
［注意］辞典に fish dealer ［monger］ が出ているが使われていない。

30 「酒屋」
（デトロイト保険の2, 3軒先に酒屋があります）
There's a
　◎ Ⓐ liquor store two or three down away from Detroit Insurance.
　△ Ⓑ liquor shop ...
　△ Ⓒ package store ...

31 「サンドイッチショップ」
（この近くにサンドイッチショップがありますか）
Is there a ◎ Ⓐ sub shop near here?

　　　　　◎ ⑧ deli near here?
　　　　　○ ⓒ sandwich shop near here?
　　[注意] ⑧はサンドイッチだけでなく，サラダやスープを売っている。

32 「質屋」
（消防署の真向いに質屋があります）
　There's a ◎ Ⓐ pawn shop across the street from fire station.
　　　　　× Ⓑ pawn store ...

33 「事務用品店」
（この先に事務用品店があります）
　There's an ◎ Ⓐ office supply store down the street.
　　　　　△ Ⓑ office supply shop ...

34 「写真館」
（市役所の近くに写真館があります）
　There's a ◎ Ⓐ photo [photographer] studio near city hall.
　　　　　○ Ⓑ photographer ...

35 「写真屋」
（角に写真屋があります）
　There's a ☆ Ⓐ one-hour photo store on the corner.
　　　　　◎ Ⓑ one-hour photo (shop) ...

36 「食料品店」
（信号の近くに食料品店があります）
　There's a ☆ Ⓐ grocery store near the light.
　　　　　◎ Ⓑ corner grocery store ...
　　　　　○ ⓒ neighborhood [small] grocery store ...

37 「紳士洋品店」
（彼は紳士洋品店で働いています）
　He works at a ☆ Ⓐ men's clothing store.
　　　　　○ Ⓑ clothing store for men.
　[注意] 辞典に haberdashery が出ているが使われていない。

38「スーパー」
　　（この先にスーパーがあります）
　　There's a ☆ Ⓐ grocery store down the street.
　　　　　　 ◎ Ⓑ big grocery store ...
　　　　　　 ○ Ⓒ large grocery store ...
　　　　　　 △ Ⓓ supermarket ...

39「寿司屋」
　　（シアトル銀行の隣に寿司屋があります）
　　There's a ◎ Ⓐ sushi bar next door to Seattle Bank.
　　　　　　 × Ⓑ sushi shop [store] ...

40「スポーツ用品店」
　　（消防署の少し手前にスポーツ用品店があります）
　　There's a ☆ Ⓐ sporting goods store a little before the fire station.
　　　　　　 ◎ Ⓑ sporitng goods shop ...
　　　　　　 × Ⓒ sport goods store [shop] ...

41「瀬戸物屋」
　　（この先に瀬戸物屋があります）
　　There's a ◎ Ⓐ china store down the street.
　　　　　　 ○ Ⓑ china shop ...
　　　　　　 × Ⓒ chinaware store (shop) ...
　　[注意] Ⓒが辞典に特記なく出ているが使われていない。但しchinaware storeはアメリカの東南部ではよく使われている。

42「セルフサービスレストラン」
　　（この近くにセルフサービスレストランがありますか）
　　Is there a ◎ Ⓐ cafeteria near here?
　　　　　　　× Ⓑ self-service restaurant near here?
　　[注意] Ⓑが辞典に出ているが使われていない。

43「専門店」
　　（ペルシアじゅうたんの専門店へ行きましょう）
　　Let's go to a store that
　　　　◎ Ⓐ sells [has, carries] only Persian carpets.
　　　　◎ Ⓑ only sells [has, carries] Persian carpets.

◎ ⓒ specializes in Persian carpets.
▽ ⓓ deals only in Persian carpets.
[注意] ⓓはいろいろな辞典に用例として出ているが，口語英語としてはあまり使われていない。

44 「デリカショップ」
(郵便局の真裏にデリカショップがあります)
There's a ◎ ⓐ deli right behind the post office.
　　　　△ ⓑ delicatessen ...
　　　　△ ⓒ sandwich shop ...
　　　　× ⓓ delica shop ...
　　　　× ⓔ side dish store ...
[注意] (1) ⓓが日本のお惣菜店の看板で広く使われているが英語ではない。
(2) ⓔが辞典に出ているが使われていない。
(3) ⓐⓑはアメリカではお惣菜そのものだけを売っているのではなく，お客の好みに応じてお惣菜をサンドイッチにして売る店。

45 「床屋」
(このビルの裏に床屋があります)
There's a ☆ ⓐ barber behind this building.
　　　　◎ ⓑ barbershop ...
　　　　○ ⓒ barber's shop ...

46 「肉屋」
● スーパーの中で店員に尋ねるとき
(肉屋はどこですか)
☆ ⓐ Where's the meat department?
○ ⓑ Where's the meat section [counter]?
○ ⓒ Where do you have [keep] the meat?
△ ⓓ Where's the meat?
[注意] アメリカでスーパーがある市や町では独立した肉屋はない。スーパーの中にある。
● 小さい町で
(役場の真裏に肉屋があります)
There's a ◎ ⓐ butcher [meat market] right behind town hall.
　　　　○ ⓑ butcher's ...
　　　　△ ⓒ butcher shop ...

47「バイキングレストラン」
　　　（あのホテルにバイキングレストランがあります）
　　　There's ☆ Ⓐ an all-you-can-eat restaurant in that hotel.
　　　　　　　◎ Ⓑ a buffet-style restaurant ...
　　　　　　　◎ Ⓒ a buffet ...
　　　　　　　○ Ⓓ a buffet restaurant ...
　　　　　　　△ Ⓔ a smorgasbord ...
　　　　　　　▽ Ⓕ a smorgasbord restaurant ...
　　　［注意］ⒶはⒷ～Ⓕより大衆的な響きがある。

48「花屋」
　　　（駅の近くに花屋があります）
　　　There's a ◎ Ⓐ florist near the station.
　　　　　　　　○ Ⓑ flower shop ...
　　　　　　　　△ Ⓒ flower store ...
　　　［注意］辞典に florist's が出ているが使われていない。

49「パン屋」
　　　（市役所の２，３軒先にパン屋があります）
　　　There's a ◎ Ⓐ bakery two or three down away from city hall.
　　　　　　　　○ Ⓑ baker's ...
　　　　　　　　△ Ⓒ baker ...

50「ビデオ屋」
　　　●売っている店
　　　（あのビルにビデオ屋があります）
　　　There's a ◎ Ⓐ video store in that building.
　　　　　　　　○ Ⓑ video shop ...
　　　●貸す店
　　　（あのビルにビデオ屋があります）
　　　There's a ◎ Ⓐ video store in that building.
　　　　　　　　○ Ⓑ video shop ...
　　　　　　　　△ Ⓒ video rental store ［shop］ ...

51「フランチャイズ店」
　　　（うちはフランチャイズ店をたくさん持っています）
　　　We have a lot of ◎ Ⓐ franchises.

　　　　　○ Ⓑ chains [chain stores].
　　　　　△ Ⓒ franchise stores.
[注意] ⒶⒸはⒷとは厳密には同じでない。しかしアメリカ人は混用し，同意語として使っている。

52 「美容院」
（角を曲った所に美容院があります）
There's a ☆ Ⓐ beauty shop around the corner.
　　　　　◎ Ⓑ beauty salon ...
　　　　　○ Ⓒ beauty parlor ...
　　　　　△ Ⓓ beautician ...
[注意] Ⓑは高級な美容院に使われている。Ⓒは米国南部では非常によく使われている。

53 「文房具店」
（この先に文房具店があります）
There's a ◎ Ⓐ stationery store [shop] down the street.
　　　　　× Ⓑ stationer('s) ...

54 「宝石店」
（アメリカ銀行の真向いに宝石店があります）
There's a ☆ Ⓐ jewelry store facing Bank of America.
　　　　　◎ Ⓑ jeweler's store ...
　　　　　◎ Ⓒ jewelry shop ...
　　　　　○ Ⓓ jeweler ...

55 「本店」
（おたくの本店はどこにあるのですか）
Where's your ◎ Ⓐ main store?
　　　　　　　○ Ⓑ head store?

56 「薬局」
（信号の少し手前に薬局があります）
There's a ◎ Ⓐ drug store a little before the light.
　　　　　◎ Ⓑ pharmacy ...
　　　　　○ Ⓒ pharmacist ...
[注意] 厳密には処方せんを扱う店がⒷで扱わない店がⒶ，しかし実際には混

用されている。

57 「リサイクルショップ」
(このホテルの裏にリサイクルショップがあります)
There's a ◎ Ⓐ thrift store [shop] behind this hotel.
　　　　　× Ⓑ recycle [recycling] store ...

58 「レンタカー屋」
(郵便局の真向いにレンタカー屋があります)
There's a ☆ Ⓐ rental car agency facing the post office.
　　　　　△ Ⓑ rental car agent ...

第19章

車に関する表現

1 「自動車」
(a) **発明**
(自動車はドイツ人によって発明されました)
☆ Ⓐ The automobile was invented by a German.
◎ Ⓑ The car was ...
○ Ⓒ Automobiles [Cars] were ...

(b) **普及させる**
(フォードが自動車を普及させたんです)
Ford ☆ Ⓐ made the automobile popular.
　　　☆ Ⓑ made the automobile [made cars] affordable.
　　　◎ Ⓒ popularized the automobile [popularized cars].
　　　◎ Ⓓ made the automobile [made cars] accessible.
　　　◎ Ⓔ made the automobile [made cars] more available.
　　　◎ Ⓕ made cars popular.

2 「エンジンをかけて下さい」
(エンジンをかけて下さい)
☆ Ⓐ Start the engine.
◎ Ⓑ Start up the car.
◎ Ⓒ Turn on the engine.
◎ Ⓓ Turn the engine on.
○ Ⓔ Get the engine going.

3 「エンジンをかけておく」
(エンジンをかけておいて下さい)
Keep the car engine ◎ Ⓐ on [running].
　　　　　　　　　　○ Ⓑ going.
　　　　　　　　　　△ Ⓒ working.

4 「車に乗る」
(あなたは車に乗れるんですか)
◎ Ⓐ Can you drive?
○ Ⓑ Can you drive a car?
× Ⓒ Can you drive an auto?

5 「車を運転する」
(駅の近くでジムが車を運転しているのを見ました)
I saw Jim ☆ Ⓐ driving near the station.
　　　　　◎ Ⓑ sitting behind the wheel ...
　　　　　○ Ⓒ sitting behind the steering wheel ...
[注意] ⒷⒸには車が止まっていて「運転席にいた」という意味もある。

6 「スピードを出す」
(a) 車の速度
(スピードを出して)
☆ Ⓐ Step on it.
◎ Ⓑ Drive [Go] faster.
◎ Ⓒ Speed up.
○ Ⓓ Gun it [Speed it up].
○ Ⓔ Hit [Step on] the gas.
△ Ⓕ Get the lead out.
△ Ⓖ Give it some gas.

(b) 数字を明示しない場合
(タクシーはトラックと衝突したときスピードを出していました)
The taxi was ☆ Ⓐ going fast when it crashed into a truck.
　　　　　　○ Ⓑ traveling [driving, moving] fast ...
　　　　　　× Ⓒ running fast ...
[注意] Ⓑは新聞では非常によく使われている。

第19章　車に関する表現

(c)　数字を明示する場合
(タクシーはトラックと衝突したとき時速100マイルのスピードを出していました)
The taxi was ☆ Ⓐ going a hundred miles an hour when it crashed
　　　　　　　 ◎ Ⓑ going at a hundred ...
　　　　　　　 ◎ Ⓒ traveling (at) a hundred ...
　　　　　　　 ○ Ⓓ driving (at) a hundred ...
　　　　　　　 ○ Ⓔ speeding along (at) a hundred ...
　　　　　　　 ○ Ⓕ moving (at) a hundred ...
into a truck.

7 「交替で運転する」
(交替で運転しよう)
Let's ◎ Ⓐ take turns driving.
　　　 ○ Ⓑ take turns to drive.
　　　 △ Ⓒ drive in turns.
[注意] 辞典に drive in turn が出ているが使われていない。

8 「クラクションを鳴らす」
(私の家に来たらクラクションを鳴らして下さい)
Please ☆ Ⓐ honk when you get to my house.
　　　　 ◎ Ⓑ honk [beep] the horn when ...
　　　　 ◎ Ⓒ beep when ...
　　　　 ○ Ⓓ blow the horn when ...
　　　　 △ Ⓔ use [sound, toot] the horn when ...

9 「車で送る」
(a)　一般的な状況の場合
(車で駅までお送りしましょうか)
Do you want me to ◎ Ⓐ take [drive] you to the station?
　　　　　　　　　 ◎ Ⓑ give you a ride [lift] ...?
[注意] ある辞典に send you to the station が出ているが使われていない。

(b)　難しい状況の場合
(心配しないで。彼が家まで送り届けるよ)
◎ Don't worry. He'll get you home.

(c)　部下，または家族などに送らせる場合

(誰かに駅まで車で送らせます)
◎ I'll have someone drive you [take you, give you a ride [lift]] to the station.

10 「車で送ってきてくれる」
(ブライアンが私をここまで車で送ってきてくれたんです)
Brian ◎ Ⓐ dropped me off here.
　　　 ◎ Ⓑ brought [drove] me here.
　　　 ◎ Ⓒ gave me a ride here.
　　　 ○ Ⓓ gave me a lift here.
　　　 △ Ⓔ brought me here by car.

11 「スピード違反で捕まる」
(ブライアンはスピード違反で捕まったんです)
Brian got ☆ Ⓐ busted [caught] for speeding.
　　　　　 ◎ Ⓑ busted [caught] for going [driving] too fast.
　　　　　 ◎ Ⓒ a speeding ticket.
　　　　　 ◎ Ⓓ a ticket for speeding.

12 「酔っ払い運転で捕まる」
(ビルは酔っ払い運転で捕まったんです)
Bill was ◎ Ⓐ caught for drunk driving.
　　　　 ○ Ⓑ arrested for drunk driving.

13 「(車庫に) 入れる」
(車を車庫に入れましょうか)
Would you like me to ◎ Ⓐ put your car in the garage?
　　　　　　　　　　 ◎ Ⓑ pull [drive] your car into ...?
　　　　　　　　　　 ○ Ⓒ put your car into ...?
　　　　　　　　　　 × Ⓓ run your car into ...?
［注意］辞典にⒹが出ているが使われていない。

14 「高級車」
(a) 車の外面を述べている場合
(ジムは高級車に乗っています)
Jim drives ◎ Ⓐ an expensive [a luxury, a fancy] car.
　　　　　 ○ Ⓑ a classy [a prestigious] car.

第19章　車に関する表現

△ Ⓒ an upscale [an exclusive, a high-priced] car.
[注意] 辞典に luxurious [high-class, high-grade, top-class] car が出ているが使われていない。

(b) 車の中で述べている場合
(これは高級車ですね)
This is a ◎ Ⓐ luxurious car.
　　　　　 ○ Ⓑ classy car.

15 「外車」
(彼は外車を運転しています)
He drives ☆ Ⓐ an import.
　　　　　 ◎ Ⓑ a foreign car.
　　　　　 ○ Ⓒ an imported [a foreign-made] car.
　　　　　 ○ Ⓓ a car from overseas.

16 「小型車」
(私は小型車を買うつもりです)
I'm going to buy a ☆ Ⓐ small car.
　　　　　　　　　 ◎ Ⓑ compact (car).
[注意] 辞典に an economy car が出ているが，これはサイズではなく燃費上から述べるのでⒶⒷとは違う。

17 「クーペ」
(ブライアンはクーペに乗っています)
Brian drives a ☆ Ⓐ hatchback.
　　　　　　　 ◎ Ⓑ coupe.
[注意] ⒶⒷは正しくは同意語ではない。しかし今アメリカでは混用され同意語になっている。

18 「オープンカー」
(オープンカーが角の店にどすんと衝突したんです)
◎ Ⓐ A convertible slammed into the store on the corner.
△ Ⓑ A ragtop ...

19 「ライトバン（軽量トラック）」
(うちには2台ライトバンがあります)

We have two ◎ Ⓐ light trucks.
　　　　　　◎ Ⓑ lightweight trucks.

20 「小型トラック」
(a) ほろ付き
(うちは小型トラックを買わなければならないんです)
We have to buy a ☆ Ⓐ smal truck.
　　　　　　　　　◎ Ⓑ small-size [small-sized] truck.

(b) ほろなし
(うちは小型トラックを買わなければならないんです)
We have to buy a ☆ Ⓐ pickup.
　　　　　　　　　◎ Ⓑ pickup truck.

21 「大型トラック」
(うちの会社は大型トラックをもう1台買わなければならないね)
Our company has to buy another
　　☆ Ⓐ big truck.
　　◎ Ⓑ heavy-duty [heavyweight] truck.
　　○ Ⓒ large-sized [large-size] truck.
　　○ Ⓓ full-sized [full-size, large] truck.

22 「大型トレーラー」
(あなたは大型トレーラーを運転できますか)
Can you drive ◎ Ⓐ an 18-wheeler?
　　　　　　　○ Ⓑ a tractor-trailer?
　　　　　　　○ Ⓒ a big rig?
　　　　　　　○ Ⓓ a semi?
　　　　　　　△ Ⓔ a semi truck?

23 「クレーン車」
(うちはもう1台クレーン車を買わなければならないね)
We have to buy another ◎ Ⓐ crane.
　　　　　　　　　　　 ○ Ⓑ crane truck.
　　　　　　　　　　　 △ Ⓒ mobile crane.

24 「ハイブリッド車」

第19章　車に関する表現

(私はハイブリッド車を買おうと思っているんです)
I'm thinking of buying a ☆ Ⓐ hybrid car.
　　　　　　　　　　　　　 ◎ Ⓑ hybrid.
　　　　　　　　　　　　　 ○ Ⓒ hybrid vehicle.
[注意] 辞典に a HV が出ているが使われていない。

25 「電気自動車」
(私は電気自動車を買おうと思っているんです)
I'm thinking of buying an ◎ Ⓐ electric car.
　　　　　　　　　　　　　 ○ Ⓑ electric vehicle.

26 「低公害車」
(自動車メーカーの生き残りは低公害車を開発できるかどうかにかかっている)
The survival of automakers depend on whether they can develop
　　☆ Ⓐ low emission cars.
　　◎ Ⓑ cars with low emissions.
　　○ Ⓒ low emission vehicles.

27 「中古」
(a) 形容詞としての「中古の」という意味で
(私は中古車を買うつもりなんです)
I'm going to buy a ◎ Ⓐ used [secondhand] car.
　　　　　　　　　　 △ Ⓑ previously owned car.
[注意] Ⓑは広告では非常によく使われている。

(b) 副詞としての「中古で」の意味で
(私はこのオープンカーを中古で買ったんです)
◎ I bought this convertible used [secondhand].

28 「ポンコツ」
(a) 普通または少し怒っているとき
(あの車はポンコツだ)
That car's a ◎ Ⓐ pile of crap [junk].
　　　　　　　 ◎ Ⓑ piece [hunk] of junk.
　　　　　　　 ◎ Ⓒ lemon [junker].

(b) 怒っているとき

(あの車はポンコツだ)
◎ That car's a piece [pile] of shit.
[注意] 気を使う必要がない場面では非常によく使われているが，下品な表現なので改まって話す場面では使わないほうがよい。

29 「燃費」
(a) **燃費が悪い**
(あの車は燃費が悪いんです)
That car ◎ Ⓐ gets bad [low] gas mileage.
　　　　 ○ Ⓑ has bad [low] gas mileage.
　　　　 △ Ⓒ delivers bad [low] gas mileage.

(b) **燃費がいい**
(あの車は燃費がいいんです)
That ◎ Ⓐ car gets good [high] gas mileage.
　　 ○ Ⓑ is a gas-efficient [fuel-efficient, fuel-saving] car.
　　 △ Ⓒ car delivers good [high] gas mileage.
　　 △ Ⓓ car has good gas mileage.

(c) **ガソリンを食う**
　●話し手が怒っているとき
(あの車はガソリンをがぶ飲みするんだよ)
That ◎ Ⓐ is a gas guzzler.
　　 ◎ Ⓑ car guzzles a lot of gas.
　　 △ Ⓒ car eats a lot of gas.
　　 △ Ⓓ car is a gas hog.
　　 △ Ⓔ car swallows up [drinks] a lot of gas.
[注意] ⒹⒺは人により使用頻度はかなり上下する。
　●客観的に述べるとき
(あの車はガソリンをすごく使うんですよ)
That car ◎ Ⓐ uses [consumes] a lot of gas.
　　　　 ○ Ⓑ takes a lot of gas.
　　　　 △ Ⓒ puts away a lot of gas.

30 「代車」
(車を修理してもらっている間，代車をお借りできますか)
Can we ☆ Ⓐ use a loner (car) while we're having our car fixed?

　　　　◎ Ⓑ borrow a loner (car) ...?
［注意］辞典に a sub car, a substitute car が出ているが使われていない。

31 「ナンバープレート」
(a) 前のナンバープレート
　　（誰かが前のナンバープレートをはずして持って行ったようだ）
　　It looks like somebody took off my ◎ Ⓐ (front license) plate.
　　　　　　　　　　　　　　　　　　　◎ Ⓑ front tag.
　　［注意］辞典に number plate を出しているが使われていない。

(b) 後ろのナンバープレート
　　（誰かが後ろのナンバープレートをはずして持って行ったようだ）
　　It looks like somebody took off my ◎ Ⓐ back (license) plate.
　　　　　　　　　　　　　　　　　　　◎ Ⓑ back tag.

(c) 前と後ろの両方を述べる場合
　　（誰かがナンバープレートをはずして持って行ったようだ）
　　It looks like somebody took off my
　　　　☆ Ⓐ license plates.
　　　　◎ Ⓑ plates.
　　　　○ Ⓒ front and back (license) plates.
　　　　○ Ⓓ tags.
　　　　△ Ⓔ license tags.

32 「フロントガラス」
　　（フロントガラスをきれいにして下さい）
　　Please clean the ◎ Ⓐ windshield.
　　　　　　　　　　 × Ⓑ front glass.
　　［注意］Ⓑは和製英語。

33 「バックミラー」
(a) 「バックミラー」そのものに言及する場合
　　（もっと大きいバックミラーを付けてくれますか）
　　Can I get a bigger ◎ Ⓐ rear-view mirror?
　　　　　　　　　　　 × Ⓑ back mirror?

(b) 「バックミラーを付ける」ことに言及する場合

（もっと大きいバックミラーを付けてくれますか）
　　Can　☆ Ⓐ I get a bigger rear-view mirror?
　　　　　◎ Ⓑ you put in a bigger rear-view mirror?
　　　　　○ Ⓒ you install a bigger rear-view mirror?

34 「カーナビ」
(a) 車を買う場合
　　●付いている
　　（あの車はカーナビが付いているのですか）
　　◎ Does that car come with a GPS?
　　●付けてもらう
　　（ナビを無料で付けてくれますか）
　　◎ Can you throw [give] in a GPS for free?

(b) 車をすでに持っている場合
　　（カーナビを付けてくれますか）
　　Can you put ◎ Ⓐ a GPS in?
　　　　　　　　○ Ⓑ a navigation system?
　　　　　　　　△ Ⓒ a car navigation system?

(c) 付いているか否かの状態を尋ねる場合
　　（あなたの車はカーナビが付いているのですか）
　　☆ Ⓐ Does your car have a GPS?
　　◎ Ⓑ Is there a GPS in your car?
　　○ Ⓒ Does your car have a navigation system?
　　△ Ⓓ Is your car equipped with a GPS?

35 「台車」
　　（うちは台車を買わなければならないね）
　　We have to buy a ☆ Ⓐ hand truck.
　　　　　　　　　　　◎ Ⓑ handcart [dolly].
　　［注意］辞典に platform truck, trolly が出ているが使われていない。

36 「乳母車」
　　（私は新しい乳母車を買わなければならないんです）
　　I have to buy a ☆ Ⓐ stroller.
　　　　　　　　　　◎ Ⓑ baby stroller.

　　　　　△ Ⓒ baby buggy.
[注意] 辞典に baby carriage, pushchair, buggy が出ているが使われていない。

37 「駐車場」

(a) **有料駐車場**
　　(LMN 銀行の近くに駐車場があります)
　　There's ◎ Ⓐ a parking lot near LMN Bank.
　　　　　　◎ Ⓑ parking near ...
　　[注意] Ⓑの parking は不可算名詞扱いのため不定冠詞は不要である。

(b) **お客・社員のための無料駐車場**
　　(LMN 銀行の近くに駐車場があります)
　　There's ◎ Ⓐ a parking lot near LMN Bank.
　　　　　　◎ Ⓑ parking ...
　　　　　　△ Ⓒ a parking area ...
　　[注意] ⒸはⒶⒷと違って「駐車場」として特に作ったものではない。従って草が生えている空き地を言うこともある。

(c) **パーキングビル**
　　(LMN 銀行の近くに大きな駐車場があります)
　　There's a big ◎ Ⓐ parking garage near LMN Bank.
　　　　　　　　× Ⓑ parking building [stall, structure] ...
　　[注意] Ⓑは辞典に出ているが使われていない。

(d) **地下駐車場**
　　(LMN 銀行の近くに大きな地下駐車場があります)
　　There's
　　　　◎ Ⓐ a big underground parking garage near LMN Bank.
　　　　○ Ⓑ big underground parking lot ...

(e) **１台ずつの仕切りのある駐車場**
　　(〈駐車場で係員に尋ねて〉駐車する所はありますか)
　　◎ Ⓐ Are there any (parking) spots [spaces] available?
　　○ Ⓑ Is there any parking (available)?
　　△ Ⓒ Are there any (parking) places?

38「洗車場」
　（この近くに洗車場がありますか）
　Is there a ☆ Ⓐ car wash near here?
　　　　　　☆ Ⓑ car washing service ...?
　　　　　　◯ Ⓒ car washing business ［outfit］...?
　［注意］Ⓐはセルフサービスである。

39「保証」
(a)　保証期間を述べるとき
　（あの中古車には１年の保証が付いています）
　That ◎ Ⓐ used car has ［carries］ a one-year warranty.
　　　 ◎ Ⓑ used car has ［carries］ a one-year guarantee.
　　　 ◎ Ⓒ used car's warranted ［guaranteed］ for one year.

(b)　保証期間を尋ねるとき
　（この車の保証期間はどの位ですか）
　☆ Ⓐ How long's the warranty on this car?
　◎ Ⓑ How long a warranty does this car have?
　◎ Ⓒ How long's the guarantee on this car?
　◯ Ⓓ How long of a warranty does this car have?
　△ Ⓔ How long (of) a guarantee does this car have?
　△ Ⓕ How long's this car warranted ［guaranteed］?

40「さびつく」
　（この車はさびついてきた）
　This car's ◎ Ⓐ getting rusty.
　　　　　　◎ Ⓑ rusting.
　　　　　　◯ Ⓒ rusting out.

INDEX

[あ]
挨拶カード会社　52
挨拶のカード店　202
赤字　144
　決算書作成直後に会社の赤字の状態を
　　述べる場合　144
　会社の赤字の数字を述べる場合　144
　会社の清算を述べる場合　144
　国の財政　144
赤字に転落する　145
あくせく働く　102
上げ相場　196
上げ局面　196
あごで使う　113
　第三者のことを述べる場合　113
　聞き手に述べる場合　113
頭の回転がいい　13
頭の回転が遅い　13
アパート管理会社　52
アパートの管理人　24
粗利　143
ありますか　200
　色　200
　サイズ　200
アルバイトをする　109
　他に定職を持っている人の場合　109
　主婦・学生が昼間にアルバイトをする
　　場合　109
合わない　142
　勘定　142
　商品と送り状　142

[い]
言い値　201
医師　24
　眼科医　24
　肛門医　24
　産婦人科医　24
　耳鼻咽喉科　25
　小児科医　25
　心臓専門医　25

　整形外科医　25
　精神科医　25
　内科医　25
　脳外科医　26
　皮膚科医　27
　美容外科医　27
　婦人科医　27
　麻酔専門医　27
　やぶ医者　27
忙しい　100
　動詞を従えるとき　101
　名詞を従えるとき　101
　スケジュール　101
　忙殺される　101
　殺人的な　101
　てんてこ舞い　102
　手が離せない　102
(仕事を) 急ぐ　119
　「急がなければならない」と述べるとき
　　119
　「急いで帰らなければならない」と述
　　べるとき　119
　命令文で述べるとき　119
　急いで何かをやってもらうとき　120
　車を運転している人に　120
　「急いでいる」と状態を述べるとき　120
委託販売　147
　製造会社　147
　小売店　147
何時まで　127
犬のブリーダー　27
医療器具工場　77
医療器具リース会社　52
医療品会社　52
医療品工場　77
(車庫に) 入れる　216
印刷会社　53
　小規模の場合　53
　中規模の場合　53
　大規模の場合　53
印刷工場　77

新聞・本・雑誌	77
チラシ	78
インターネット会社	53
インターネットカフェ	202
インターネットサービス会社	54
インターネット接続会社	54
インターネットバンキング	177
インターネットをあちこち見て回る	161

[う]

上の人	11
動く	162
裏書きする	145
エアコン取付け会社	55
営業拠点	140
営業部	85
営業を拡大する	140
多めに見る	137
ウイスキー会社	55
ウイスキー工場	78
内金	147
乳母車	222
売掛未収金	148
売り出す	128
新製品を発表するだけでなく市場に出すというニュアンスの場合	128
消費者をあっと驚かせる従来にない新製品を発表して売り出すというニュアンスの場合	129
新製品を市場に出すというニュアンスの場合	129
どこの国の市場で売り出すかを明示する場合	129
売りに出すものが主語の場合	130
売りに出すものが目的語の場合	130
売れそうな	166
消費者が述べる場合	166
業界人・ビジネスマンが述べる場合	166
運送会社	55
勤めていることを述べる場合	55
会社の所有・経営・売買を述べる場合	55
運送屋	202
運転資金	128
運動器具工場	78
運動器具の会社	55

[え]

営業マン	28
一般的に述べる場合	28
相手に聞こえよく言おうとする場合	28
栄養士	28
エステ	202
エンジンをかけておく	214
エンジンをかけて下さい	213

[お]

置いている	127
店を主語にして述べる場合	127
社員（They）を主語にして述べる場合	127
大型トラック	218
大型トレーラー	218
大口投資家	195
オープンカー	217
大物	22
実業界・政界の場合	22
スポーツ界の場合	23
お菓子屋	202
お気に入り	159
マイクロソフト	159
ネットスケープ	159
織り込み済みです	195
下ろす	179

[か]

カーテン工場	78
カーナビ	222
車を買う場合	222
車をすでに持っている場合	222
付いているか否かの状態を尋ねる場合	222
カーペット工場	78
海外事業部	85
皆勤手当	124
会計事務所	73
外国為替銀行	176
買い占める	193
（市場を）買い占める	171
会社	50
小さい［大きい］会社の場合	50
ホワイトカラーの会社の場合	50
法人組織になっている会社であること	

を明示する場合	50	株を持っている会社の数に言及する場	
くだけた調子で述べる場合	50	合	192
場所として述べる場合	51	漠然とある会社の株に言及する場合	192
形容詞的に使われる場合	51	株式会社にする	51
会社案内	114	株式を公開する	192
会社・商店売買仲介会社	56	カメラ会社	57
会社の清算を述べる場合	146	カメラ工場	79
外車	217	カメラマン	28
改装する	135	新聞・雑誌	28
大規模の場合	135	ビデオ	28
小規模の場合	135	映画	28
店の正面だけの場合	135	がむしゃらに働く	102
解体会社	56	ガラス会社	57
会長	5	ガラス工場	79
男性	5	カリスマ性がある	14
女性	5	画廊	204
回転がいい	131	皮製品工場	79
解任される	111	観光ガイド	29
開発部	85	監査部	85
解約する	181	缶詰工場	79
化学会社	56	監督	29
価格競争	146	スポーツ	29
化学繊維工場	79	映画	29
かぎ屋	203	看板屋	68
家具屋	203	管理職の下っ端	11
架空名義口座	178	官僚	29
隔週5日制	107	単に官僚と述べる場合	29
掛売りする	147	高級官僚と述べる場合	29
貸し衣装会社	56	下級官僚と述べる場合	30
貸し衣装屋	203		
男女対象	203	[き]	
女性対象	203	企画部	86
男性対象	203	機関投資家	195
貸倒れ	148	企業再建屋	31
（銀行の）貸付係	31	貴金属会社	57
ガソリンスタンド	203	生地屋	204
肩書き	12	技術提携している	139
片付ける	116	技術部	86
カタログを改訂する	141	お客様と接触する	86
合併する	138	お客様と接触しない	86
家電工場	78	傷がある	169
金物屋	204	汽（客）船会社	71
かなり（いい収入）	125	客	114
株	192	キャッチコピー	174
株数を述べる場合	192	休暇	108

一般の人	108	クラクションを鳴らす	215
軍人・公務員・医師・看護婦	108	車で送ってきてくれる	216
求人サイト	158	車で送る	215
求人情報誌	91	一般的な状況の場合	215
給料	122	難しい状況の場合	215
「給料が安い」と述べる場合	122	部下，または家族などに送らせる場合	215
「給料がいい」と述べる場合	122	車に乗る	214
強化する	141	車の修理工	31
競争力のある	166	車の修理所	204
共同出資する	140	車の販売店	205
小規模	140	車のリース会社	58
大規模	140	車のレンタル会社	58
競売	183	車を運転する	214
競売にかけられると述べる場合	183	クリーニング屋	204
競売で買った（売った）と述べる場合	183	クレーン車	218
（電話が）切れていました	191	クレジットカード会社	58
きれる	15	黒字	143
特別高い地位でない人の場合	15	会社	143
高い地位の人の場合	15	会社の黒字の数字を述べる場合	143
切れる	150	国の財政	144
銀行員	31	国の貿易黒字	144
銀行家	31	詳しい	21
銀行の頭取	6	専門的知識を持っているという意味で	
銀行名に言及しない場合	6	の「詳しい」	21
銀行名に言及する場合	7	名詞の前で使う「詳しい」	22
金属会社	57	軍需工場	80
勤務	99		
時間帯	99	[け]	
体系	100	経営コンサルタント会社	58
金利	181	経営者	32
金利を尋ねる場合	181	オーナーを指す場合	32
金利が高い（安い）に言及する場合	181	経営だけに言及する場合	32
		計画性	20
[く]		「計画性がある」と述べる場合	20
空席	94	「計画性がない」と述べる場合	20
クーペ	217	経済記者	32
（会社の成績が）下り坂	132	計算が速い	14
クツ下製造工場	80	刑事	32
クツのメーカー	58	携帯電話会社	59
首になる	110	芸能プロダクション	75
社員に落度があった場合	110	警備員	33
社員に全く責任がなく会社の都合でリ		警備員だと述べる場合	33
ストラされた場合	111	警備を担当していると述べる場合	33
社員に責任があったときと会社の都合		警備会社	59
でリストラされた場合	111	契約	149

INDEX

ビジネス	149	
賃貸借契約	150	
契約違反	151	
契約している	150	
経理	33	
経理事務所	73	
経理部	86	
外科部長	10	
決算	142	
普通に述べるとき	142	
粉飾決算	143	
化粧品会社	59	
決裂する	154	
原価	141	
生産原価を尋ねる場合	141	
仕入れ原価	141	
原価計算	142	
減給	125	
給料をカットする	125	
給料をカットされる	126	
現金の振り込み	180	
検索エンジンで調べる	161	
検索エンジン名を特定しない場合	161	
検索エンジンを特定する場合	161	
研修	97	
建設会社	59	

[こ]

コインランドリー	205
効果	175
降格	106
高級車	216
車の外面を述べている場合	216
車の中で述べている場合	217
高給取り	125
航空会社	60
漠然と述べる場合	60
会社名として述べる場合	60
広告する	172
テレビ・ラジオ	172
新聞・雑誌	173
広告代理店	75
（得意先を訪ねる）広告取り	33
口座	177
口座の名義人	178

口座番号	178
工場長	8
自動車・鉄鋼・びん詰・缶詰などの工場	8
製紙・繊維・製粉などの工場	9
工場の設備	149
工場の設備投資	149
興信所	75
企業の成績を調べる	75
個人のクレジットカードの支払いを調べる	75
個人の素行調査	75
交替で運転する	215
公定歩合	180
口頭契約	150
公認会計士	33
購買部	86
合弁会社	51
広報部	86
公務員	34
国家公務員	34
県庁	35
市役所	36
工務店	60
合理化する	134
経費の削減を意味する場合	134
改良を意味する場合	135
声を大きくする	191
コーヒー工場	80
コーヒーショップ	206
子会社	51
小型株	194
小型車	217
小型トラック	218
ほろ付き	218
ほろなし	218
国産品	170
個人投資家	195
固定費	141
誤作動	162
ごみ	117
事務所	117
「ごみが散らかっている」と述べる場合	117
ごみ箱	118
ゴミ回収会社	60

ゴム工場	80
小物	23
主語が単数の場合	23
主語が複数の場合	23
コンピューター恐怖症	164
コンピューター工場	80
コンピューター修理会社	54
コンピューター通	163
主語が3人称の場合	163
主語が1人称の場合	163
会社・営業部・人事部のような場所を限定して述べる場合	163
コンピューターに入力する	157
コンピューターの調子	162
コンピューターは苦手	164
コンピューターは全く使えない	164
コンピューターを使える	162

[さ]

債権がある	183
事実だけを述べる場合	183
債権を放棄する旨を述べる場合	184
最高管理職	10
在庫がある	168
在庫が少なくなってきている	168
在庫がたくさんある	168
在庫を切らしている	169
在庫を切らして注文してある	169
（比喩的な意味で）財産	15
祭日	108
最先端	155
在宅勤務	100
サイト	157
新製品紹介	157
求人	158
才能	16
科学上の才能	16
インテリア・デザイン・ファッション・音楽などの才能	16
人の上に立つ才能	16
裁判官	36
最高［控訴］裁判所	36
最高［控訴］裁判以外の裁判所	36
財務部	87
サインペン	118

魚屋	206
酒屋	206
下げ相場	196
（値段を）下げる	134
大幅に下げる場合	134
普通に下げる場合	134
値下げのパーセンテージを述べる場合	134
作曲家	36
クラシック音楽	36
ジャズ音楽	37
ロック音楽	37
指図される	113
さびつく	20
さびつく	224
さぼる	107
サンドイッチショップ	206

[し]

時間稼ぎをする	153
資金運用部	87
資金を出す（スポンサーとなる）	140
仕事	93
ブルーカラー・臨時の仕事の場合	93
ホワイトカラーの場合	93
医師・弁護士・大学の教授の場合	93
専門職の場合	93
重役の場合	93
「一生の職業」という意味で大学生などが言う場合	94
保険・出版・新聞・株式市場・不動産・広告業の場合	94
仕事が速い	13
仕事中毒	102
否定的に述べる場合	102
冗談として述べる場合	103
仕事を紹介する	93
仕事を転々とする	112
市場	171
「市場に出ている」と述べる場合	171
「市場に出す」と述べる場合	171
市場がだぶついている	171
市場調査部	87
下っ端	4
1人しかいない場合	4
2人以上いる場合	5

INDEX

質屋	207
(市場は) しっかりしている	198
実業家	37
一般的	37
製造業	37
失業者が増える	112
失業率が悪化する	112
室内装飾会社	60
実力	103
支店長	7
どこの支店ではなく広く一般的に述べる場合	7
支店内，または支店外でも特定の支店を頭に入れて述べる場合	7
支店名と共に述べる場合	7
自動車	213
発明	213
普及させる	213
自動車組立て工場	80
自動車工場	81
自動的に振り込まれる	180
品薄です	170
老舗の	202
支配人	8
中西部・東部・南部などの大きな地域の支配人	8
中西部・東部・南部などのある州の支配人	8
都市・町などの支配人	8
(信用調査機関による) 支払い能力評価	146
よい場合	146
悪い場合	147
支払う	153
地元の銀行	176
事務機器製造会社	61
事務職	100
現在	100
未来	100
事務用品会社	61
事務用品店	207
シャープペン	118
写真館	207
写真師	37
写真屋	207
社長	5

週休2日制	107
就職する	95
高い地位	95
高くない地位	96
就職することが難しい	92
就職説明会	91
就職で苦労している	92
受注残	138
出勤する	97
時間が逼迫している場合	97
習慣的なこと	97
ちょうど出勤してきた場合	98
出勤しているか否かを尋ねる場合	98
出世	105
事実だけを述べる場合	105
比較して述べる場合	106
出世頭	106
出版社	61
需要が多い	170
受話器を口に近づける	190
小規模で	128
昇給してもらう	123
普通に述べる場合	123
先月，去年の昇給を述べる場合	123
昇給のパーセンテージに言及する場合	123
昇給すると述べる場合	123
昇給のスピードを述べる場合	123
昇給が遅いと述べる場合	123
証券会社	61
小さい会社	61
大きな会社	61
上司	1
一般的に述べる場合	1
くだけた口調で述べる場合	1
直属の上司	1
昇進が遅い	107
昇進する	104
「そろそろ昇進していい頃だ」というニュアンスの場合	104
(昇進が発表された後) 昇進することになっている	104
昇進が発表されていない場合	104
昇進する地位を明示する場合	105
すごく昇進したとき	105
上手です	18

[231]

語学の場合	18	製品が主語の場合	137
演説の場合	18	生産部	88
楽器の場合	19	正式契約書	150
スポーツの場合	19	政治記者	38
扱い方	19	製紙工場	81
上層部	3	（会社の）成績はいい	131
消費者金融会社	62	清掃会社	63
商品券	201	製造部	88
商品の回転が速い	168	製粉工場	81
消防士	37	製本会社	63
情報部	87	税務会計事務所	73
照明係	38	税務官吏	38
職業紹介所	92	税務署員	38
職業別電話帳	159	税務署長	39
食料品店	207	税務調査官	39
私立探偵	38	製薬会社	63
ジン会社	62	製薬工場	82
ジン工場	81	セールストーク	17
人材銀行	91	一般的に述べる場合	17
審査部	87	特定な場面を述べる場合	18
人事部	88	設計事務所	74
人事部長	7	規模が小さい場合	74
紳士洋品店	207	規模が大きい場合	74
新入社員	97	石けん工場	82
		接続する	157
		設立する	128
[す]		瀬戸物屋	208
推奨株	194	ゼネコン	60
水道会社	62	セメント会社	63
スーツ（ドレス）縫製工場	81	セメント工場	82
スーパー	208	セルフサービスレストラン	208
（電話が）すぐつながる	190	繊維会社	64
すごい降格	106	繊維工場	82
寿司屋	208	洗車会社	64
スピード違反で捕まる	216	洗車場	224
スピードを出す	214	前任者	11
車の速度	214	支配人	11
数字を明示しない場合	214	大統領・首相など地位の高い人	11
数字を明示する場合	215	専門店	208
スポーツ用品店	208		
		[そ]	
[せ]		造園会社	64
製菓会社	62	造園技師	39
製菓工場	81	総辞職する	111
生産に入っている	137	総代理店	74
工場が主語の場合	137		

[232]

INDEX

贈答品として包装する	200
相場	153
買う場合	153
借りる場合	153
（株の）相場	196
総務（庶務）部	88
創立記念日	117
測量会社	64
測量士	39
素質	16
素質を求められる職業に言及する場合	16
戦力になる期待を見せている場合	17

[た]

代休	108
代金引換えで払う	148
大使	39
代車	220
台車	222
退社する	99
タイムレコーダー	98
（出勤して）押すと述べる場合	98
（退社するときに）押すと述べる場合	99
機械を述べる場合	99
大量売却による株価急落	197
高値で引ける	198
高値をつける	196
タクシー会社	65
タクシーの運転手	39
宅配会社	65
（会社の経営が）立ち直る	132
（電話で）誰々が話し中	190
人を主語にして述べる場合	190
電話機を主語にして述べる場合	190
話し中が長く続いていることを述べる場合	190
炭酸飲料会社	65

[ち]

地方銀行	176
中間管理職	10
中古	219
形容詞としての「中古の」という意味で	219
副詞としての「中古で」の意味で	219

駐車場	223
有料駐車場	223
お客・社員のための無料駐車場	223
パーキングビル	223
地下駐車場	223
１台ずつの仕切りのある駐車場	223
駐車場の係員	40
駐車ビル	40
地上の駐車場	40
駐車場の係の責任者	40
（高級ホテル・レストランなどの）駐車場の車の出し入れ係	40
一般的に述べる場合	40
ホテル名・レストラン名を明示する場合	40
注文	132
「注文する」と述べる場合	132
注文を明示する場合	133
「注文してある」状態を述べる場合	133
注文が本当にじゃんじゃん入ってきている	133
製品を明示しないで述べる場合	133
製品を明示して述べる場合	133
注文がものすごく入っている状態	133
調査会社	65
調停人	40
貯金する	178
未来の内容	178
過去から現在まで	179
習慣的内容	179
隠して貯金しているというニュアンスで	179
貯蓄銀行	176
賃金凍結	125

[つ]

通勤手当	124
通信社	66
通販で	201
通訳	41
ただ通訳であることを述べる場合	41
何語の通訳であるかを述べる場合	41
同時通訳	41
通訳会社	66
（電話を）つなぐ	189

[233]

[て]

ディーエム会社	66
低公害車	219
定着率	109
「定着率が高い」と述べる場合	109
「定着率が悪い」と述べる場合	109
抵当銀行	177
デスクトップパソコン	155
鉄鋼工場	82
鉄道会社	66
出て行く	115
一般的に述べる場合	115
ちょっと出て行くと述べる場合	115
怒って出て行くと述べる場合	115
出て来る	116
建物から	116
入口・裏口から	116
駅の東口・西口・南口・北口から	116
手取り	124
手の平サイズパソコン	156
デリカショップ	209
テレアポ会社	66
テレビ広告	173
テレビ局名を明示しないとき	173
テレビ局名を明示したとき	174
テレビ工場	82
テレビタレント	41
テレビの総合司会者	41
手を引く	154
店員	41
コンビニ・スーパーのように店員が買物客を説得する必要のない店	41
デパートの婦人服売場、宝石店など店員が買物客を説得する必要のある店	42
ガソリンスタンドの店員	42
電気会社	67
電気技師	42
電気自動車	219
転勤になる	107
伝言	114
伝言をするか否かを尋ねる場合	114
伝言があることを述べる場合	114
誰かが伝言を残していったことを述べる場合	114
電子会社	67
電子工場	83
電子商取引	152
電卓	118
店頭株（非上場株）	194
電力会社	67
電話	185
鳴っている電話に「出る」と述べる場合	185
電話をかけた先に「…のお宅ですか」と尋ねる場合	185
かかってきた電話に対して「…です」と述べる場合	185
電話で話をしたい人を呼び出す場合	186
電話をかけてきた人の名前を尋ねる場合	186
呼び出してもらうとき	187
電話に出た人が当人の場合	187
切らないで待ってもらいたい場合	187
「誰々から電話です」と伝える場合	188
電話をかけてきた人が誰であったかを尋ねる場合	188
「電話で話す」と述べる場合	189
電話をひくと述べる場合	189
もう一度電話をかけ直すと述べる場合	189
番号が間違っている場合	189
電話取付け会社	67
電話のセールスで	201

[と]

当座預金	178
統率力がある	14
統率力を見せる	104
同僚	3
管理職の場合	3
非管理職の場合	3
非管理職で似た仕事に従事しているが依存してはいない場合	3
同じ会社で働いている場合	3
時計会社	67
時計工場	83
時計の修理士	42
床屋	209
（左官会社の意味での）塗装会社	67
飛ぶように売れている	167
動詞で述べる場合	167

INDEX

名詞で述べる場合	167
取締役	5
一般的に述べる場合	5
「会社の取締役」と述べる場合	6
会社名を明示して述べる場合	6
政策を決定する「取締役理事会の一人」	
の意味の「取締役」と述べる場合	6
取締役理事	42
取次業者（会社）	68
取引	151
特定の取引	151
継続的な取引	152
取引高の多い株	195
取引をまとめる	152
取引の条件・契約書の交換・金銭の授	
受を意味する場合	152
契約書の署名・交換・金銭の授受だけ	
を意味する場合	153
トリマー	43
ドル箱	165
問屋	68

[な]

中吊り広告	174
ナンバープレート	221
前のナンバープレート	221
後ろのナンバープレート	221
前と後ろの両方を述べる場合	221

[に]

肉屋	209
にせもの	169
絵	169
ダイヤモンド	169
（署名が）にせもの	151
…に向いている	17
入金する	180
入社する	96
平社員	96
役員・管理職	96
乳製品会社	69
庭師（植木屋）	43
人気株	193

[ね]

ネット	160
ネットショッピングをする	160
ネットで買う	160
ネットで注文が入る	160
ネットで株の売買をする	161
ネット利用者	159
年功序列	103
念書	150
燃費	220
燃費が悪い	220
燃費がいい	220
ガソリンを食う	220

[の]

農機具工場	83
農機具製作会社	69
能力開発部	88
ノートパソコン	155
（会社が）伸びている	131
普通に述べる場合	131
強調して述べる場合	131

[は]

バイキングレストラン	210
買収する	139
ハイテク会社	69
ハイテク株	194
配当	198
廃品回収会社	69
ハイブリッド車	218
パイロット見習い	43
破棄する	151
法律違反になる場合	151
法律違反にならない場合	151
派遣会社	70
派遣社員	2
派遣する	148
派遣している会社数のみを述べる場合	148
派遣している人材の内容と会社数を述	
べる場合	149
派遣部	88
破産する	145
客観的に述べる場合	145
会社更生の破産申請をしていることを	
述べる場合	146

バスの外側の壁面広告	174
バスの中の広告	174
パソコン接続業者	43
パソコンの修理士	44
パソコンのスイッチを入れる	157
パソコンメーカー	54
パソコンを消す	162
裸一貫	106
バックミラー	221
「バックミラー」そのものに言及する場合	221
「バックミラーを付ける」ことに言及する場合	221
発送部	88
花形株	193
花屋	210
はやっている	130
店	130
法律事務所	130
経理事務所	130
班長	9
販売管理部	89
販売促進部	89
販売代理店	75
パン屋	210

[ひ]

ピアノの調律師	44
ビール工場	83
引ける	198
飛行機の修理士	44
必需品	165
ビデオ屋	210
（解雇される意味での）ひまを出される	111
美容院	211
病院長	10
経営及び治療の両方に携わっている、またはどちらか不明の場合	10
経営には関与していない場合	10
評価する	103
過大評価する場合	103
過小評価する場合	103
病気で欠勤する電話をかける	191
美容師見習い	45
秘書	44
重役の秘書	44
社長の秘書	44
一般的に述べる場合	44
平社員	2
ホワイトカラー	2
ブルーカラー	2
びん詰工場	83

[ふ]

（株式市場の）不安材料	197
部下	4
1人の部下に言及する場合	4
複数の部下に言及する場合	4
副会長	5
副工場長	9
自動車・鉄鋼・びん詰・缶詰などの工場	9
製紙・繊維・製粉などの工場	9
副支店長	7
副班長	9
部長補佐	8
普通預金	178
不動産会社	56
不動産サイト	159
船（船舶）会社	72
フランチャイズ店	210
フリーダイヤル	191
振り込む	180
不良債権	183
ブロードバンド	156
パソコンにブロードバンドが付いていると述べる場合	156
ブロードバンドが付いたアパートと述べる場合	156
（ホテルの）フロント	46
フロントガラス	221
不渡り手形を出す	145
会社	145
個人	145
文書部	89
文房具店	211

[へ]

ヘアダイ会社	70
ヘアダイ工場	83
壁面広告	174

INDEX

（ホテル内で客の荷物を運ぶ）ベルボーイ	46
ベルボーイの責任者	46
ペンキ屋	68
弁護士	45
客観的に述べる場合	45
上品な響きを出す場合	45
否定的なニュアンスで述べる場合	45
編集主幹	45
編集長	46
社内で述べる場合	46
社外で述べる場合	46
編集プロダクション	76

[ほ]

貿易会社	70
法人組織になっている	128
縫製工場	84
宝石店	211
暴落する	197
法律事務所	74
ボーイ長	46
ボールペン	118
保険会社	70
保険の代理店	74
保険引受会社（業者）	70
保証	224
保証期間を述べるとき	224
保証期間を尋ねるとき	224
ボディーガード	47
ホテルの予約カウンター	47
保留になる	119
期限を明示しない場合	119
期限を明示する場合	119
ポンコツ	219
普通または少し怒っているとき	219
怒っているとき	219
本社	51
本店	211

[ま]

任せる技術	14
（…割）増し	124
5割増し	124
2割増し	124
マジックペン	118

窓際族	106
マニア	163

[み]

見積り	135
普通に述べる場合	135
概算の見積り	135
正確な見積り	136
最初の見積り	136
最終的な見積り	136
低めの見積り	136
見てまわる	199
何かを探して，または時間つぶしに	199
時間つぶしに	199
目的に関する含みのない場合	199
未払い金	148
未払い給料	126

[む]

向きである	170

[め]

名目上の	11
目方をごまかす	200
目玉商品	165
めどがつく	137
目のこえたお客	201
目を通す（検索する）	161

[も]

もう少し	116
売上げのノルマ・目標達成に近い人を励ます場合	117
仕事が終了したか否かの質問に対して	117
持ち直す	197
（売り上げが）持ち直す	132
もちろん	94
丁寧に言う場合	94
少しくだけて言う場合	94
親しい友人同士の場合	95
モデル派遣会社（プロダクション）	70
（株価が）ものすごく上がる	195
木綿工場	84

[や]

[237]

薬剤師	47
薬局	211
雇う	95
雇ってもらえる	95
辞める	110
普通の人	110
部長・社長など高い地位の人	110
長官・首相など高い地位の公職の人	110

[ゆ]

有給休暇	109
融資する	181
融資の係	47
2人以上いる場合	47
1人の場合	47
融資の責任者	48
優先株	193
有線テレビ会社	71
有望株	194
遊覧船会社	71
優良株	193
輸出入銀行	176
輸送会社	71
輸入部	89

[よ]

用件	114
用件（店で）	199
羊毛工場	84
預金通帳	177
銀行外の場合	177
銀行の中の場合	177
（電話で）よく聞こえる	190
予算を組む	137
酔っ払い運転で捕まる	216
予約係の責任者	48

[ら]

ライトバン（軽量トラック）	217
ラジオ広告	174
ラジオタレント	48

[り]

利益	138
投資・株などが主語の場合	138

ビジネス・商品が主語の場合	138
リサイクル工場	84
リサイクルショップ	212
流通部	89
新聞・雑誌	89
新聞・雑誌以外	89
領事	48
旅行業者	48
旅行代理店	74

[れ]

レストランの客席への案内係	48
（駐車違反）レッカー移動会社	72
連帯保証人	182
一般に	182
親子など親密な間柄	182
連帯保証をする	182
レンタカー屋	212

[ろ]

労働条件	92
労務部	90
ローンの支払いが遅れている	182
単に遅れていると述べる場合	182
遅れている日数・月数を述べる場合	182
（新聞の）論説委員	49

著者紹介

ボストンアカデミー校長　市橋敬三

　長年の滞米生活によりアメリカ英語を身につける。
　英会話上達の秘訣は「英文法を知っているではなく、使い切れるようにすることにある」と、英会話にとって英文法の不可欠性を、1984年に刊行した著書の中で、日本の英会話教育史上初めて唱えたこの道の草分けであり、現在も第一人者的存在。
　話すための英文法シリーズ4冊(研究社出版)は「英文法イコール英語の長文読解をするためのもの」という長年の誤ったイメージを根底からくつがえし、日本の英会話教育に大きな影響を巻き起こした。
　オハイオ州の名門校のマウントユニオン大学を優等(cum laude)で卒業。
　言語であるアメリカ英語を研究するだけでなく、アメリカ研究学を専攻し、アメリカの歴史、政治、社会、地理、宗教などを研究した後、ニューヨークでビジネス界に身を投じ、これらの体験によりアメリカの真の姿を知悉している数少ない知米家の一人。
　著書に新聞、雑誌の書評欄に掲載され大好評を博し、またAmazon.comで何度も好反響を得た「最新アメリカ英語表現辞典」(大修館書店)など約60冊あり。

アメリカ英語ビジネス会話辞典

2005年2月28日　1刷

著　者——市橋敬三
　　　　　ⓒ Keizō Ichihashi, 2005
発行者——南雲一範
発行所——株式会社 **南雲堂**
　　　　　東京都新宿区山吹町361（〒162-0801）
　　　　　電　話（03）3268-2384（営業部）
　　　　　　　　（03）3268-2387（編集部）
　　　　　FAX（03）3260-5425（営業部）
　　　　　振替口座　00160-0-46863
印刷所／図書印刷株式会社

Printed in Japan　〈検印省略〉
乱丁、落丁本はご面倒ですが小社通販係宛ご送付下さい。
送料小社負担にてお取替えいたします。

ISBN 4-523-31044-0　C0582 〈D-44〉

アメリカ英語日常会話辞典

市橋敬三 著　A5判　定価2625円（本体2500円）

他の辞典にはない表現を満載！

本辞典では他の辞典に収録されていないが、
現代のアメリカ本場で使われている表現を豊富に収録した。
その使用頻度も明示し、利用者の便を図った。

- 第1章　あいさつ・ちょっとした一言・呼びかけの表現
- 第2章　天気に関する表現
- 第3章　時間に関する表現
- 第4章　感情・気持に関する表現
- 第5章　性質に関する表現
- 第6章　人間関係に関する表現
- 第7章　容姿に関する表現
- 第8章　服装に関する表現
- 第9章　男女間に関する表現
- 第10章　暮らし・住居に関する表現
- 第11章　レストラン・ホテルに関する表現
- 第12章　食事・料理に関する表現
- 第13章　買い物に関する表現
- 第14章　道順に関する表現
- 第15章　交通機関に関する表現
- 第16章　健康・病気に関する表現

TOEICテスト 700点突破大作戦

市橋敬三著　A5判　定価1890円（本体1800円）

耳を鍛えるナチュラル・スピード

そのスピードについていくシャドーイングで、口を慣らす。

- 第1章　意外と使える人が少ないThisとThatの7つの意味
- 第2章　現在進行形と過去進行形の作り方
- 第3章　未来の意志と無意志を表す時に使うWill
- 第4章　助動詞
- 第5章　動名詞
- 第6章　不定詞
- 第7章　役に立つHow…？の12の表現
- 第8章　名詞節
- 第9章　付属疑問文
- 第10章　副詞節